Computer Security
Risk Management

Computer Security Risk Management

I. C. Palmer
G. A. Potter

VNR VAN NOSTRAND REINHOLD
_____ New York

First published in Great Britain in 1989 by
Jessica Kingsley Publishers Ltd
13 Brunswick Centre
London WC1N 1AF

First published in the USA in 1990 by
Van Nostrand Reinhold
115 Fifth Avenue
New York, New York 10003

ISBN 0 442 30290 8

Book design and illustrations by Richard Varley
Text set by Logotype Data Services, Bath
Printed and bound in Great Britain

Contents

Illustrations, charts and diagrams

Introduction

The growth of organised crime in the computer world, coupled with the new threat of extortion and politically motivated attack requires new levels of security in all computer installations. Attacks from professional groups are a function of the attractiveness of the theft and the vulnerability of the system.

Thus a bank is attractive because it deals in money and is a symbol of capitalism. Similarly, if its system security thresholds are low it becomes vulnerable. It then meets the two fold requirements of attractiveness and vulnerability which will ensure criminal penetration.

It has been argued that highly organised computer crime is largely a phenomenon of the USA and a peripheral activity in Europe and that the rest of the world is largely free from computer crime. However, modern communications largely nullify this hypothesis. A foreign gang can operate successfully in any town in any country with collusive support from two or three employees of the target company.

Similarly, the growth of the political left and its associated terrorist fronts gives rise for concern. A computer is a soft target offering little danger to its attackers and maximum effect and publicity, to the terrorist group, if they succeed in blowing it up.

Extortion and blackmail using computer viruses will become the crime of the 1990s. There is little chance of the criminal being caught and maximum returns for the blackmailer or extortionist if the virus is difficult to stop or if the afflicted computer belongs to an organisation which would suffer from a public scandal.

The USA keeps records of attacks on computers, very few other countries are so honest in public. The FBI estimate that only 1% of computer frauds are discovered in time to bring a prosecution. According to the Stanford Research Institute, only 20% of those discovered are actually prosecuted for fear of scandal affecting the computer owner's business, and of those prosecuted only 5% are convicted.

In other words, the odds are 10,000 : 1 in favour of the computer criminal. Three years ago the odds were 200:1. Is it any wonder that the criminal fraternity have turned their attention to computers?

The objective of everyone concerned with computer security is to have a totally secure system. Yet, despite the threats already discussed few installations are even modestly secure.

Security Officers and Security Managers without an information processing background close their eyes and ears as soon as computer security is mentioned. "Not my field" they say, "I leave that to the data processing boys". A basic fear exists of computers. This fear is based on a lack of knowledge brought about by the technical jargon used in the industry. Computer systems are simply tools, the purposes of which are easily understood. Remove the mystique of the technical jargon and the security of computer systems becomes much easier to plan.

Protectionism has existed in civilized societies since history began. Strong unions have never existed in the world of computers and so the founder members of the profession unconsciously establish a priesthood. After all, priests have always worked with esoteric languages and complicated ceremonial, and this has proved a most successful way to make their position in the society secure. Computer systems are exactly the same. They have their high priests and acolytes and their own esoteric language.

By making even the simplest operation seem difficult and complicated, computer people have established their own territory from which the less informed have been deliberately excluded. The net result is that salaries have become higher in computing than in the rest of the company and the computer department tends to work in isolation, with little or no interference from management. This process is self-generating, so that now even user-friendly microcomputers have their own jargon.

With the growth of professional protectionism has come unparalleled technological advances in the field of computers, communications and data processing. Concurrent with these advances, a new field of crime with a formidable set of problems has emerged.

Top management concern about computer security is increasing and is stimulated by numerous well publicised incidents of computer related fraud and embezzlement, terrorist attacks, Hacking, industrial action and natural disasters such as fires and floods. Top management has also begun to realise that they can expect to suffer financially from legal action if imprudence or negligence in security planning causes the company financial loss.

Computer security is the protection of the computer resources against accidental or intentional disclosure of confidential data, unlawful modification of data or programs, the destruction of data, software or hardware, and the denial of one's own computer facilities irrespective of the method together with such criminal activities computer related fraud and blackmail.

The American Institute of Certified Public Accountants in 1984 surveyed 6,359 banks and insurance companies and found 119 frauds. The American Law Association surveyed 1,000 companies and found 480 had experienced fraud. The losses ranged from $2 million to $10 million per respondent. The conclusion is that fraud by computer has reached new heights.

The emergence of hackers is also presenting new problems with disclosure, modification and destruction of data. Hackers are defined as complete outsiders who with technical know how and cheap equipment attack computer systems. In 1983, in the USA the National Bank System, the Security Pacific and Los Alamos Nuclear Laboratory Systems were penetrated. In 1984, NASA, the US Defence Department, the Naval Oceans Centre, the French Atomic Energy Commission, the Sparkasse Space Bank and the TRW Systems were penetrated. In all cases an attempt was made to disclose confidential information or to modify existing data.

Clearly any form of alteration can be expensive to correct and embarrassing if it is exposed.

Who then is responsible for preventing these attacks on computer systems? Rarely does anyone in the computer department take responsibility except in the barest of token senses. Security in a systems environment is often regarded as counter productive and inefficient. This attitude tends to result in installations being highly vulnerable to attack. At the other extreme systems are designed with such a high level of security as to be too expensive to implement and consequently risks are taken for financial reasons.

So often, companies will erect "Great Walls of China" around their installations and then go into the market place and buy programs from unknown suppliers or, to show their sophistication, allow contractors on their premises to write software for them without checking the individuals and, almost invariably, with no supervision at all. To be fair, it can be argued that a minimum of supervision is necessary since payment is made by results and if the contractor does not work he does not get paid.

It can also be argued that there are not resources to check contractors. These arguments are made despite the fact that a Trojan Horse, Virus or a Logic Bomb can easily be placed in the software during a development period for use at a much later date. It is as well to bear in mind that these devices are put into the operating systems or application programs and do not appear when the computer checks the system, only to emerge when perpetrator actuates them. He may do this months or years after the event; he may do it from a remote terminal or a distant country; he may do it whilst still an employee or as the hired hand of a gang. By triggering the device he will usually allow himself total coverage and be exempt from all authorisation within the process. Clearly the sky becomes the limit.

The following represent typical questions that should be raised by management in respect of their computer installations:

1. Is the company aware, in actual cash terms, of the value of its data base?

2. Is the computer installation vulnerable to embezzlement, fraud or other acts of misuse and abuse?

3. Are the computer personnel security conscious and is there an overriding security policy?

4. Is the security policy up to date and has it kept up with hardware and software advances?

5. Does the security programme cover all essential computer operations?

6. Are the levels of insurance commensurate with the risks that exist?

7. Have the security measures in place been quantified accurately enough to justify the cost of counter measures?

8. If the computer operation was destroyed or damaged what plans exist to carry on operations? Who would be responsible for coordinating activity? What would be the overall cost to the organisation?

Security in the computer world is logical and cost effective to implement, providing that countermeasures are built into the system from the data base outwards and not cobbled on to a working system as an after thought.

This book begins with security of the data base, since all security must work from the centre outwards. It begins with the company's prime asset and works from there outwards looking first at software, logical access controls and then personnel, finally examining physical security and other relevant considerations, in mainframe, micro and network environments. It will show those concerned with security how to take meaningful decisions on countermeasures in a structured, logical and cost effective manner.

Modern Attacks

1

Computer Fraud

The fraudulent misuse of computers is now a major criminal activity. The increased requirements of business, with its sophisticated technology has brought even greater opportunities for the dishonest. Most companies depend heavily on old management practices and will admit to having little knowledge of information processing. They show little interest in acquiring knowledge and perhaps for this reason trusted junior employees are able to perpetrate large value frauds.

In 1984 the FBI estimated that only 1 out of 22 apprehended computer criminals went to prison. In 1989 the estimated figure is 1 out of 10,000. The Stanford Research Institute in California calculates that the average computer fraud costs a major company $425,000, a bank $132,000 and a public authority $220,000 and that criminal proceedings are only instituted in less than 1% of computer related crimes.

The 'take' from computer fraud in the U.S. alone is put at $3 billion per year. In the U.K. The Daily Telegraph speculated in June 1983 that the crime was costing business $2.5 billion. Will computer crime grow? The question can be answered by the following proposition:

a. Computer frauds are related directly to the number of computers in use.

b. Computer fraud is directly proportional to the number of people who have knowledge of and access to computers.

c. Computer fraud is directly proportional to the number of terminals that access computers.

All three conditions are in a state of growth and it follows that all major fraud will be computer fraud before the next century.

The following factors make a computer system susceptible to fraud:

a. The complex nature of the data processing systems

b. The concentration of information on the company into a small area

c. The knowledge belongs only to a few selected members of the company

d. A system which is designed for speed and efficiency and not security

e. Personnel who operate the system are usually not security conscious

f. Management and auditors do not understand the computer system

g. There is usually an absence of recognised audit role.

More simplistically computer fraud is a function of the attractiveness to the thief combined with the vulnerability of the system to be robbed. All the thief needs are the resources, knowledge and the opportunity.

The Security Officer should be aware that sufficient knowledge is present in Middle Management, for example records, layouts, descriptions, etc., of any given system and an understanding of the way that data is organised, to be able to effect change. Programming knowledge can also be acquired with ease making most systems vulnerable to attack.

Resources to perpetrate fraud means equipment: A simple program and a computer. Add to this the chance to borrow the firm's magnetic media and the fraud is underway.

Perhaps there will be outside collusion, even financial backing if the return on effort is high enough. All this makes the Security Officer's job more difficult and emphasises the need to understand how frauds are committed and the basic security thresholds that can be put in place to protect the system.

Fraud Techniques

The Trojan Horse

The Trojan Horse method is the most common method of computer program based frauds and sabotage. Instructions are placed in a system so that they will be executed in the protected or restricted domain of the program and have access to all of the data files that are assigned to that program. The computer then performs unauthorised functions but continues to allow the program to perform its intended purposes.

If the fraud is engineered by a person of ability it will be extremely difficult to detect Trojan Horse methods. For example, a typical program can consist of 2,000 to 3,000 computer instructions and data. The Trojan Horse can also be concealed in the 5m. or so instructions of the operating system and intrinsic software where it waits for execution of the target application program, inserts extra instructions in it for a few mini seconds of execution time and removes them with no remaining evidence.

A suspected Trojan Horse is extremely difficult to validate. The most effective method is by comparing a copy of the operational program under suspicion with the master copy known to be free from unauthorised changes. However, it must be remembered that the perpetrator might very well have altered the master copies as well. The best method of validation is by testing the suspected program with data and under conditions that might reveal the purpose of the Trojan Horse. The main disadvantage is that the exact conditions for discovery must be known. The Trojan Horse may also reside in the source version of the program or only in the object form and may be inserted in the object form each time it is assembled or compiled.

If the Trojan Horse is discovered it is then necessary to narrow the search to those programmers who have the necessary skills, knowledge and access. These could be employees, former employees, contract programmers or consultants. The method of detection would be program code comparison or the testing of a suspect program or the tracing of gain from the act.

The Salami Technique

As with salami, this fraud involves taking small slices from the whole without noticeably reducing the total. This might be the rounding down of pence in a banking system and adding them to a special account, from which withdrawals can be made. The success of this type of fraud is based on the idea that each account customer loses so little that it is of no consequence. Many variations are possible and can be applied to interest rate calculations where a decimal part of a penny is added to a special account or to the simplistic removal of two or three pence from each account. The small amounts when multiplied by several thousand accounts and many thousands of transactions can result in a sizable fraud.

The main problem with this fraud is that the victims have usually lost so little that they are unwilling to expend effort to catch the thief.

A good auditor will look for this type of fraud by checking for deviations from standard accounting methods before rounding calculations. The life style of the employees who have the skills to perpetrate this fraud should be watched for deviations from the accepted norm. The fraud has to continue for some period of time to be of any value and it is usually only by undue financial activity on the part of the suspect that the fraud can is revealed.

It is usually the financial system programmer who can start this fraud but it must be borne in mind that former employees can be benefiting many years after initiating the fraud and therefore feedback information on life style could be very important. The cost of detailed data analysis, transaction audits and program comparisons would be very high. Perhaps it is because of this that most financial institutions encourage their employees to hold their banking accounts in house. This then allows the institution to closely watch the movements of the account. However, it does not stop the perpetrator from opening an account in a false name.

Superzapping

The name derives itself from a utility program developed by IBM. This program would by-pass all controls to modify or disclose any of the contents of the computer. It would be used when a computer had stopped or malfunctioned or entered a state that could not be overcome by normal recovery procedures. Superzap, in effect, is a universal access program. In the right hands it is a godsend; in the wrong hands a powerful and dangerous tool.

The use of Superzap programs to change data files that are normally only updated by other programs is well known. Thus outstanding balances on a debtors account cannot normally be accessed except by postings. Superzap can give immediate access and alteration to these otherwise protected fields.

A Bank in New Jersey authorised its Manager of Computer Operations to use Superzap programs to make changes to account balances. Because the demand deposit accounting system had become obsolete as a result of inattention in a computer changeover the Operations Manager was able to discover how easy it was to make changes without the usual controls or journal records. He promptly began to make changes transferring money to three friends' accounts. The fraud would not have been discovered since Superzap programs make changes to data files without leaving evidence of the alterations, had not a client found a shortage in his account and the Bank taken quick investigative action.

Similarly, frauds of this type are usually detected when management are notified that discrepancies have occurred. In these circumstances, if it is conclusive that the discrepancy is not a data error then a search of all computer usage journals might reveal the use of a Superzapp program.

Sometimes, there may be a record of a request to have a file traced on line in the computer system if it is not normally in that mode. If this has not happened then the changes would have to occur when the production program using the file is being run. The potential perpetrators are, of course, programmers and computer operation staff with applications knowledge. A comparison of current files with the father and grandfather copies of files, when no up-dates exist to account for suspicious changes might provide evidence of discrepancy. Otherwise an examination of the computer usage journals or a report of discrepancy are the only lines of defence.

Logic Bombs or Time Bombs

A logic bomb is normally a time triggered device. Secret operating instructions are inserted in a computer operating system and the programs instructed to take action at a specific time or period frequency. However, time is not the only factor, it can be triggered by any specified condition or by a form of data that might be introduced to the system. Naturally, a logic bomb has to use the Trojan Horse technique. Consequently the methods used to discover logic bombs in the computer system would be the same as for Trojan Horses.

Trap Doors

This system derives its name from the programmer's skill in providing breaks in the code for insertion of additional code and intermediate output capabilities. Most intrinsic software is designed to prevent this type of operation but system programmers will sometimes insert code that allows compromise of these requirements during the debugging phase of program development. These facilities are called Trap Doors. The unscrupulous introduce Trap Doors to later compromise security of the computer programs. It is also possible for the unscrupulous to find weaknesses in design logic which inadvertently provide Trap Doors.

When functioning for fraud or malicious purposes the norm is for the Trap Door to transfer control from a program into a region of data or into the field of operation of a second program. This would then obviously cause the computer to start executing program codes secretly whenever the program containing the Trap Door was run. Viewer systems are the most vulnerable in that they can provide free of charge service or data and programs that belong to their other time-sharing clients. Additionally, it may allow the intruder to search for passwords and, having obtained these, to gain access to all manner of privileged information.

There is no known method that can be judged to be technically competent for use against Trap Doors. However, when the nature of a suspected Trap Door is ascertained there are tests of varying degrees of complexity that could be performed to discover hidden functions used for malicious purposes. It goes without saying that suspicion must fall on systems programmers and very expert applications programmers; in other words the most highly qualified available experts. To discover whether a computer system is performing outside its specification, exhaustive testing is necessary together with comparison of specification to performance.

Piggy Backing

Piggy backing occurs when a terminal and individual have been accepted as genuine by the computer system. A hidden computer terminal is connected to the same line through the telephone switching equipment and used when the legitimate user is not using his terminal. The computer system will not be able to differentiate or recognise the two terminals.

Impersonation has very much the same effect as piggy backing but usually a second terminal is not employed nor are the lines tapped. Physical access to computers or computer terminals and electronic access is all that is required.

Potential perpetrators might be almost anybody and methods of detection could only be by examination of journals and logs and the use of specialised programs that analyse characteristics of on-line computer user accesses.

Scavenging

Scavenging is a matter of obtaining information on a system after the event. This might involve collecting discarded computer listings or carbon paper from multi part forms. Electronically, this occurs when data or programs that were due to be overwritten have not been eliminated or when the operating system has not properly erased buffer storage areas used for temporary storage purposes. Thus it is possible for the scavenger to read the entire storage area before he himself overwrites it.

The detection of scavenging usually occurs as a result of discovering suspected crimes involving information that may have come from a computer system or computer media. Usually, the information has been obtained from manual scavenging rather than electronic scavenging. Once a shredding policy has been adopted and all documents are shredded before being dumped then it only remains to ensure that scratched discs and unwanted development areas are always overwritten before being passed to anyone else for use.

Data Diddling

This is always the simplest and most common method used in computer related crime. It involves the changing of data before or during the time it is being input to the system. It can be effected by almost anybody who has access to source data files or is involved in the process of creating, encoding, checking or converting data that would go into the computer.

The potential perpetrators would be data preparation clerks, user departments that provide source data, computer operators or indeed anyone who has access to the raw data in its information flow. The ways of detecting have to be data comparison, document validation and integrity tests.

Root Causes

Before investigating one of the more complex frauds that have been described it is as well to discover whether the circumstances which contribute to fraud actually exist. In fact, the water of the computing department should be tested periodically to ensure that root causes, which will culminate in fraud, do not exist.

There are seven main areas which permit the perpetration of fraud. In any installation if five of these areas are obvious then a question mark should be placed against the security of the present system. Even evidence of weakness in one or two of them should be cause for concern and remedial action. The seven areas are:

a. Segregation of duties
b. Alterations to programs
c. Overtime
d. Salary structures
e. Operations management
f. Documentation
g. Data control.

a. Segregation of Duties

It goes without saying that there should be segregation of duties between operators and programmers. On large systems it is important that operators do not run the same files day in and day out. It is imperative, therefore, that rotating duties be performed to prevent any operator dominating a particular file.

Source programs and listings should not be made available to operators and there should always be a casual check on the programming ability of the operations staff. When it becomes clear that they have such skills they should be moved to another department.

Wherever practicable, when overtime is worked, at least two operators should be on duty at any one time or an operator and a member of management staff.

With modern mini computers, programmers and analysts tend to run and test their own programs and files on their own visual display units. In this situation programs and jobs must be clearly and definitely segregated and the auditors appraised of all program alterations and changes. To counter security threats during program testing the following should be followed:

a.   Sign out verification procedures for real live test data.

b.   Controlled or simulated testing of security routines and tables.

c.   Rigid program update procedures.

d.   Control of manual files when conversion to computer environment is involved.

The biggest security problem resulting from program testing is that security may be breached at some time during this procedure. However, with many computers, it is possible for the analyst or programmer to build in his fraudulent "loop" to be triggered at a later date ("The Trojan Horse Technique"). If a triggering is dependent on a time factor the device becomes known as a "Time Bomb". Similarly a device for gaining unauthorised access to restricted areas of the computer's memory is known as "The Trapdoor". The latter type of fraud is usually not committed through an absence of segregated duties, but rather through Operating System controls which are discussed in a separate section.

In summary, segregation of duties amongst all members of the organisation must be clearly defined and rigorously applied. If duties and responsibilities are sufficiently divided the chances for collusion and embezzlement to occur are minimised. It is important that no single group has full responsibility for the protection of the computer system.

An illustration of this type of breakdown is that of a director of a brokerage house who used his position to get access to the computers after hours and at weekends, there being little effective control over his actions in this area. He embezzled an identified #100,000 over a period of time by punching fraudulent input cards and having them processed together with the regular input data.

b. Alterations to Programs

Programming languages are relatively easy to learn. Once they are learnt other members of staff beside programmers can patch or suppress printing, or write new programs etc. A separate section discusses the control of program alterations. However, auditors must take strong and responsible action in developing standards for their clients or their own organisations to ensure that the threshold for this type of crime is so high as to be not worthwhile. Control documentation must be in existence. Alterations to programs must be a difficult procedure and access to source documentation must be lengthy and time consuming.Auditors should always be kept advised of all the modifications so that they can be validated during spot audits which should include Parallel

Simulation. Under Parallel Simulation duplicate live transaction data would be run through a standard and duplicate application program, the output being compared with the same data from the standard program. This will detect program manipulation and unrecorded changes.

Documentation covering program modification should begin at the library, extend to user departments and involve senior management. Back up copies of programs should be securely held in an outside installation and should be held in such a way that descriptions, block diagrams and source statement listings are available on issue only on senior management authorisation.

When copies of program modifications are sent to auditors or to internal auditors it is important that the auditor be seen to check and verify the alterations that have been made.

c. Overtime

Overtime in the computer room or on program development always presents the opportunity for fraud. During unsociable hours most laid down procedures are waived in the interests of efficiency with the result that the thief has the freedom, the time and, inevitably, the machinery at his disposal. When pressure of work has produced overtime the more spectacular frauds have come into existence. Dishonest staff have not wasted the opportunity to manipulate files in the hours of freedom during night or weekend working.

Payroll should always be run during the working day as an absolute rule. The secrecy that is implicit in running a sensitive software suite like wages during the lunch hour, is totally fallacious.

If consistent overtime is necessary, extra staff should be employed. If a programming effort must be carried on into the night then management with programming skills should always be present. Auditors, or security personnel, should spot check during this time.

The best precaution is, however, not to work overtime on a computer installation.

d. Salary Structures

Salary structures are all important, since low rates of pay will inevitably ensure the perpetration of fraud. Most companies try to battle with the computer department to hold down the pay levels, arguing that operations managers, chief programmers, assistant managers and data processing managers should not earn more than their own branch or work manager. This of course will always receive a sympathetic Board "aye". Yet a man who feels himself underpaid will become a breeding ground of resentment and if he has access to sensitive files which he can manipulate, will result in theft.

Paying by internal policies should never apply to data processing staff. Payment of management and senior personnel should be based on the average of nationwide earnings. The men themselves will be aware of the correct levels and should be paid accordingly. It must always be kept in mind that data processing personnel are nomadic mercenaries who have a loyalty only to themselves and their disciplines and rarely owe the same level of devotion to their employers.

A useful ploy to persuade data processing staff to take personality tests would be to disguise these as an evaluation procedure for pay increases. With this possibility of increased pay at the end of it most staff members will willingly take them.

e. Operations Management

Operations management in this context must be defined as the implementation of integrity of equipment, programs, people and operating procedures. Physical security would be placed in this latter category.

Controls should be established for the modification of hardware and software and also for the integrity of the hardware and software to be verified after the repair or modification process is complete. Control should also be exercised over programs, data, documentation and contingency plans and to ensure that duplicate copies are kept locked in safes or vaults.

When communication channels are used, procedures should be developed to protect against wire taps and related techniques.

In terms of physical access outsiders should not be permitted in the computer area and maintenance and repair personnel should only be permitted with authorisation. Security must be designed into the system such that NO ONE is able to bypass security procedures, security logs and audit facilities.

Standard operating procedures should include provisions for:

a.   maintaining logs that record the running of sensitive jobs;

b.   manual and automatic restart and recovery procedures for hardware and software failures;

c.   the physical transportation of sensitive data, including core dumps and file maps.

d.   restrictions in the use of stand alone programs that bypass the security controls of the system and operations management approval of the level of authorisation to access files and the ability of the authorised individual to manipulated these files.

To assess the level of controls in most organisations it is first of all necessary to inspect the documentation; if this has been slackly maintained then control is weak. If no formal authorisation is necessary to modify existing programs or data files then control is probably absent altogether. In distributive systems if satellite devices join the processor without record or have unlimited access to files then management must be regarded with the deepest of suspicions.

f. Documentation

Computer programmers and analysts are creative individuals who turn their minds eagerly to the problem and delight in solving it. Like all creative people they hate the chore of documentation, but documentation is vital to the security of the installation. In small mini computer installations there is invariably no documentation at all and in the larger more professional organisations documentation is often inadequate. The following represent the basic requirements for all installations:

a.   The old manual system is documented.

b.   The system specification is up to date and amendments are clearly visible and readable.

c.   Programs and course listings are available in neat and orderly form.

d.   Operation procedures are fully documented

e.   A full disaster plan exists.

f. Security methodology is documented and available to all staff, telling them the procedures for altering programs, removing discs or tapes from the computer area and gaining access to source listings.

All documentation should be available in duplicate form in a secure location.

The absence of documentation makes life very easy for the computer thief.

g. Data Control

This may be defined as the need to ensure the completeness, accuracy and integrity of prime data as it is processed by the machine, brought to the machine, or taken from the machine; in other words, the data process through the entire computer system taking into account the hardware, software and clerical control procedures. Often there is little or no control in evidence; users access files on a random basis; no record is kept of the access of the files; prints can be called off at any time and no record is kept of these documents. Disc volumes are moved in and out of the computer room or loaded on the machine without computer personnel logging times on and off together with disc volume reference numbers.

Controls must exist to safequard assets and ensure reliability of accounting records. The first step of any organisation in this direction must be the appointment of a Security Manager/Officer. Depending on the size of the installation this may be part time or full time, within the organisation, and may or may not involve auditing functions. The security manager should have overall responsibility for ensuring that data control is 100% secure.

As a basic requirement each system should provide the following:

a. Access Management which will prevent the user from accidentally accessing another users program or data.

b. Processing Restrictions to prevent a user from accidentally addressing into the program space of another user or from executing a privileged instruction that could adversely affect other programs and data that reside in the system.

c. Prevention of Accidental Infiltration in a physical sense by adequate locking devices. Procedures should be such that a person wandering into a computer room should not be exposed to a sensitive print out and similarly controls should be such that sensitive print outs are not delivered to the wrong person.

d. Level of Authorisation and data file protection procedures operating in conjunction with all the above techniques to prevent the user from being accidentally provided access to sensitive programs and data. Correct authorisation and lockable protection will inform the system and the user that restrictions are in operation.

e. Procedures to prevent browsing. Individuals should not be permitted to use time to browse through files on visual display units. Processing restrictions should apply to main storage protection and further to eliminate the possibility of the user accessing a program to gain casual information. Auditing of the system should provide a log of unsuccessful attempts to access files that will identify the browser. The ideal access to files should include pass words or mathlocks accompanied by the individuals security code.

Espionage

All electronic equipment produces electro magnetic fields which may cause interference to radio or television. These emanations can be picked up and monitored, amplified and decoded. This is especially the case with digital equipment and presents a major problem since, from the emanations of computer installations, it is possible to reconstruct the data the equipment is processing.

It was believed for a considerable period of time that eavesdropping on digital equipment could only be performed by professionals with access to very sophisticated detection and decoding equipment. This unfortunately, is no longer the case and eavesdropping of a video display unit can be achieved with a modified TV Broadcast Receiver.

The signal that is received by a TV receiver monitoring a VDU will not contain the synchronisation information. The quality of reception can be improved by externally generating the necessary synchronisation signals and feeding them into the TV receiver. The cost of this equipment is approximately £15. With this equipment any VDU can be eavesdropped providing the radiation level is sufficiently high. Eavesdropping on a VDU is possible at several hundred yards distance, using a normal black and white TV receiver, a directional antennae and a signal amplifier.

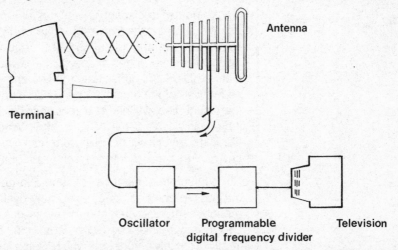

Terminal · Antenna · Oscillator · Programmable digital frequency divider · Television

It has been variously argued that the problem can be solved by using types of VDUs with synchronisation frequencies outside the normal television range. However, the would be spy who is determined to copy the VDU screen has many ways of adjusting the synchronisation frequencies at very low cost.

The easiest and cheapest way of reconstructing the synchronisation in the TV receiver is the use of a device containing two oscillators:

a.   One adjustable oscillator for the frequency range 15 to 20 kHz to generate the horizontal synchronisation signal.

b.   One adjustable oscillator of the frequency range 40 to 80 Hz to generate the vertical synchronisation signal.

Both signals are then combined into the synchronisation separator of the TV receiver. It is slightly difficult to adjust both oscillators to the VDU synchronisation frequency but it can be achieved.

An antenna can be mounted on top of a van and equipment installed inside the van. The van can be parked almost anywhere and since with sophisticated equipment it is possible to pick up transmissions over half a mile away industrial espionage may very well be a real problem. The obvious target for this type of snooping would be the offices of Investment Managers and Merchant Banks responsible for take over bids or stock exchange flotations. Clearing Banks would be another target where encryption keys are transmitted via visual display units.

Solutions

Where extremely sensitive information is being processed, the whole VDU system should be electro magnetically shielded so that no radiation is possible. A metal shield would have to constructed around the visual display unit with all cables entering the shield through glands and part of the screen transparent so the operator can see the screen. There are a vast range of shielding materials that will aid the function described above, these include:

> Gold coated cathode ray tube screens;
>
> Meshed wire nettings placed before the cathode ray screen;
>
> Cable shields for the interconnection of the VDU and the keyboard;
>
> Electric filters to prevent radiation from penetrating cables;

A cryptographic display is another alternative. A basic factor that leads to eavesdropping is the similarity between the VDU and the TV receiver in its image build up. Therefore, a solution is to change the sequence in which the successive display lines are written on the screen of the VDU. The TV receiver expects the picture build up to start at the top line and to end at the bottom line in a normal sequence but the digital image build up could be changed to a random one on the Visual Display Unit. The sequence obtained would be dependent on a code key which is fed into the VDU circuitry. When the radiated signal is picked up by the TV receiver it will not be readable. To further protect the installation the code key can be made to change semi-randomly after a specific time interval.

Another solution might be to place a large number of VDUs in one room thus making pin point accuracy extremely difficult. However, VDUs have different resonance frequencies and it may be possible to isolate a single VDU from a considerable distance. Sound common sense can be applied by not using a family of digital components which switch faster than necessary for the operation of the circuits. This limits the high cut off frequency of the radiated spectral intensity. In addition, the radiating area of any electric circuit loop should be made as small as possible and inter connecting leads should be kept as short as possible.

Emission monitoring will be the growth computer crime in this decade and will take over from wire tapping. The advantage of having a mobile TV receiver is obvious. It will be necessary for Security Officers to be cognisant of this fact and also of the relatively low cost of protective measures that are generally available.

Extortion

Terrorist attacks on computer installations can be of a destructive physical nature, an attack on data or an attempt at extortion. Terrorist organisations, like any others, need to be funded and one way of acheiving this is by coercion of company employees.

This type of fraud will generally benefit an outside organisation and it may be that a customer always receives a preferential discount of 99%, pays his bills promptly and settles the account with a completed audit trail. Alternatively, an organisation could receive numerous high value credit notes generated by falsified documentation.

This type of crime will be the most difficult to discover since the individual who has occasioned it will be protected or eliminated by the group that he is financing. He is unlikely to be a financial beneficiary of the embezzlement.

Computer Blackmail

A new crime is computer blackmail. In the USA an Organisation manufacturing armaments for the Defence Department was held to ransom by an outside organisation that had implanted a Virus in their software. The difficulty of eliminating a Virus was borne out by the fact that the organisation, are very well known computer consultants, could not eliminate the virus. Since they were involved in government work, and the system had been penetrated by an outside organisation, this was bound to cost them governmental confidence. In the final analysis they had to pay to have the virus removed.

Home Office statistics show a growth in the number of cases of blackmail. This is certainly made possible by the growth of information processing which facilitates the holding and manipulation of personnel records. The Data Protection Act has been brought in to try and protect the individual but where security controls are weak, unauthorised access is always possible. With conventional blackmail, the blackmailer is usually known to his target. With computerised blackmail he can be totally anonymous and, as a result, will in the next decade become an accepted part of criminal life.

Hackers

The basic characteristics of a successful hacker are determination, alertness, opportunism, analytical ability and the equipment necessary to penetrate someone else's system. Hackers fall into four categories as the illustration below shows:

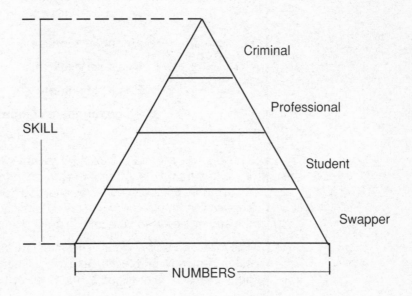

A Swapper may start with a Sinclair or a ZX81, both of which are cheap, plus an acoustic coupler and this is usually sufficient to get the innocent started on a career of computer crime. Later he might aspire to an IBM PC with hard disc for speed.

IBM now offer packages that will integrate the PC and mainframe into one huge set of systems. It follows that the increased power will work to the more sophisticated hacker's advantage. Products are becoming available in plug-in board form which will support a variety of key synchronous communications, for example 327x. They will also handle high speed file transfers in CICS, TSO and CMS.

Other cards can handle the smaller IBM minis. This type of equipment is expensive, costing anything from £6-7000 and is strictly for the experienced and very "professional" hacker who is turning to fraud. However, the increasing use of remote workstations will mean more and more remote attacks.

Recently Prince Philip was embarrassed by the penetration of his Prestel System. TRW, far more sinisterly, were penetrated on a computer system that held the credit ratings of 44 million people and whether the attack was for gain is still not known. It is almost certain that this attack was criminally backed.

The world wide network of Computer Sciences was penetrated, NASA has been penetrated, and recently an American boy was charged with hacking the computer of the USA Congress.

ATM have always been a target and recently were cheated by users decrementing the amount the machine had refused to give them in lots of £5 and when the figure was low enough they cancelled the last transaction and the machine paid the full amount. This has since been corrected.

Accepting the skills of these young men and their growing numbers, what are likely targets? Generally for the experienced hackers the following are thought of as fair targets:

Credit worthiness companies;

Credit agencies;

University facilities;

Banks;

Financial services;

News services;

Electronic mail;

All government computers.

The US Navy found a winking eye in its secret computer system. The eye appeared from time to time, winked and then disappeared. No damage was done but the computer had to be shut down and the implanted patch found. The cost was enormous but worse, after it was thought to have been eliminated and the system powered up again, the eye reappeared!

The message is very clear. This threat will continue to grow and will cost large sums of money. Protection is essential before an attack takes place and the protection can be provided by the Security Officer.

Industrial Action

A recent strike within the DHSS was concentrated on the computer department. The effect was one of public embarrassment and heavy costs at the end of the day. The white collar unions are aware of the serious damage they can cause by bringing only the computer department out on strike; the company cannot function, it must continue to pay the rest of its staff and the union need only give strike pay to a minority.

It may not only be the computer department going on strike that can destroy business flow. A strike by telephone engineers could have the same effect, perhaps not immediately, but once equipment breaks down and needs repairs.

The Contingency Plan must allow for this eventuality. The first precaution would be to employ non-union data processing staff only. The second precaution would be to have a back-up site where processing can continue in the event of a strike using outside contract labour. This illustrates the need for first class documentation so that outsiders can carry on processing with a minimum learning curve. Secrecy would be of the essence and the Security Officer should be the principal custodian of the plan to preclude sabotage.

Micro computers should be brought into the company's strategy to process information at the user's workplace. There may be problems associated with this policy but at the end of the day it will make life easier for the company when there is a strike if critical documents, for example invoices and statements, can be produced without delay.

Success in this situation can only be achieved by thinking and planning ahead

Summary

Modern computer crimes are becoming more and more sophisticated. If the Security Officer has sound security thresholds in place he has discharged to the best of his ability his employers interests. To discover the specialised fraud where there is no recognisable individual beneficiary will certainly require outside help, as will attack via a Trojan Horse mechanism. Knowing who to go to get the best results will be part and parcel of the modern Security Officer's armoury. Consequently, no questions are offered the for the Security Officer's use at the end of this section.

Database

2

All too often security consultant's reports begin with the statement on the data base:

" No policy of formal data classification exists and no value has been put on the constituent parts, making it impossible to use security risk management methods to define appropriate security measures."

The data base is often an organisation's prime asset. This is rarely appreciated by senior management who seldom have any idea of the financial value of the data base, in terms of investment already made in its creation, or the consequential cost to the organisation if the data base were completely lost in a disaster. Perhaps, because of this, data bases are not protected in the manner which they deserve.

All logical security must begin at the data base.

Should there prove to be inadequate security for a data base it can result in unauthorised modification of data, disclosure of the contents, even destruction of data and the possible denial of the facility. Any one of these threats might disrupt the continuing well being of the organisation. It follows that if data can be modified or disclosed then the risk of fraud is extremely high.

Establishing an effective policy to protect the data base is a multi-faceted operation involving senior management, users, computing management and the Security Officer. Data base security considerations must be part of the systems life cycle methodology. Security measures should never be added as an after thought but should be planned from the operational requirements stage and implemented at the beginning of the development phase.

Data Ownership

The beginning of security is with the definition of data ownership. Without a policy or definition of data ownership it follows that rules cannot be effectively established detailing how each item of data may be used and the extent and type of protection required.

In real life the owner of the data is the organisation. However, in terms of accountability, the responsibility for data lies with the individual who will be required to explain a major penetration of the data base caused by weakness of the protective methods. In reality there is a delegation of responsibility in this respect. As a result individuals in an organisation can be Data Owners without actually knowing it.

The Data Owner has the responsibility of defining how sensitive his data is and by whom it should be accessed and updated. The level of sensitivity which he defines will automatically define the level of protection the computer system should contain. Therefore, the Owner will provide a base from which rules can be established for delegating the responsibility for data and establishing the security standards.

Often, a Guardian is spoken of in terms of data. Generally, he is defined as being responsible for the accuracy of the data and the issuing of licenses for data usage. His responsibility extends upwards to the Owner of the data. In terms of security this is an over-refinement and often results in access and definition of sensitivity being ignored as someone else's responsibility.

In general, the Owner will specify the requirement for data protection and the Guardian must satisfy the Owner that he is capable of implementing security measures which are cost effective and efficient. Thus the Guardian becomes accountable for the security of the data in his charge.

The Owner will specify which users may access his data. He thus issues a license. The license specifies which items the licensee may access and the conditions under which they can be used. The Licensee is the person or group authorised to use data according to the Owner specified licence. His or their activities are limited by access control software implementing the conditions and specifications of the license.

Having defined the principles of data ownership it will now be possible to move to the next stage of data base security, that of classifying the data held in the data base.

Data Classification

The number of levels required in a classification system will depend upon the data being processed. For illustrative purposes, a very sensitive environment may very well require four levels of classification and these might be defined as follows:

a.   **Level One** - highly sensitive data requiring special protection measures. Access to data at this level can only be allowed when specifically authorised by the Owner. Generally, this will be top secret information, the disclosure of which would cause extremely serious damage to the organisation. For example, Password files, Encryption keys etc.,

b.   **Level Two** - medium sensitive data requiring more than normal protection and would be used when access is to be restricted to specific individuals or sections. Disclosure of Level Two information would cause serious damage to the organisation. For example, personnel data, operating systems utilities, sensitive programs, etc.

c.   **Level Three** - low sensitive data which should not be released without the authorisation of the Guardian. This could be described as confidential information the disclosure of which would be detrimental to the interests of the organisation. This level should be used when access is allowed to all staff with a need to know and would include items such as ledgers, input data controls etc.

d.   **Level Four** - would include non-sensitive data and would have no access restrictions. In other words the information used lies in the public domain.

   However, care must be taken to ensure that the combination of various items of Level Four data does not increase the level of sensitivity.

It must be stated that the four levels of classification described above will rarely be implemented as most organisations can generally classify their data in two levels:

a.   Data which must be protected at all costs to ensure the continuing well being of the organisation.

b.   Data which is sensitive but not vital to the well being of the organisation.

To determine the classification of data it is necessary for a review to be conducted of the data in the data base. This review should take the form of analysing the impact that disclosure or denial of the data would have on the organisation to determine the classification into which the data falls.

Having done this it is then possible to determine the type and nature of controls that should be implemented.

Security Controls

Once the possible levels of sensitivity have been defined it becomes necessary to specify the minimum security control requirements for each level. The following represents a general overview and example:

Classification Level Four (Non-Sensitive Data)

This is data that falls into the public domain, knowledge of which will not dramatically effect the organisation.

    a.   Access controls. Generally, none required.

    b.   Input data controls. Data that is manually input should be validated and checked for consistency.

    c.   Output control**s**. None required.

    d.   Communication controls. None required.

Classification Level Three (Low Sensitivity Data)

At this level are items of data the disclosure of which would be detrimental to the well being of the organisation. The data is not restricted, but it should not be readily available to personnel of the organisation. An example of this would be supplier identity, value of an account etc.

Non-sensitive programs, that is programs that do not handle financial transactions or update important financial data base information, would also be defined at this level.

    a.   Access controls. Each user of the computer system would be identified to that system by unique user identification. This need not be secret but would serve mainly to identify whether the individual has a right to use that terminal.

    b.   Input data control. As level four.

    c.   Output controls. Identity of the recipient should be printed on relevant output reports.

    d.   Communication controls. As level four.

Classification Level Two (Medium Sensitivity Data)

This is data which if it were revealed would cause serious damage to the organisation. The first type of information would be personnel data which is covered by the Data Protection Act disclosure of which might result in legal action against the responsible director. Additionally, sensitive programs and utilities would fall into this section as would financial data and confidential data.

    a.   Access controls. These will include those specified for levels three and four plus the following:

        i.   Password control. Each user of the system will have an individual and unique password which would define his rights of access to a specific area of the system and access rights to specific areas of data (that is read only, read and write, write only, access to particular data items, records, sub schemas etc.)

        ii.   An individual terminal would be restricted to accessing specific areas of the system.

  iii. Terminals would be equipped with key locks and strict security procedures maintained over these keys.

  iv. Physical access to terminals should be restricted.

 b. Input data controls. These should include those specified for lower levels plus:

  i. For financial transactions responsibility for input should be shared; possibly by a system of confirmation to the system by someone other than the person who originally entered the data.

  ii. Record counts, hash totals and financial totals should be used as a means of control.

  iii. An audit trail of all input transactions should be used which will of course, contain the user identification and the terminal at which the data was entered.

  iv. Check digits should be in use for sensitive static data, such as client number, account number etc.

 c. Output data controls. These will include controls for lower level data plus:

  i. Sensitive reports should be securely hand delivered to the recipients.

  ii. The policy should be in place to shred documentation at the end of retention periods.

 d. Communication controls. Data being transmitted should be protected by encryption or authentication. An authentication feature would have the advantage of highlighting tampering by third parties.

Classification Level One (Highly Sensitive Data)

As such, requiring special protection measures.

 a. Access controls. All access controls defined for lower level data would apply plus the following:

  User identification and password entry plus additional verification such as tokens or personal information. For example, a randomly selected personal question and answer session. For very sensitive information a 'one off' password could be used and then destroyed.

 b. Input data controls. Data items should be validated and consistency checked on entry to the system and when ever any program access those data items.

 c. Output data controls. Controls for lower levels would apply to level one data plus:

  i. Printed outputs should be marked as 'confidential' and hand delivered to recipients who should sign a receipt. These should be in sealed envelopes marked "to be opened by ...... or authorised deputy."

  ii. At the end of a document retention period it should be disposed of by first shredding and then chemical disposal or burning.

 d. Communication controls. All Level One data transmitted over communication lines should be encrypted and authenticated.

Security can now move out from the data base. Thus programming changes on code that access highly sensitive data will have different and more rigorous standards than code that access data in the public domain. Similarly terminals accessing highly sensitive data will have greater physical security than those accessing less sensitive information, and so on.

Another important consideration with data bases of all types is recovery when they get out of step, or when incorrect data is input or the power fails.

Recovery Issues

Data base management systems (DBMS) work with the operating system to protect the data base from hardware and software failure. Manufacturers provide sets of recovery tools but even possession of a comprehensive set of recovery tools will not in itself provide data base security. There are many other areas that will need to be examined before it can be said that an acceptable recovery system exists.

Recovery Software. The extent to which recovery software can be trusted will depend completely on the vendors reputation. Despite the efficacy of the software or the hardware design it will be necessary to involve a software specialist in each recovery situation and job descriptions should be ear marked with this function.

Recovery Data. It is good practice to maintain duplicate copies of all dumps and journals. These should be retained as long as possible. The constraints that will affect retention are, of course, cost and available space. Each organisation must make its own decision in this respect.

It is important to check that the recovery data produced can be used and that creeping corruption is not present. In most cases a simple read can be used when creating a second copy. Naturally an integrity test should be made on the data base before it is dumped. Special integrity checks should also be utilised where software is used to compact journals in order to reduce space requirements.

Three questions that must be answered by the systems security officer are:

How many copies of the data base is it economic to maintain?

What length of time can they be retained?

What methods do you use to ensure they are not corrupt?

Other problems need to be considered in the administration of security with a data base. For example, the length of time it takes to create a security dump. This may mean to effect a dump other procedures have to be implemented and probably more complex software bought in. Clearly, in this situation it is possible to have a complete disaster in a recovery situation purely by the knock on effect. The number of tapes, discs and cartridges which are necessary to provide back up also needs to be considered. To reduce costs the retention period is often reduced. This may mean that all or part of the data may not be recoverable. The length of time it takes to carry out an integrity checking process on the data base may mean that the job is either skimped or ignored. The danger is that corruption may occur and remain undetected for the period of time between integrity checks. In the final analysis the data may be so corrupt that it would be valueless in recovering the data base.

Creeping Corruption

Application programs and systems software may corrupt the data base. This will always be unintentional and often not discovered in its infancy. Clearly, this may result in gradual degradation of the contents. A similar problem can occur with duplexed data bases. These are used to improve reliability but it is possible for the two plexes to get out of step producing conflicting data.

Software can be written to carry out integrity checks. However, it must be borne in mind that this type of software can involve large amounts of memory and time and is probably only practical to write as a background job, usually overnight.

Another threat to the data base is during problem solving events. This always involves systems programmers who for speed and efficiency bypass the normal systems controls. The utilities employed are powerful and, if a mistake is made, it may prove to be disastrous. At this time it is possible to add, delete and modify application code as well as modifying data base indices.

To avoid this situation changes made in problem solving sessions must be subject to change control procedures. All transactions must be logged and the logs duplicated and maintained to provide an audit trail. These should be scrutinised by the systems security officer and data processing management after the event to ensure that no misdemeanour has taken place.

Tapes and discs which fail must be disposed of in a manner that totally destroys the media. It is recommended that degaussing should take place before the media is disposed off. The most secure policy is to incinerate the tapes and to break up hard discs and then incinerate these. An organisation should never return discs to the manufacturer for refurbishment when they have been used on the data base. Since even if they have been degaussed very sensitive equipment can read the disc service and it would take very little to interpret what has been written there.

Users

The modern trend is for users to have powerful microcomputers which can spin off part of the data base, process it and then return it to the data base. The effect in terms of corruption could be horrendous. The only way to deal with this situation is to create independent files for these users from the main data base and still subject them to data sensitivity rules.

There is also a danger of the data becoming out of date because a user holds it on his micro computer and returns it to the system at a much later date than would have been the case in a pure data processing environment. With this system data from a number of sources may be combined in a way which changes the nature of the data base since the moves have not been anticipated. There is also the real danger that data spun off to micro computers can be copied onto a micro computer and then taken home for further processing on a personal computer.

The systems security officer will need to define procedures to prevent all these eventualities which are necessary to ensure the data base should not be corrupted.

Questionnaire

1. What is the financial value of the data base to the organisation?

2. Is there a corporate awareness of the data base as a major asset?

3. Does the organisation have a policy for managing data in an organised way?

4. What measures are taken to protect sensitive data?

5. Is there a scheme for assessing and ranking the sensitivity of data and the data base?

6. What policies exist to prevent the aggregation of insensitive data to produce highly sensitive information?

7. If sub-contractors are employed are they carefully vetted, and subject to controls which only allow them to be involved in certain types of work? Are they also required to work to the organisation's standards?

8. Are checks made on the methods that programmers use to access the data base?

9. Are dumps for the data base and journals properly secured by holding two or more copies?

10. What procedures are in place for checking that recovery data can actually be used?

11. How long are copies retained for recovery of the data base?

12. Is there a defined policy for data retention? Does it take into account business requirements? Or operational requirements?

13. Is there a policy for controlling the import and export of data to and from micro computers?

14. Is there a programmable access to Data Dictionary data? Can it be disabled?

15. Is an audit trail of Data Dictionary System modification kept?

16. Will the Data Base Management System allow the Administrator to control access to the data at:

        a) program level?

        b) level of the programmers local view of the data base?

        c) record level for retrieval and update?

Programming Practices

3

Creating the data base or operating system or indeed any application program is a very expensive undertaking. Unauthorised modification, deletions or destruction of contents or codes can result in major problems. Few companies or computer departments take this into account since meeting deadlines is always the priority for the company and the goal on which the computer department is judged. Security is seen as a delaying nuisance.

Programming practices must be in place at the beginning of any project. The level of detailed control required will depend on the level of sensitivity of data that these programs will access. However, irrespective of the criticality of the program, all actions must be fully accountable.

The key to success in this area is the employment of a proven structured design methodology. Programming practices that are based on the best software engineering and control methodologies are vital to security since programming errors are a common cause of serious losses.

At the very outset it is necessary to identify sensitive data and the programs that will interact with the sensitive data. If the classification is of the highest then the Systems Security Officer should designate the program as "sensitive" and the program specification should be marked as such. Procedures must be defined which must be adhered to throughout the life of the program or until the classification of the program is changed by the Systems Security Officer.

As a matter of course the name of the original author of the program should be part of the embedded source code documentation. After each routine has been coded, or on completion of coding of the program, a walk through of the code should be performed by the responsible programmer with another programmer of equal or greater ability. The results will verify not only that the code does not contain any security errors but also that:

    a.   it satisfies all design specifications;

    b.   it is efficient;

    c.   it is easily maintainable.

It is important that the reviewer should understand completely the purpose of the code and what is expected of the code from a user stand point. This is the most effective technique for preventing a programmer making fraudulent modifications to the code.

Generally the procedure should follow the following routine:

The following diagram represents the simplest method of ensuring that all development or patch work holds the programmer accountable for his actions. It also ensures that Users do not request frivolous changes to existing programs or irresponsibly request new application programs since they will be held financially accountable.

Departmental Responsibility	Action	Auditable Record
User	Document requirements	Yes
User	Cost	Yes
User and Computer Committee	Priorities	Yes
Internal Audit	Check for security implications	Yes
Computer	Allocate programmers	Yes
Computer	Request listings (if program already exists)	Yes
Computer	Request copy program (if program already exists)	Yes
Computer	Write Program	Yes
Computer	Test program and sign off	Yes
Computer	Peer audit	Yes
User	Test and sign off	Yes
Computer	Take image of program and store for future comparisons	Yes
Computer	Take into library	Yes
User	Verify cost justification	Yes

Program Peer Audits and Test Results should be checked as correct by another programmer(s) of equivalent or better standard. Prior to system testing the Systems Security Officer should check the program code. Also, during systems testing, the Systems Security Officer will test all security features and controls in the program and will check all test results.

As a matter of course, if a sensitive program is processing confidential data, then the program should clear data areas after use of the data and prior to the programs termination. Ideally the relevant areas should be filled with zeros to prevent browsing.

Documentation of Security Related Code

Program documentation is needed during any software development and especially when patches or changes are being made. Security related modules or sections of codes must be clearly identified and completely documented. The following are the elements of security related code:

a. Code that implements security related controls

b. Code that performs critical processing

c. Code that has access to critical or sensitive data during its execution.

Program Changes

All user requested changes or error correction changes should be checked by the Systems Security Officer to ensure that they do not violate security controls. Each source code update should be uniquely identified and that identification should include the name of the programmer coding the update.

When a code change is made, as already described, the Systems Security Officer should check it prior to testing. The analyst/project leader should certify as correct system test results. These should be checked by the Systems Security Officer to ensure validity. Prior to going live the code should be checked and, if correct, authorised under signature to be transferred to the Live Program Library.

Program Libraries

The Program Library will catalogue the control access to all versions of program modules as they are being developed. Under normal conditions there should be no sensitive program source code in a development library once the program is live. Where it is necessary to make authorised code changes to a sensitive program the Systems Security Officer should copy the live source code to the development library and authorise access to the program by a programmer.

The program library can provide the following types of security controls during the programming stage:

a. Permit only authorised persons to access program modules

b. Record all access to program modules

c. Associate control data with program modules to facilitate detection of changes

d. Enable comparison of current versions of modules with previous versions to identify code that has been changed.

Program Development Tools

Program development tools can help to increase the reliability and correctness of the final product. For example, preprocessors; a preprocessor accepts programs written in an improved dialect of a language and translates them into the language. Preprocessors can be used to eliminate some of the more restrictive conditions in an existing language and provide automated quality control by checking that program modules meet the coding standards of the project.

Testing Procedure

It is important to ensure that unauthorised code is not introduced into the system with the separation of units and system testing. Programmers should be responsible for unit testing where the size of the unit can be as large as a transaction or a batch program. After this it should be passed into a library controlled by the independent body normally referred to as Configuration Management. This body or group is responsible for the integrity of all source and object code which has been formally approved. Programmers will only have access to this code after it has entered the library and, when changes are made, must formally hand over any altered source code.

A separate group of people will be responsible for testing the system. This group will ensure the system is:

> reliable
>
> meets the specifications
>
> meets the requirements of the user.

Thorough evaluation will improve systems security by uncovering errors, omissions and other flaws in the applications systems design and code. Security requirements are usually stated in terms of events which must not occur under any circumstances. Full proof of correctness requires that very general and even even negative requirements are evaluated.

Test Plan

A test plan should be in position which will describe what is to be tested and what methods and tools will be needed. These tests will identify the system's response to abnormal, unusual, improbable and illegal circumstances. There are three possible types of static evaluation:

> **Code review**
>
> **Penetration studies**
>
> **Source code analysers.**

With **Code Review** portions of the source code are evaluated to determine if they implement the design specification and are free from errors. The entire system code cannot be reviewed for very obvious practical reasons, for generally samples of the code will be reviewed and especially if critical modules or critical portions exist. The code review can be done by an entire test and valuation team involved in development or by an independent third party team. Code review differs from peer review in that code review is performed by individuals who were not involved in the design and programming of the application.

Penetration studies are conducted by a group of individuals who try to find unknown weaknesses in the security controls. However, the failure of a penetration study does not demonstrate that the application is secure nor does success mean that the application is totally insecure in any practical sense and therefore the results have to be weighed with great care.

Source code analysers aid the evaluation process by providing details of the specific characteristics of source programs. They cross reference listings and identify suspicious variables and source statement references. They will also identify variables which can influence control decisions and variables which could be read before any value has been assigned to them can be identified.

Dynamic testing is another form of review. It breaks down into two basic forms:

> **Program analysers**
>
> **Flaw hypothesis.**

The **Program Analyser** is a computer program that collects data about another program's operation while it is executing. For example, the Analyser can determine whether test inputs have caused all the program statements to be executed and maintain a record of the number of times each statement of a program has been executed.

The **Flaw Hypothesis** method is based on analogous flaws found in other systems and then tested for existence on the current system. This is an effective approach for selecting test cases to see if any security flaws exist.

It goes without saying that all test groups should be completely separated from the individuals who build the system. The necessary code should be delivered to them in object form by the Configuration Management Section. Ideally this code will be compiled from the Configuration Management libraries.

Test data should be as realistic as possible. It is quite common, therefore, to use live data for this purpose. Unfortunately, this creates confusion when discs are compared at later dates. It also introduces a significant risk of data being inadvertently disclosed. To obviate the threat careful control of the media must be implemented and all redundant output documents should be shredded.

Third Party Software

This represents a significant problem for the data processing department. Often, insurance companies will not offer cover against third party developed software. It is, therefore, imperative that the following steps should be followed:

a.   Validate the design;

b.   Review the code;

c.   Ensure that no unauthorised code exists;

d.   Subject the code to in-house rigorous program tests;

e.   Ensure that it is easy to maintain.

The testing procedures described above, if applied to external software will validate it as closely as in-house developed software.

Designing Security

The design stage is the point in time when decisions are made regarding individual verification, use of tokens, use of encryption, etc. However, security designing is not just a case of adding controls to a system design. It is not necessary for every design decision to take the most secure approach. There will be alternative ways to make adequate levels of security and these should all be backed by detailed risk analysis. This must be performed at the beginning of the design phase so that it can be ensured that appropriate cost effective controls are integrated into the systems design.

Unnecessary Programming

Terminals should be interfaced with the application system so as to minimise the danger that users can get unneeded program capability. The fall back is always that operating systems will prevent this; however, users who have the potential to execute their own programs can, as a rule, bypass any security control. The track inserted almost anywhere in the code of the application or the operating system and triggered by some designated event could cause data entered from the terminal to be executed as a program. The effectiveness of the control depends upon the integrity of the program developers who might have had an opportunity to embed traps in the code.

Restricted User Interface

The greatest danger occurs when users are given unnecessary access to general purpose programming language. In this instance, it would be very difficult to analyse on a "risk management" basis, the possible ramifications. Once the users actual needs are understood interfaces should be designed to meet these needs as simply as possible with no unnecessary capabilities to complicate things both for the users and for the analyst. Interfaces must be designed so that they are easy to understand and to use. Whilst the task is difficult and deserves careful thought it does ensure users will not neglect or bypass controls which they view as cumbersome and annoying.

System responses to the user must be clear and presented in a way that the user will easily understand. Ideally, the user should not be required to enter excess information or repeatedly answer questions.

Isolation of Critical Code

The code and system data that is critical to security should be well identified so that it can be more easily ordered and protected. Security controls should be isolated in modules and have few interactions with the rest of the application software.

If the security related code always resides in a fixed area of memory then special problems arise and it is necessary to examine **disc residue** and **memory residue** as separate subjects.

Disc residue is a problem of data residue on disc and is one of the more insidious of security problems, especially with small computer systems. For example, when a file is erased or deleted the data contained on disc for that file is not actually erased or otherwise deleted; rather a bit set in the directory entry associated with the file. This bit indicates the file spaces available for reuse. The data itself is not over written or affected. Even if part of the file space is reallocated and overwritten, many sectors remain unchanged for long periods of time. Thus, a subsequent user often finds previous file data by simply dumping disc content sector by sector. It is important that with this type of security requirement a sub routine should be written that over writes the area with x's or 0's.

Memory residue presents another problem since the previous content of memory is often available to subsequently running programs or tasks. If sensitive information is being processed at any time it should be cleared before a subsequent task is given control. Indeed, exposure of previous memory contents exist to varying degrees in each of the following situations:

Power Up. Any information in non volatile writeable memory is readable.

System Coldstart. Many systems do not clear memory as part of the coldstart process they simply reload and initialise the operation system and its tables.

System Warmstart. This usually involves reloading only selected parts of the operating system and tables and therefore most of the memory remains unchanged.

Program Initiation. Except for the areas of memory into which the actual program code is loaded the entire portion of memory allocated to program execution is usually unchanged.

Program Termination. Virtually all of memory remains unchanged.

Access to previous contents of memory is easily obtained through the System Debugger or by the use of Peek and Poke Routines. This latter routine simply allows for the beginning and ending address to be specified and to print out. When designing a system great care must be taken in making provision for these types of activities.

Consideration should also be given to safe languages. Comparison of these languages can protect modules and their data from erroneous unauthorised interaction with other modules. Also, hardware protection states or protection domains can protect data critical to security. Even so, without very careful planning all system code and data may very well be relevant to security because errors or deliberate traps elsewhere cause security failure. This other software includes:

the operating system and other software that supports any of the security functions;

all parts of the application system needed to guarantee that the security controls are invoked at the appropriate times;

compilers and software used to maintain any security irrelevant software.

Use of Available Controls

The operating system and facility management may also provide a variety of controls such as:

user identity verification

authorisation for access to system files

journalling of operating system activities

back up and recovery procedures

real time logging

authorisation

hierarchies, components and strata, etc.

Clearly available controls should be used to the fullest extent possible. Other counter measures should be considered and a risk management basis utilised where appropriate. These might include:

    a.   Encryption

    b.   Security packages such as:

        i.   RACF

        ii.   ACF2

        iii.   SECURE

        iv.   TOP SECRET

        v.   PADLOCK

    c.   Audit packages

    d.   Data traps.

Operating System Countermeasures

Operating System Countermeasures include the following;

    a.   Store zeroise

    b.   Memory protection

    c.   Memory segmentation

    d.   Access mediations

    e.   Prohibition of patches

    f.   Plugging channel leaks

    g.   Non monopolising of system resources

Program Flow Analysis

Program flow analysis offers three methods and these are:

    a.   Control flow analysis

    b.   Data flow analysis

    c.   Information flow analysis

The control flow analysis will check that conventions relating to control structure have been respected. Data flow analysis allows the programmer to check that such things as variables are defined before being referenced, or defined and not used. It also involves a consideration of the sequence of events in executing program paths.

Information flow analysis will verify the dependencies of output variables and input variables of procedures and identify the statements whose execution may effect specific output variables. From a set of definitions of information flow relations, the technique forms tables of the said relations which it has found in the program and then carries out a number of tests on these tables to reveal specific kinds of errors such as ineffective statements, ineffective imported values, undefined variables and unstable repetitive statements.

Design Review

The design review is the last reasonable opportunity to identify weak points in the security plan. After this time weak points that are not identified will require costly software modification. Ideally, the entire security plan for the application should be reviewed by a team of experts who have not been part of the early design effort.

Questionnaire

1. Have you developed systems test routines or programs which:

   a. try to read the content of memory outside its assigned area?

   b. check that the bounds limitations for addresses below its address space are handled the same as above its address space?

   c. dynamically get additional memory allocated and read-out of that address space before storing anything into these locations?

   d. check the address bounds are still inviolate after overlay?

   e. determine the address bounds have behaved differently if the entire address is manufactured after execution starts versus if the address constants are stored prior to execution?

   f. are able to dynamically open files during execution which were not declared at log on time?

   g. are able to read from a file before writing to it?

2. Have you exercised the authorisation control system by trying:

   a. to gain access to a safeguard program or file while not on any list?

   b. to use an illegitimate name and an illegitimate password in the attempt to get to a legitimate program or file?

   c. to use an obsolete password the day after it was changed?

3. Have you tried to access files without leaving audit trail records in the security log or accounting file?

4. Have you tried to catalogue a program onto disc that has the same program ID or name as a system module routine or utility?

5. Are your tests designed or directed towards testing in your unique environment:

   a. known loop holes?

   b. local security loop holes?

   c. other local system modifications?

6. Are programmers provided with source data definitions automatically generated from the data dictionary?

7. Are checks made on the methods that programmers use to access the data base?

8. If sub contractors are employed are they:

   a. carefully vetted?

   b. subjected to controls which will only allow them to be involved in certain types of work?

   c. required to work on the installations standards?

9. Are programmers restricted to unit testing?

10. Is there a policy that programmers only hand over source code to the person who will test the code, and that he does not test himself

11. Before the start of systems test, is the application source compiled against the data dictionary?

12. Are master copies of source and object code maintained in an independent library?

13. Is a rigorous systems test performed against a realistically sized data base?

14. Are all new releases of systems software only installed after a validation exercise has been successfully performed against a representative workload?

15. Are patches and fixes subject to a validation exercise before they are applied?

16. Do you accept that a new utility which is designed to run against the data base will work or do you subject it to an exhaustive test?

17. If the application software is developed by outside organisations do you:

    a. insist that it is produced according to your standards?

    b. take part in designer reviews?

    c. have control of the data dictionary and the data base design?

Micro Computers

4

Micro computers present a very special security problem since they are ordered by user departments becoming more and more computer erudite, and are then distributed throughout the organisation. As a result normal physical data processing controls cannot apply. Yet someone must be responsible for security and for producing a simple, concise manual of guide lines which will take the users through the principles of micro computer security.

It is argued that micro computers do not need a complicated security mechanism and that users need only remove and lock away their discs. This concept of a single user micro computer has resulted in a general lack of security awareness which is compounded by the very user friendly software used by these systems. However, most micro computer systems are often too expensive to be used by just one person and are shared among several users, making them even more vulnerable.

User departments buy micros that appear to them to meet their needs. This results in micro computers not being serviced (because the manufacturer has gone out of business), and a proliferation of non standard operating systems and application programs. Security under these circumstances becomes a nightmare.

Micro security should follow the following schematic:

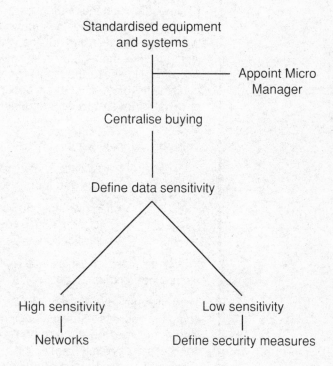

The computer department must take the decision on equipment since only they have the sufficient background and technical knowledge to intelligently standardise on equipment. Once this decision has been taken an analyst should be given the responsibility of analysing the proposed applications into "high" and "low" sensitivity data classifications.

Highly sensitive data should be secured by networking and lesser sensitive data should be put on to stand-alone micros. The Manager will now have to define security measures for these devices but this will be done as a strategy exercise rather than in detail. The following diagram is an illustration of the way that this might be followed:

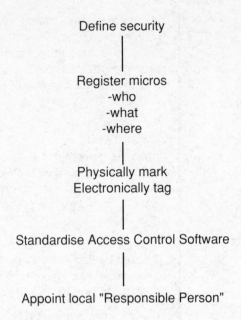

Define security

Register micros
-who
-what
-where

Physically mark
Electronically tag

Standardise Access Control Software

Appoint local "Responsible Person"

It is important that the Manager should draw up a register of all the micros in the organisation. This should state who is principally responsible for the machine, the model, software and application programs in use and where the machine is located. Once the register is in existence it can be maintained, if necessary, by Security. However, the Registrar, whoever this may be, must be advised if a machine is moved. It must become a disciplinary matter if a machine is physically moved or a user acquires new software without advising the Registrar.

This policy serves two purposes:

a.   It facilitates contingency planning as a fall back for network users and for other stand alone micro users.

b.   It allows the Registrar to monitor application programs being bought-in and to see if any user's machine is increasing its data classification.

In large organisations this can be painstaking work but it is a policy that will make a direct contribution to security.

The machines should be physically stencilled with the department's name and company address. Stolen machines thus become less easy to dispose of and less attractive to the sneak thief. As an added precaution the machine and discs can be electronically tagged, in much the same way that large stores tag merchandise, so that their removal sounds an alarm at the door.

Depending on the level of sensitivity, a policy will be in place covering access control and authorisation mechanisms. Products like "Watch Dog" or "PCLock" should be considered, among others that are available. On sensitive data that does not qualify for networking but risk management studies indicate that a higher form of protection is necessary, then "dongles" might be considered, which require a card to activate them and disable the micro once the card is removed.

A local "Responsible Person" should be appointed by the Manager. The Responsible Person will produce the local security manual based on pre-determined policy. He will be responsible for ensuring that security matters are complied with and that machines are not removed from his area without advising the Registrar. All security breaches will be investigated by the Responsible Person and if necessary the Security Manager should be brought in on an advisory basis.

By following this methodology micro users can maintain their autonomy; they can process work where it is generated and also be secure.

Cryptology

The normal manner in which cryptology is used in a micro computer environment is to encrypt and decrypt entire files. In a normal working environment an entire file is presented for encryption. The original file is then overwritten. Before using the file again, the utility program must be used to decrypt and produce a clear text version of the file. Generally speaking, the user is responsible for the key that is used in encryption and decryption. Various software packages are available that will provide for bulk file encryption and decryption as well as utility to overwrite old files.

The problem with cryptology is that of general inconvenience. An alternative is to use a cryptographic facility. With this facility each block of data to be written to disc is first encrypted and also any block read from disc is decrypted before it is passed to the existing program. Thus, the entire process is totally transferred to the user and eliminates the inconvenience and dangers associated with bulk file procedures.

Generally speaking, the Data Encryption Standard (DES) is the cryptographic standard for non classified application. In the UK DES is not used in government or military applications but is generally accepted for commercial applications. The DES is a private key crypto system. DES has undergone extensive critical analysis which has provided a high level of understanding of the level of protection that it provides.

A number of commercial cryptographic products, both private- and public-user systems, use proprietary (secret) cryptographic algorithms and a single integrated chip is available with DES on it.

The following software products are generally available:

      a.   General purpose cryptographic facilities.

      b.   Bulk file encryption utilities. These are programs which enable the user to encrypt or decrypt a specific data file. The user must enter the cryptographic key.

      c.   Integral disc encryption systems. These cause all disc write operations to be encrypted or decrypted, thus eliminating clear text on disc, while not changing the application interface.

      d.   Communications encryption systems.

Validation and Verification

Viruses have become a major problem and especially with micro computers where they can lie dormant for a considerable period of time and then activate once the stand alone micro has been networked or communicates with the mainframe.

It follows that Software should only be bought from reputable suppliers and should be tested by a central group who are skilled in machine architecture, operating systems and assembly language. In other words a Verification and Validation Group.

Only when programs have passed this agency should they be used on the system.

Other more practical steps can be taken which include making employees aware of the potential damage that a virus might cause.

As a normal security feature employees should be prohibited from bringing into the work area outside programs for installation on the business system. This should especially apply to Bulletin Board Software.

Once software is released a master copy should be retained by the Validation and Verification Group and comparisons should be made periodically of known, clean software with existing software. All differences should be thoroughly investigated. Files kept on the system should be reviewed at regular intervals.

Consideration should also be given, after a Risk Management study, of system software that will form cryptographic check sums of files in a computer system in order to allow their integrity to be validated. The program will form cryptographic check sums of files and programs and verify the cryptographic check sums, particularly prior to the execution of a program or the modification of a file.

Similarly, the length of each clean program can be stored and kept for comparison at the time of execution. Differences in size will indicate program modification. If this is cumbersome a test can be made on part of the program.

There can be no doubt that all present computer installations are vulnerable to attack. The situation can be improved by implementing strong personnel procedures coupled with programming and operating procedures.

Local Security

The security policy document should contain notes along the following lines. This will allow the local Responsible Person to modify the notes to suit local needs.

Physical Security

Suggestions might include a simple cover lock or lock down device. This will not prevent a determined thief stealing the equipment, which after all is portable but it will deter him and electronic tagging might facilitate his apprehension. Additionally the equipment will prevent him gaining access to the interior of the equipment without being observed or detected. Sophisticated lock-down devices are available which will protect system security mechanisms and specialist circuit boards.

However, protecting the micro computer from theft and physical damage is not a new problem; it has been necessary to protect office equipment for years. Therefore, it has been argued that physical protection needed for micro computers is the same as other valuable equipment in the work place. This is not the case. Micro computers are the only pieces of office equipment with detailed and logical memory that can be unravelled at will once they are removed.

Generally, micro computers should not be placed in areas which have no physical access controls such as locks on doors or are unoccupied during normal working hours. Where equipment and information is of such value that additional precautions are necessary and the entire area cannot be made secure, the micro computers and their devices can be placed in special work station enclosures which can be closed and locked when the equipment is not in use. It will also provide protection for other items such as documentation, discs and printers.

Micro computers are designed to operate where people work. It is therefore argued if the people are comfortable the micro computer will be comfortable. Despite this, attention should be given to minimising the environmental hazards to which the equipment is exposed.

Power and Atmosphere

Micro computers are sensitive to the quality of power that is available. If there are power surges, spikes, or frequent power loss situations then battery back up, constant voltage units, or uninterrupted power supply systems should be considered. It will always be helpful if micro computers can be placed on separate ring mains, especially if there are welding devices or other high inductive loads on the the power supply.

The temperature and humidity of the average office are usually adequate for a micro computer; however, air contaminants have a much more dramatic effect on a micro computer which like all electronic equipment will naturally attract charged particles in the air. Eliminating contaminants such as smoke and dust will certainly have a beneficial effect on the equipment and magnetic media as well as the people who operate it.

Fire and Flood

Micro computer equipment does not represent any more of a significant fire hazard than does any other item of office equipment. It is normally unnecessary to install extra equipment when micro computers are bought, but it is worthwhile looking at the value of the equipment and information that is processed in a specific area, and then re examining the fire detection and suppression facilities.

Possible water leaks are always a problem and consideration should be given to inexpensive plastic equipment covers. These covers will also provide protection from dust and other air borne contaminants during periods of non-use.

Static electricity may present a problem since this can build up in personnel especially if carpeting made of nylon is used. A discharge occurs when a person touches the micro computer, this discharge may cause damage to integrated circuit components or semi conductor memory. Anti static sprays and carpeting and placing the micros on an insulated mat should rectify the problem.

Magnetic Media Protection

The common micro computer back-up medium is a floppy disc. With a Winchester disc drive, a full file back up may require more than 20 discs. A streamer can be used for incremental back ups where disc copying is too time consuming.

Regardless of the type of back up only high quality media should ever be used. Assurance of successful back up can be achieved by forming file comparisons of original and back up copies. Most micro computer systems provide disc and file comparison utility programs and users should be shown how to use these.

The Responsible Person should give special attention to the protection of magnetic media. These may be discs, tape or cartridges.

Fixed discs, or rigid discs, are usually contained in sealed units that are well protected from environmental constraints. The most important thing to remember with a micro computer with hard discs is that moving it may cause damage to the disc units. The manufacturer's instructions will give detailed information on securing the disc before it is moved.

Every magnetic computer system has at least one "floppy" disc drive. Flexible discs, or floppies, are the most prevalent medium for distributing software and data. With flexible discs the actual magnetic disc is contained within a protective jacket. There are openings in the jacket for access by the read/write heads of the drive mechanism. The exposed surface of these openings presents a major problem. Potential dangers and proper handling techniques for flexible discs should be made known to all users. The following are the main means of protection:

> The disc should be properly stored and protected from bending or similar damage.
>
> Direct contact with magnetic devices should be avoided.
>
> All forms of exposure to contaminants such as smoke, hair, crumbs, coffee, etc. should be avoided.
>
> Do not write directly onto disc jacket or sleeve. Labels should be written before applying.

Most of these precautions are common sense. However, many micro computer users are careless and the Security Officer has the responsibility of providing training and discipline in this area.

In general:

> Beware of magnetism - keep discs away from magnetic sources, but it is worth noting that airport X ray devices pose no danger, despite concern to the contrary;
>
> Avoid touching the shiny exposed surfaces.
>
> Do not jam discs into slots.
>
> Do not use clips to fasten anything to a disc.
>
> Do not use a hard pencil or ball point pen when writing on a sleeve.
>
> If the data is important, copy it.

With the increased use of hard discs, or Winchester drives, there are one or two other precautionary notes which must be added and these are:

> Before shutting the system down, use the PARK program to store the head on the hard disc;
>
> Use an automatic back up system to ensure recovery in case of a crash;
>
> If an automatic back up system is not in use frequent regular back ups and saves should be made;
>
> Always provide a hard disc system with a stand by uninterrupted power supply (or UPS) system for an orderly shut down.

Data Residue

It is a common failing that users inadvertently leave sensitive "residue" on discs or in memory. It follows that this information can be read by subsequent users. Delete commands generally only remove the file header but leave the information unaltered on disc or disc. There are many available software utilities which will then read the discs or discs after the file header has been erased. It is clearly dangerous, therefore, to pass files to other users which are on disc or disc with erased files.

This problem can be easily solved by using an "overwrite" on all file data as part of a deletion process. If such a utility is not available then sensitive disc media should not be shared amongst users.

Electro Magnetic Emanations

All electric equipment emanates electro magnetic signals. In the case of computers the emanations carry information which can be detected by an appropriately placed monitoring devices. Various counter measures exist which are discussed elsewhere (Chapter 2: Modern Attacks).

Identification

In the micro computer environment user identification may be implicit or explicit. Typically, a user establishes authority to use the system simply by being able to turn it on. If such implied identification is to mean anything the system must be a true "personal" system and there must be adequate controls to ensure that only that user can gain access. In a shared system simple identification procedures are inadequate.

User identification must always be authenticated in some manner. Let us assume the system is powered up. The process of application should parallel that of a mainframe. The user will log on by putting in his name or number; he will be asked for a password and perhaps for personal details before being given access to the total machine. This type of authentication is usually accomplished by a program which interrupts the system initialisation process and requires each user to complete a log-on process. "Log on" procedures are commercially available and highly effective.

There is an extreme amount of youthful interest in micro computers and consequently the protective software that is available is highly interesting. CompuLit Incorporated, 562 Croydon Road, Elmont, New York have a specialised package where failure to enter the password correctly or answer any of the prompt questions specifically will result in the execution of an alarm. The screen is automatically filled with the words "You are an illegal user", a bell or buzzer is then sounded for one minute. In some micro computers it is possible to replace the existing buzzer by a small radio speaker which will alert the Security Officer.

Conclusion

A City Investment Manager had vigorous control systems which applied to members of staff. Part of these were that staff members should instruct their stock broker to copy all contract notes to the company secretary. This was an intention to prevent insider dealing and is acceptable in the city.

It was pointed out to the Directors that even their clerks might have two stock brokers dealing for them, one that provides copies for the secretary and one that does not. The Directors responded with a statement that clerks did not have two stock brokers.

In fact the clerks did have two stock brokers. In fact they all dealt with the same stock brokers. They had no way of knowing what their elders and betters might decide in terms of take over bids but they were able to operate micro computers. The secretarial staff who used the micro computers always went to lunch at the same time and were punctual time keepers, always going from noon until 1.00 p.m. The clerks went from 1.00 p.m. until 2.00 p.m. From noon until 1.00 p.m. they sat at the micro computers and called up all the letters that the Senior Partners had written. When they were in doubt they consulted the user manuals that had been provided by the manufacturers and been left by the secretaries beside the word processors. Whenever they were in doubt they were able to refer to the conveniently left books. Indexes, meticulously kept by the secretaries, were also left beside the machines. They were thus able to browse through all the correspondence of the directors. They were able to find the impending take over bids or flotations and recommended prices. They were able to make a very large profit.

It goes without saying micro computers do not in general have the type of hardware and operating support system necessary for sophisticated security and access control. In the example given above rudimentary controls would have prohibited these young men from making large and satisfactory profits. Defence mechanisms are developed by the user or can be acquired initially. It is important, for the Security Officers to determine the type of control actually necessary for a given system rather than arbitrarily installing costly access controls.

More and more micro computers will be used in commerce. Linked micro computers will offer unimaginable power in terms of processing. User friendly systems will make this a fraudster's delight. Security is almost exclusively in the hands of the Security Officer, who with a little imagination is capable of working wonders.

Questionnaire

Micro Strategy

1. What defined strategy exists for micros?

2. Has a policy of standardisation been implemented? What happens if a non-standard machine is bought?

3. Has data being processed by micros been classified?

4. Is a single individual made responsible for micro policies within the organisation?

5. Is a register of hardware and software maintained?

6. Has a validation and verification procedure been adopted for bought-in software?

7   Has security strategy been defined?

8. What policy exists for encryption and authentication?

9. Are micros incorporated into the network security plan?

Micro Strategy

1. What policy is in place to keep equipment free of excessive dust, ashes, smoke and combustibles?

2. Is the equipment covered when it is not in use?

3. Do staff eat, drink and smoke near equipment?

4. Is the micro computer secured to the work surface?

5. Is the unit locked at the end of the day?

6. Is the equipment left unattended when it is operational?

7. Are the spare units located where unauthorised persons can observe the operation?

8. Are passwords shared with others?

9. Are passwords displayed on equipment so that others may see?

10.   Are all sensitive files password protected?

11.   Does the user log off before leaving the terminal?

12.   Do you use sewage suppressers ie. filters on equipment?

13.   Do you use anti static sprays on equipment?

14.   Do you use anti static mats under equipment and operators chairs?

15.   Have you located alternative equipment for use in the event of equipment failure?

16.   How do you store back up copies of discs outside the area and offsite?

17.   Who in your installation loans or borrows back up copies of discs?

18.   What period is required for the cleaning of read/write heads?

19.   Do you cover the machine when it is not in use?

20.   Do you periodically clean the printer of dust and paper particles with a vacuum cleaner?

21.   Do you make a print out of discs direct?

22.   Do you maintain a documentation of all working files?

23.   Is the individual responsible for all work done under his password?

24.   Do you keep the floppy discs in protective envelopes or vinyl sleeves when they are not in the disc drive?

25.   Do you store the disc in an upright position in a dust proof case or box or special plastic sleeve?

26.   Do you use a felt tip pen to write lightly if you must write on the label of the disc?

27.   Do you turn the power off for the micro computer before you insert any discs in the disc drives?

28.   Do you remove all discs before you switch off power from the micro computer?

29. Do you fold or flex a floppy disc?

30. Do you bring a magnet or magnetic object near the disc?

31. Do you use rubber bands to hold several discs together?

32. Do you allow discs to be excessively exposed to direct sunlight or extreme cold or heat?

Ledger Systems

5

An accounting system is made up of records of business transactions, called journals, together with summary information of account balances, called ledgers. The main ledger systems in commercial use are Sales, Purchase and Nominal Ledgers.

Sales Ledgers hold details of the transactions between the organisation and its customers. Purchase Ledgers hold details of transactions between the organisation and suppliers. Both are kept on the basis of individual customer or supplier name and account number. The Nominal or General Ledger reflects current balances in the form of a summary by asset, liability, revenue and expense. Variance from budget values are also itemised in the ledger.

Micro computers lent themselves easily to modelling and then to spread sheets. Until proven networks were extensively used the ledger functions, especially in the larger company, remained confined to minis and mainframes. However, with networks, it is possible to run ledger systems on micros and pass relevant management information to other appropriate individuals on other systems. This is illustrated below.

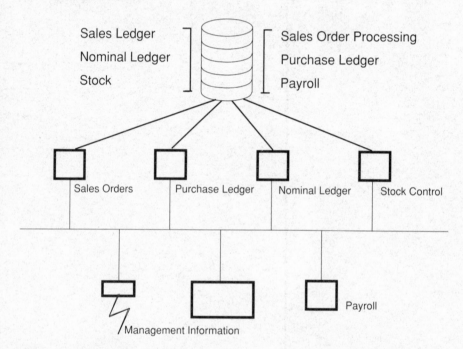

Double-entry book-keeping began in Italy in the 15th century. Three hundred years later the Industrial Revolution provided a stimulus to this method of accounting. This was because industrial expansion required more accurate financial records to assist the decision making process. Expansion in the 20th century, latterly with the aid of computers, brought the double entry system into its own.

Double entry book-keeping largely means that each transaction is divided into two equal parts: a debit entry and a credit entry. When an asset is acquired an appropriate debit is made in an expense account and an offsetting credit entry is made to a liability account. When an asset is sold a credit entry is made to a revenue account and an offsetting debit entry is made to an expense account.

The process begins with the purchase of an asset or the acquisition of an expense or alternatively the sale of an asset or the incurring of a liability. These transactions are then summarised in ledgers and result in a balance sheet showing the degree of profit or loss. At a simplistic level this might be as follows:

```
BALANCE SHEET AS AT (DATE):

ASSETS
Cash                    £20,000    Accounts Payable    £25,000
Accounts Receivable     £40,000    Notes Payable       £10,000
Inventory                £5,000    Taxes               £30,000
Buildings               £85,000    Equity              £85,000
            Total      £150,000              Total    £150,000
```

This type of accounting came into its own with computers, especially as computers are designed to speed up repetitive business transactions. This is accomplished by:

Automatically making entries in daily journals and ledgers - simultaneously.

Eliminating paper flow by eradicating multiple postings.

Reducing human controls to a minimum and applying computerised controls, to verify accuracy and validate data.

Various checks can be applied automatically to data being input to a computerised double-entry system. These include:

Batch totals; totalling all the sums of all the amounts to be entered.

Item counts; the totalling of all items to be entered.

Hash totals; adding all the numbers of a series of transactions.

In all three cases comparisons are made by the machine to pre-entered numbers. For example:

```
            VENDOR NUMBER              VOUCHER AMOUNT
                 1234                      £10,000
                 4321                      £70,000
                 5678                      £20,000
                 8765                      £25,000

Hash Total    19998       Batch Total     £125,000
Item Count 4 (Vouchers Processed)
```

Sales Ledger

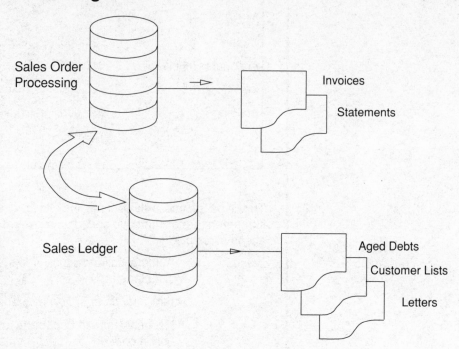

Sales Order Processing

Invoices

Statements

Sales Ledger

Aged Debts

Customer Lists

Letters

ATTACKS

MODIFICATION

Illegal discounts.

False credit ratings.

Aged Debt List Deletions.

Unauthorised Credit Notes.

Inflated sales for company loan purposes.

DISCLOSURE

Customer lists.

Customer payment records.

Customer credit ratings.

Pricing structures.

DESTRUCTION

Deletion of debts.

Deletion of names.

Overwriting files.

Purchase Ledger Attacks

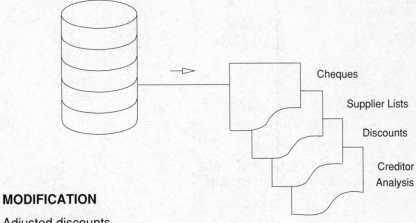

MODIFICATION

Adjusted discounts.

Erroneous creditors

False cheques.

DISCLOSURE

Discounts.

Pricing.

Customer sales.

DENIAL

Overwriting files

Payroll Attacks

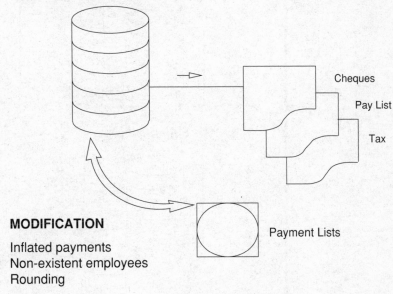

MODIFICATION

Inflated payments
Non-existent employees
Rounding

DISCLOSURE

Pay rates.

DESTRUCTION

Overwriting files

Stock Ledger Attacks

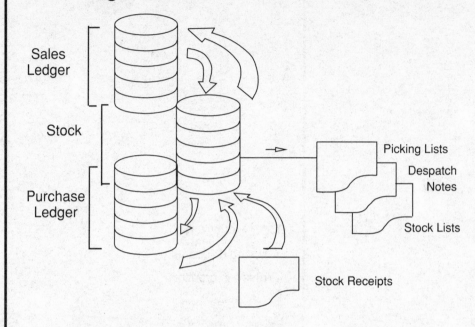

MODIFICATION

Deliveries received.
Stock values.
Write-offs.
Interbranch transfers.
Samples.

DISCLOSURE

Pricing structure.

DESTRUCTION

Over-writing files.
Altering files.

Nominal Ledger Attacks

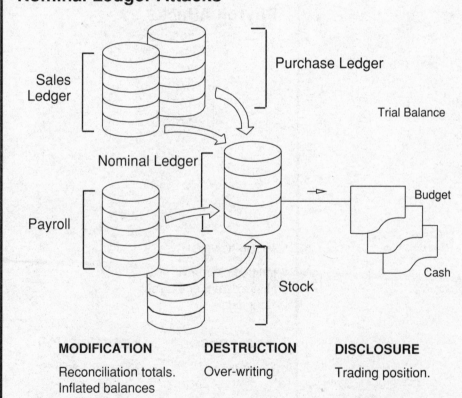

MODIFICATION

Reconciliation totals.
Inflated balances

DESTRUCTION

Over-writing

DISCLOSURE

Trading position.

Audit Trails

When the Renaissance Italians sat on high stools and filled in their ledger systems, auditing their activity was fairly simple. A trail of paper linked activities. For example:

> approval of actions,
>
> approval of new suppliers,
>
> approval of new customers,
>
> oversight mechanisms with accountability,
>
> and dual responsibility.

All these provided an audit trail that highlighted errors, omissions and misdemeanors. The system worked very well and it was hoped to imitate it on computer systems. Problems arose because of the speed of the new machines; processes could not be held up because the Sales Department was slow in authorising new customer accounts, or Engineering was slow in authorising credit notes for faulty equipment. So new audit trails and controls came into existence, structured in quite a different way:

> history files,
>
> password authorisation,
>
> programs and flowcharts,
>
> input/output records,
>
> computer activity logs.

These were supported by:

Range checks;	the computer ensures a sum is within a specified range.
Parity checks;	which ensure data is transmitted around the system correctly.
Limit checks;	which ensure sums do not exceed a specified amount.
Echo checks;	which play back a transmission for comparison with the original.
Sequence checks;	which determine if any alterations to the sequence have occurred.

These checks when combined with Hash, Batch and Voucher Totals should be enough. However, because of original programming problems and the delays in paper work catching up with the system various error accommodations have been designed. These include:

> suspense accounts,
>
> unresolved differences,
>
> unclassified expenditures,

unknown payees,

unknown vendors,

inventory variation accounts,

receivables suspense accounts,

payables suspense accounts.

At any one time in large volume systems there will be high value assets not fully accounted for and, almost certainly, languishing in one of these accounts. Clearly the fraudster can use these to manipulate reconciliations and cover his handy work. This presents probably the greatest weakness in the computerised double entry book-keeping system.

Systems often run late. Patching programs keeps the data processing department busy, so that the ultimate system of controls is never developed. The computerised system presents an easy target, especially if the internal audit department cannot audit "through" the system.

Auditors tend to audit "around" a system. That is, they verify that data entering the system bears a logical relationship to data leaving the computer. If totals agree, in this circumstance, the auditor will assume that all is well. However, as shown above, information can be manipulated within a computer system and the output falsified.

To overcome this, the auditor should audit "through" the system. This means understanding the logic of the system and following transactions through each process.

In a "through" audit a transaction should be traced through its processing cycle to see that it was entered correctly and processed correctly. Authorisation steps should be followed and activity logs evaluated. The logic of the process can then be followed through operator instructions, flow diagrams, layouts, input/output controls, program listings and system controls.

Generally the system works but control has passed from church going clerks on high stools to programmers and analysts who seldom have an ethical belief. This combined with inherent weaknesses can result in fraud, disclosure of confidential information, modification of critical data and denial of service.

Communications & Networks

In the area of communications, the Security Officer will need to work with others and probably act as a co-ordinator. As a co-ordinator he can act as a prompter by promoting security awareness to influence design and practices. A Security officer with a knowledge of Local Area Network (LAN) or Wide Area Network (WAN) techniques will be readily accepted by both the computer centre personnel and the communications network engineers. Security is not a high priority in their work load if only because the work load in modern networks always exceeds the available resources.

The future of information and data processing depends heavily on communications. Already the financial world uses communications systems to transfer their funds (e.g., SWIFTS, CHAPS, EFTPOS etc.). In commercial organisations remote terminals linking subsidiary companies to holding companies are commonplace and within both organisations Local Area Networks are becoming commonplace, whilst company and home banking terminals increase in use and information processing men talk continually of "**Downsizing**". For the future there will be an increasing requirement for security against fraud in systems employing remote access from terminals, where valuable information is carried or valuable transactions are performed.

Two major factors will give added impetus to data security precautions in the next decade. The first is the provisions of the Data Protection Act and the second is the needs of commerce and industry, as witnessed by the City's growing concern over computer fraud and the recent failure of SEAQ, (the Stock Exchange Automated Quotation System) just when it was most needed. Whilst this latter situation is to do with recovery and resilience there can be no doubt of future demands for security standards for what better time can there be to make an illegal implant in a system for the purpose of fraud than when it is down and confusion reigns?

Principles of Communications.

In its simplest form a terminal communicates with a computer over a public telephone line. Most communications which can be used for data transmission are designed to carry analogue signals but the computer is a digital device. The process of converting digital data to analogue form is called modulation. The reverse process of converting analogue signals to digital is called demodulation. A small hardware device performs this function and is called a modem. A typical example of a VDU. connected to a central processor is shown below . . . .

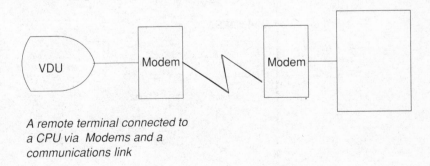

A remote terminal connected to
a CPU via Modems and a
communications link

A more complex system using many devices and terminals at several locations might also use datasets. A dataset establishes fixed connection between one terminal and telephone line. To establish contact the computer is dialled in much the same way as an acoustic coupler . Datasets at the computer end will lead into a Transmission Control Unit (TCU) and Front End Processor as illustrated below.

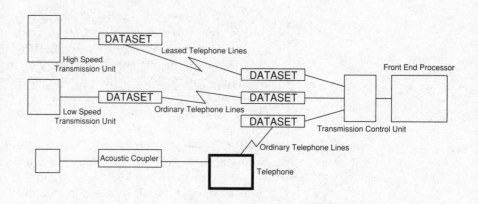

Clearly a network communicating throughout the country might employ acoustic couplers, data sets and modems. However, the tendency is towards modems and tied lines, for security reasons, and away from dial up lines.

Local Area Networks

There are three common layouts or topologies used in LANS:

BUS

The most widely used layout topology is the BUS. In the BUS topology, the LAN provides a single, multi point physical channel that is shared by a number of nodes (endpoints). In this type of configuration, a node will recognise its own address (as far as the computer is concerned) and will receive a message with its address on but if the address is absent will broadcast it to another node over the channel. An illustration of this topology is given below.

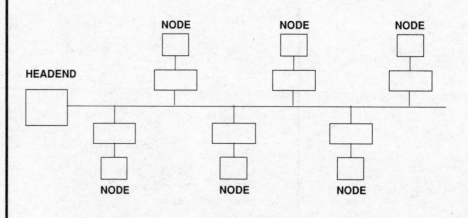

STAR

Star Topology is a radial layout and is a method of joining all the nodes to a single point, called a central node. The central node usually controls the whole network. A frequently encountered application of star topology is in clustered word processing.

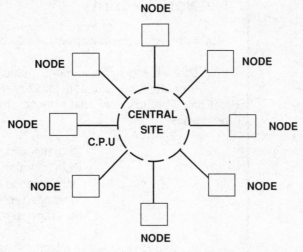

A Star Network

RING

Ring topology occurs where nodes are arranged in an unbroken loop configuration with each node connected by a point link with another node. A message moves from node to node around the ring until it is recognised by the node to which it is addressed. When a node does not recognise the address on the message then it serves as a repeater or transmitter of the message. Most popular is the IBM Token Ring system which is rapidly becoming a communications standard.

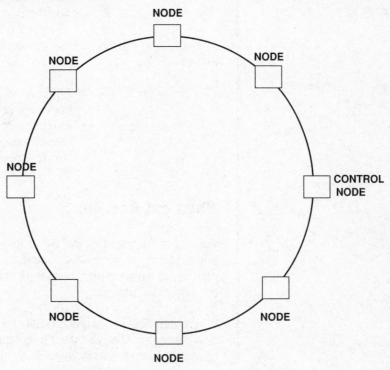

Failure may occur in this system if an active component (repeater) breaks down. A systems ability to overcome this type of problem and continue processing is known as **resilience**.

Network Security

Attacks on computer networks fall into two categories; Passive or Active.

In a passive attack, the intruder is able to read data from a communications system or store, but is unable to change it. An active attack differs in that it is not only able to read data but to amend it, allowing any of the following processes:

- Data modification
- Data insertion
- Data deletion or destruction
- Message replay or delay
- Message re-routing

A broad solution to passive attack is message encryption and to active attack is message authentication. Neither of these solutions will prevent an attack with complete certainty, but will considerably reduce the possibility and attractiveness of achieving success.

Principles of *stand alone* computer security might be summarised as:

- Personnel controls
- Physical security
- Access and authorisation controls
- Software controls
- Operation controls
- Audit features

All these apply to the network system but with special and additional attention to:

- Physical access
- Logical access
- Message integrity
- Network control
- Network resilience

Physical Access

The understanding of the need to provide physical security in a network environment is less well understood than in a conventional computer environment possibly because the individual units pass out of the control of the computer department.

Where terminals or microcomputers are connected to the network the same high standards of physical security should be applied to these devices as are applied to the mainframe. Access to the office area should be via locked doors and preferably with some form of automated access monitoring.

The development of LANs has produced cable systems capable of carrying a high volume of traffic of different types and Local Area Networks are more difficult to protect because:

a) connection to the line is standard making ease of connection by a wide variety of devices possible; facilitating privacy violations;

b) lines are often fitted with spare access points, ready for future use; facilitating a tap to be made without breaching the cable;

c) on a token ring system where a message is looking for an address, a listener at a hidden access point can monitor every transmission;

d) masquerading on temporarily abandoned terminals is aided by the user friendly prompts.

A typical example of the vulnerability of these systems is a case study using Ethernet; a LAN protocol. All the micros were distributed over two floors but were protected by a password control feature. However, a vampire clamp operated by an intruder equipped with an Ethernet Monitor could tap the cable and record every message sent over the network. In this case, besides physical security procedures governing access to terminal areas the solution would be to use optical fiber for the segment linking floors (the obvious area of attack).

LAN protection should commence with risk management studies. When information does not need to be used by terminals, then these should be isolated by using secure gateways. A typical LAN might be the one illustrated below. This is an open multifunction LAN which is almost as impossible to protect as a concentrated system, where inter floor or section is validated by gateways.

Network monitoring equipment and software is becoming increasingly available. A network which has these facilities and, more importantly, is known to use them, is less likely to be penetrated.

An illustration of the vulnerable system is given below:

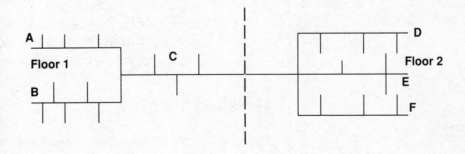

A more secure system using gateways to protect the network between floors is shown below. (Gateways are able to exercise all the access controls normally associated with mainframe software systems).

Whilst restricted access to these systems is axiomatic other measures are also required. These are:

Micro processors stencilled with the company name
Micro processors fixed to the desk
Fully operative gateways.
Defined and identifiable users.
Full configuration management preventing illegal joiners

Logical Access

All the password related preventive measures that apply to minis and mainframes apply to networks. Authorisation tables also apply. The security principles that refer to these larger machines apply to the more sophisticated networks.

Once access has been granted then software mechanisms must be in place to determine the mode of access - read, write, create, update, delete. Software must then determine:

· Partitioning and classification.

· Reconciliation of users with equipment and software , for example, data base privileges, programs and files.

· Access to individual files and programs.

Message Integrity

Message integrity invokes three main elements:

- **Encryption**
- **Authentication**
- **Key Management**

Encryption

To ensure that messages transmitted via the PTT are secure, a form of encryption is necessary. The most widely accepted is the Data Encryption Standard (DES).

DES was developed jointly by IBM and the USA Bureau of Standards. The algorithm is strong and the key excellent. Indeed it is now accepted as an international standard.

Consider the example of the encryption of "Cancel Contract".
Using the Caesar 3 character shift and two alphabets:

ABCDEFGHIJKLMNOPQRSTUVWXYZ

3 character Caesar Shift

DEFGHIJKLMNOPQRSTUVWXYZABC

The encoded message becomes:

FDQFHO FRQWUDFW

or run together:

FDQFHOFRQWUDFW

and divided into groups of five:

FDQFH OFRQW UDFW

and transposed, back to front:

HFDQF WQRFO WFDU

DES is programmed to perform this sixteen times over

This is converted into binary and then run together becoming page after page of 0 and 1's, for example:

0101000101110101001010100011111010100101000010101010 etc.

If this is combined with a key which will take the same form, for example:

01010101011010101101010001101010001 etc.

Then the resultant binary number would take up to two years using the most powerful computers, coupled with the most favourable information, to unscramble.

It must be concluded that this binary statement cannot be unscrambled except by possession of the binary key.

Encryption is usually achieved using a special device known as a "Black Box". It does not burden the operating system system but occurs remotely from the Central Node. The message arrives at the black box in clear and is encrypted prior to transmission. Any attempt to break into the box or even to X-Ray it results in self destruction. All messages after the box are in encrypted form.

Authentication

This means checking that the user is who he claims to be, or ensuring the origin and validity of an incoming message. Part of the authentication procedure would be the use of proven and established methods for guarding access to secure material. These would be selected on the basis of a risk management study and could include:

a) Something the user knows; e.g. a password or Personal Identification Number.

b) Something carried; e.g., a physical key or a card, either of which could be inserted in a terminal to activate it, or an electronic token which emits a short-range radio signal detectable by a sensor within the terminal.

c) Calling the terminal back to ensure that it is authentic.

To ensure that the message was indeed transmitted by the authorised source it is necessary to authenticate each important message, or indeed off-line files and live data bases. In this instance off-line files are held on magnetic media and usually, for the sake of security, in a remote location. Should an intruder tamper with the information that the devices hold then the data signature produced by the algorithm will change. Live data bases can also be protected in the same way so that information called from the data base can be validated, by the user, prior to use.

Generally, authentication is required to;

· determine the origin of the message,
· confirm the integrity of the message,
· check information loss or addition within the message.

Authentication works in much the same way as encryption except that a data signature is added to the message.

A key for the algorithm is generated. Its use might be, as an example, date dependent:

21st Dec'87   123456123456789789123451234512
10th Feb'88   987654321123456768900988776788

So that at the appropriate time the key comes into effect and is known by both sender and receiver. The sender applies the algorithm to his message, which might be to debit account number 7364312082 by $125,000, $124,999 to be paid to account 2398346780 and $1 to be paid to account 2804782138.

The data signature when added to this transaction will be:

29451759307187581 0356301E

Should the message be intercepted and modified so the the sums are reversed between the accounts, the hash total of money remains the same at $250,000 and of transactions at 2. As a result the amounts would normally be paid but , had the authentication algorithm been applied it would have shown:

Calculated data signature; 899932 312036 913965 7497 01E
Signature actual;   294517 593071 875810 3563 01E

The difference is so dramatic it would be noticed and payment stopped.

The weakness with this type of authentication is "key management" and the transmission in plain text. The latter can be overcome
by encryption but the former depends on the procedures in place within each company.

Key Management

New, or daily keys, can be transmitted under the protection of the encryption and authentication mechanism. Once received under these two constraints it must be assumed to be uncompromised. A further protection mechanism would be to transmit the key in two halves. This has the benefit of ensuring that the entire key is not discovered in one event.

Keys may be date activated but require specific passwords to access them in an encrypted data base. This is the policy demonstrated in the example on authentication.

At the set up of the system, keys are usually distributed by hand and acknowledged and logged by signature. Thus accountability for security violations is auditable. Following set up, subsequent keys are normally transmitted to users using encrypted messages.

The key should never stay in use long enough for a cryptologist to be able to determine its value. In the banking system using DES it should be changed every four months. This rule should be applied commercially.

Public Key

This form of cryptology requires no prior exchange of keys , thus enabling a user to communicate securely with many others. The public key may or may not be known. Indeed, anyone can encrypt using a public key but only a specific person can decrypt this.

The example normally used to illustrate the methodology would be User A has an English to Portuguese dictionary and this is known. He transmits his message in Portuguese. B has an English to Portuguese key and a Portuguese to English key. The eavesdropper also obtains the key, ie. the Portuguese to English dictionary but when the message reply is transmitted in Portuguese translation presents time consuming problems.

The advantage of this form of encryption is the length of time needed to decrypt the message. In some instances this can be longer than the life of the universe when conventional means are used.

Network Control

Responsibility for control of LANS or linked LANS should be vested in a senior member of staff. His responsibilities will include maintaining registers of units on the network, authorising devices which can join the network, giving users logical access and the preparation and maintenance of standards for all users on the network. His responsibilities also include preparation and maintenance of restart and recovery procedures in the event of failure of the network, the starting up and closing down of the network and the resolution of any problems encountered by users.

The Controller will need to determine the level and type of security to be applied in any system. Recent developments in computing and communications have resulted in powerful and cheap micro computers and high bandwidth local area networks, broad band and baseband networks. Broadband transmission uses radio frequency modems to convey digital information over the network and by operating modems at different frequencies a single transmission medium is able to support a number of simultaneous channels without disruption. Baseband transmission uses direct encoding to convey digital information over the transmission medium (radio frequency modems are not used). At any time only one signal can be present on this bandwidth. Generally, baseband transmission is the one encountered in the office environment.

Multi-level security on modern networks is a prime consideration. In any system the Controller will have to classify information depending on its sensitivity and define security for each classification.

A methodology for achieving this end has been defined by enforcing security between information compartments and then to add a trusted control sharing mechanism to implement the security policy. Isolation can be provided by four separation mechanisms:

> 1. Physical separation preventing information flow between the elements to be separated.

> 2. Temporary separation where information is processed in one area of the system and then purged of all information and used subsequently to process data in a different set of compartments.

> 3. Logical separation by means of algorithms implemented in a combination of hardware and software.

> 4. Crypto separation that ensures data can only be read by approved recipients. Different crypto keys are used in different departments.

A typical network is on the next page:

In the second system shown below the Controller might choose to interpose Network Interface Units (NIU) between users and the system. The use of an Access Control Centre may also be deemed appropriate to maintain security

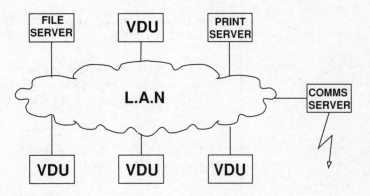

and as such is also shown:

In this system the Controller might allocate one or more security compartments. this allocation would then be stored in the appropriate NIU. The task of the NIU would then be to ensure that data can only flow between users with the same level of security clearance. This is achieved by labelling all data flowing

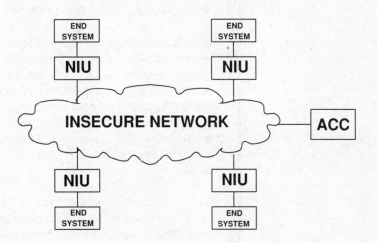

from users to the network with its security rating and by passing data to users only if their NIU accepts the label on the data as of the correct security rating.

The network software must be capable of labelling its outgoing data correctly, maintaining the labeling of incoming data and apply the approved security policy. This greater level of flexibility could be provided by an Access Control Centre (ACC).

The ACC will verify the identity of the user and verify that he is allowed access to the desired level of security and issues the appropriate label to the NIU. The user can then communicate with all other users of the same classification and receive appropriate information from the data base. In this system, the NIU will purge the workstation, once a user has finished his work so that residual information is not available to the next user of the terminal. The next user is of course free to log on at his appropriate level. This allows workstations to be used for various levels of security.

The ACC will also have a printer and possibly disc storage facilities to record security level activity.

This type of system security allows the Controller to provide multi-level security based on simple principles achieving user separation by appropriately manipulating the four basic separation techniques described above.

Network Resilience

The Mean Time Between Failure is higher on networks than on minis and mainframes. However, equipment and systems are becoming more robust as design and construction techniques improve. The Network Controller must determine effective recovery procedures involving the use of adequate check points and log files in order to limit the amount of data that must be reinput after failure.

In the event of failure it may be necessary to install additional lines and equipment. The nature of the system will determine whether additional communications controllers or file servers are held.

Properly selected and installed a local area network can be extremely reliable. Poor installation, however, is very common and the supplying organisation rarely installs the system, the user falling back on cable supplying companies who have little or no experience of networks. Cable paths shown on designs are often ignored and connections and cable lengths vary from specifications. This not only presents a security problem but also maintenance problems in emergencies. There are also restrictions on cable lengths between stations for correct operation. This could be infringed where incorrect cable runs are installed.

Power spikes and induced currents also present a problem. Unless an Automatic Voltage regulator is installed power glitches may cause NIUs to re-initialise their memories to default values.

Ring LANs send messages through every node. Node failure may result in the user being unable to process on that device. If the system allows for various levels of security the user may be able to use another terminal thus increasing the resilience of the system. The problem may worsen where a master station is used. All ring systems can detect and react to node failure. However, data in transit ,when failure occurs, is normally corrupted.

Security of Networks

Networks have twofold security problem areas:

a) the micro computers and terminals that operate on their systems
b) the communications lines that carry data and programs. Each requires different forms of protection. The Network Controller will need to ensure that protection exists to prevent the many forms of intrusion that can occur.

For example the controller will need to ensure:

> 1. that the level of security is appropriate by classifying data sensitivity and authorisation rights: He must be able to protect resources and assets against accidental or deliberate damage.

> 2. that the information being transmitted is accurate, complete and protected from unauthorised intruders;

> 3. that appropriate software security aids but does not affect the performance of the system by the burden these aids may place upon it.

> 4. that the security techniques selected can be implemented and controlled with a minimum of disruption and maximum commitment from staff;

> 5. that systems resilience can ensure effective and economic recovery from a system crash, especially systems using ring topologies.

The basic security mechanisms to protect LANs divide into the two areas described below:

> **a) Communications security:**

> > i.   Physical security.
> > ii. Emission security.
> > iii. Crypto security.
> > iv. Transmission security.

> **b) Micro computer security:**

> > i.   Physical security and access controls
> > ii. Software controls.
> > iii. Hardware access and control.
> > iv. Audit features and operational controls.
> > v.   Clearance and access controls.

As a result the problem of securing LANs is multifaceted and whatever countermeasures are selected these should be supported by a full security risk management study (showing adequate returns on the countermeasures selected).

An analysis of security countermeasures indicates that there are eight security characteristics necessary for a secure protocol set, and these are:

1. Secrecy.
2. Authentication.
3. Privacy.
4. Integrity.
5. Message preservation.
6. Confinement.
7. Authorisation.
8. Delivery assurance.

Failure to provide all of these characteristics will limit dramatically the security of the network.

Network Threats

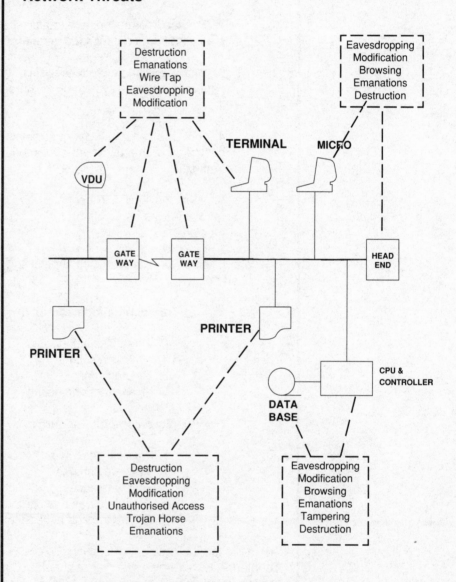

Bus Network Threats

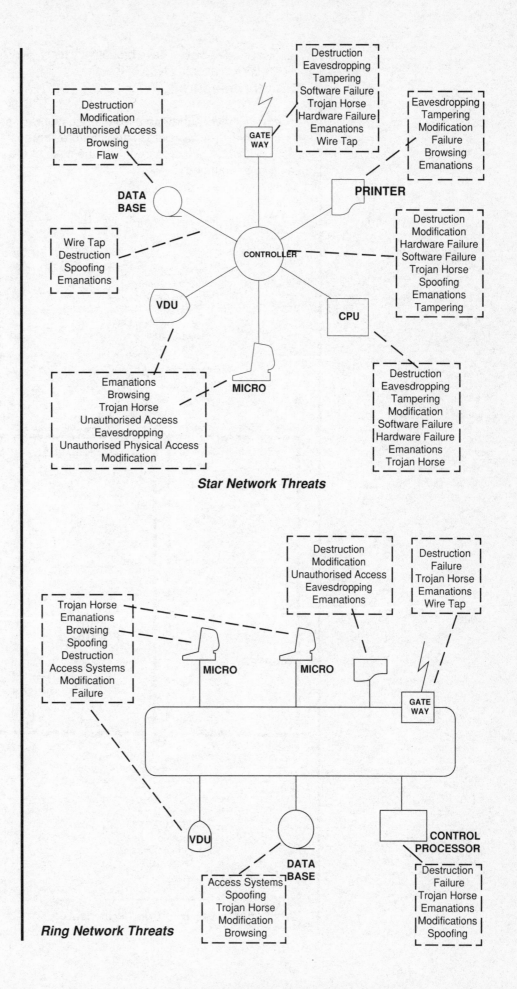

Star Network Threats

Destruction
Eavesdropping
Tampering
Software Failure
Trojan Horse
Hardware Failure
Emanations
Wire Tap

GATE WAY

Destruction
Modification
Unauthorised Access
Browsing
Flaw

Eavesdropping
Tampering
Modification
Failure
Browsing
Emanations

DATA BASE

PRINTER

Wire Tap
Destruction
Spoofing
Emanations

CONTROLLER

Destruction
Modification
Hardware Failure
Software Failure
Trojan Horse
Spoofing
Emanations
Tampering

VDU

CPU

Emanations
Browsing
Trojan Horse
Unauthorised Access
Eavesdropping
Unauthorised Physical Access
Modification

MICRO

Destruction
Eavesdropping
Tampering
Modification
Software Failure
Hardware Failure
Emanations
Trojan Horse

Ring Network Threats

Destruction
Modification
Unauthorised Access
Eavesdropping
Emanations

Destruction
Failure
Trojan Horse
Emanations
Wire Tap

Trojan Horse
Emanations
Browsing
Spoofing
Destruction
Access Systems
Modification
Failure

MICRO

MICRO

GATE WAY

VDU

DATA BASE

CONTROL PROCESSOR

Access Systems
Spoofing
Trojan Horse
Modification
Browsing

Destruction
Failure
Trojan Horse
Emanations
Modifications
Spoofing

Sophisticated networks have brought a variety of threats and the chosen type of network will alter the type of threat:

Countermeasures

All threats have appropriate countermeasures that will raise the security thresholds of networks. Clearly, before any countermeasure is chosen its' cost will have to be compared with the cost to the organisation of the threat being consummated.

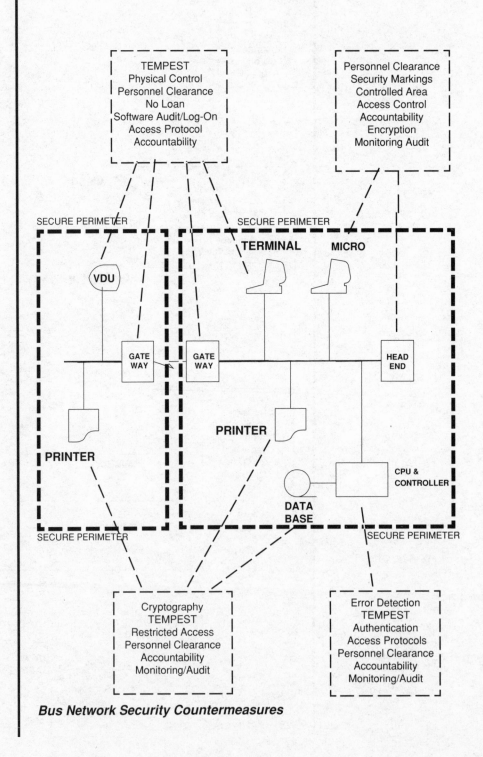

Bus Network Security Countermeasures

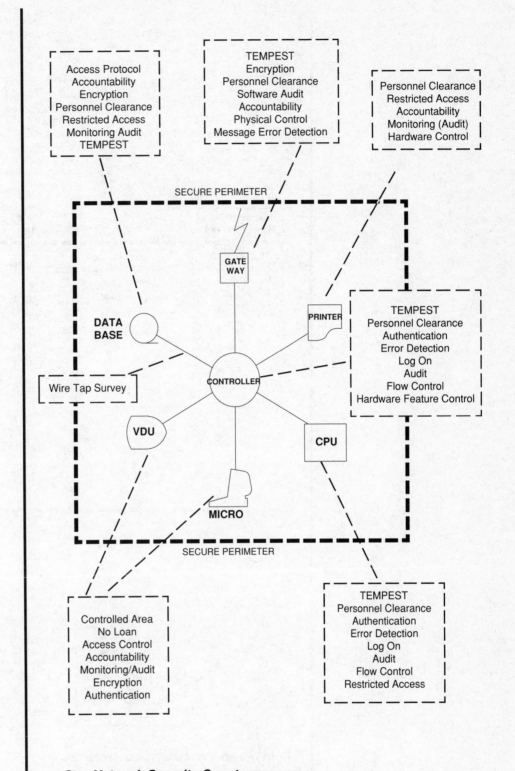

Access Protocol
Accountability
Encryption
Personnel Clearance
Restricted Access
Monitoring Audit
TEMPEST

TEMPEST
Encryption
Personnel Clearance
Software Audit
Accountability
Physical Control
Message Error Detection

Personnel Clearance
Restricted Access
Accountability
Monitoring (Audit)
Hardware Control

SECURE PERIMETER

GATE WAY

PRINTER

DATA BASE

Wire Tap Survey

CONTROLLER

VDU

CPU

MICRO

TEMPEST
Personnel Clearance
Authentication
Error Detection
Log On
Audit
Flow Control
Hardware Feature Control

SECURE PERIMETER

Controlled Area
No Loan
Access Control
Accountability
Monitoring/Audit
Encryption
Authentication

TEMPEST
Personnel Clearance
Authentication
Error Detection
Log On
Audit
Flow Control
Restricted Access

Star Network Security Countermeasures

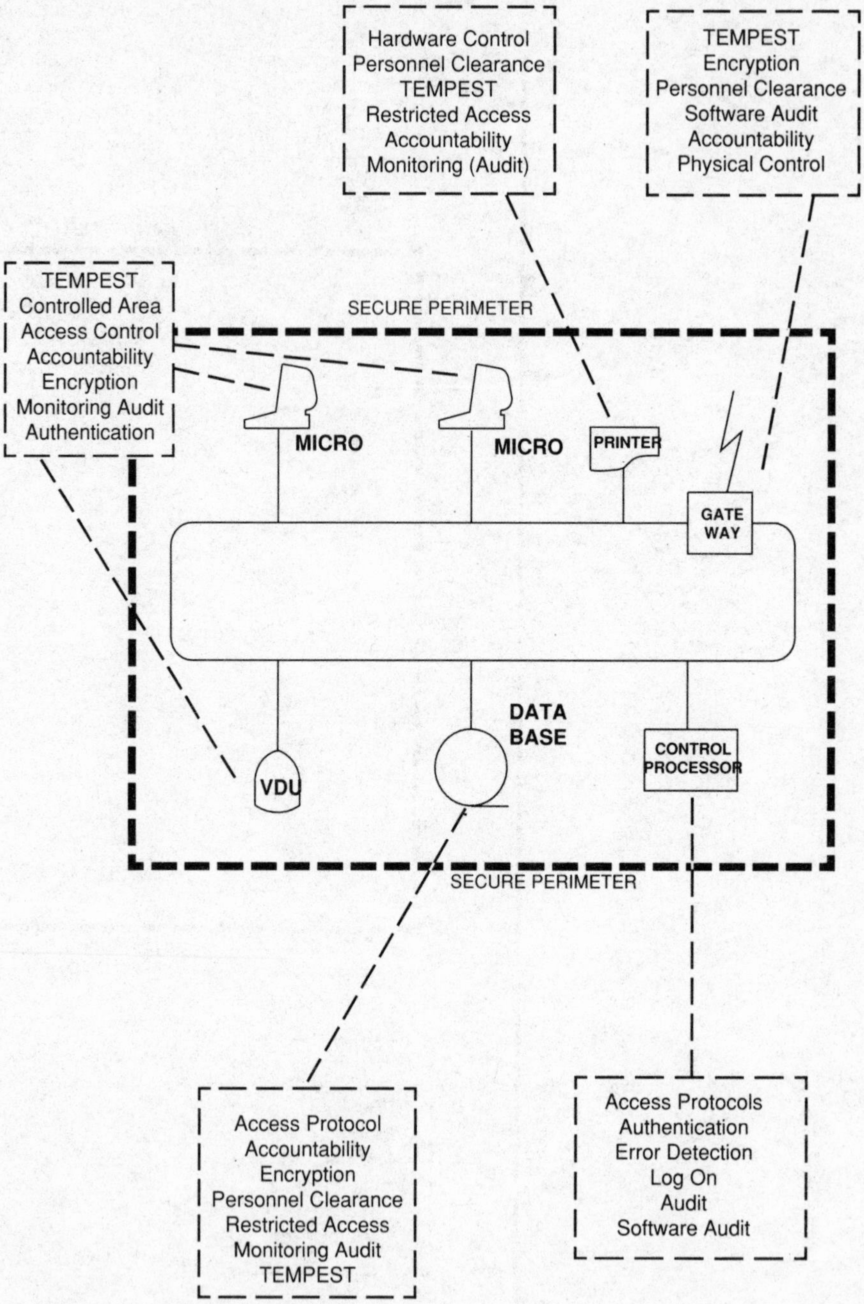
Hardware Control
Personnel Clearance
TEMPEST
Restricted Access
Accountability
Monitoring (Audit)
TEMPEST
Encryption
Personnel Clearance
Software Audit
Accountability
Physical Control
TEMPEST
Controlled Area
Access Control
Accountability
Encryption
Monitoring Audit
Authentication
SECURE PERIMETER
MICRO
MICRO
PRINTER
GATE WAY
DATA BASE
VDU
CONTROL PROCESSOR
SECURE PERIMETER
Access Protocol
Accountability
Encryption
Personnel Clearance
Restricted Access
Monitoring Audit
TEMPEST
Access Protocols
Authentication
Error Detection
Log On
Audit
Software Audit

Ring Network Security Countermeasures

The Society for World Wide Inter-bank Financial Transactions

SWIFT is a bank owned, non-profit co-operative society with 1,000 shareholding banks in 50 countries. The costs of its messages are paid for by members using a tariff designed to cover the costs according to numbers of connections, addresses and volume of message traffic.

All messages are processed on a store and forward basis through one of three centers located in Belgium, Holland and U.S.A. SWIFT installs in member countries regional processors which are connected by leased lines to the centers. All connections to the network go through the regional processors which act as concentrators.

The majority of users have a SWIFT Interface Device or SID, which can be a stand alone micro operated by software provided by the society. Others use a Direct Swift Link or DSL on an IBM mainframe.

SWIFT reports the number of messages received and transmitted allowing banks to resolve any difficulty about message content and completeness.

It is possible to have strict standards of message format. Each message format is denoted by a message type, for example MT100 which is a Customer Transfer. A message will contain a number of fields some of which are mandatory. The demarcation of each field is by a message tag. For example, with MT100 messages the mandatory fields are:

20	Reference Number
32a	Value date, currency code, amount
50	Ordering Customer
52	Ordering Bank
53	Senders Correspondence Bank
54	Receivers Correspondence Bank
57	Account With Bank
59	Beneficiary Customer

and so on.

These fields are sufficient for customers with member banks and those with accounts that have to use a correspondent bank. Where a bank is not a member fields 53, 54, 57 and 59 would be used. Formats are defined in a similar way for some 63 message types. Free format is also possible by using 99 to signify free format. Therefore, to commit an acceptable fraud a knowledge of the way messages are constructed is a pre-requisite.

The most important security attribute between banks is authenticity. Details of the SWIFT authentication algorithm are not in the public domain. However, the key is 16 hexadecimal characters in length. and the sharing of this key between sender and receiver, is the key to security of the system. Keys are exchanged bilaterally and are not known to SWIFT.

To prevent replication, alteration or deletion and then the re-transmission of messages all messages are sequentially numbered. The connection between SWIFT and its users is safeguarded by input and output sequence numbers. The centers check the format and input sequence numbering. The output from the center contains a sequence number which must be verified by the receiver. The transaction reference number provides an end-to-end sequence control for each pair of banks and is included in the part of the message to which the authenticator is applied.

The interface between SWIFT and a member bank is protected from the introduction of false messages, that have the correct sequence numbers and authenticators, by various security procedures that are recommended by SWIFT but are the responsibility of the member to implement. The recommendation is that one person should assemble the message with a second checking the message and releasing it for transmission.

Terminals coming on line to the system verify their identity by a password. The passwords are issued by SWIFT and are received in the form of a table. The table is sent to the user in two parts to prevent unauthorized penetration of the system. Once received they are acknowledged to SWIFT before they can be activated on the system. Each table consists of a sequence of passwords listed against a sequence number. Thus each "log on" continues a numeric sequence. To prevent "piggy backs" by a fraudster impersonating SWIFT to the SID to obtain the password, each password is given a response number which the user must check before beginning his transmission.

Lines and centres are the responsibility of SWIFT; procedures of the users. Messages between centres are encrypted. Again, each bank must decide whether to encrypt its transmissions.

The Clearing House Automatic Payment System

CHAPS carries payments between 13 settlement banks. In turn they offer the facility to some 300 other banks in the UK. The system provides same day settlement between users using accounts they hold at the bank of England.

The format of the message is the same as for SWIFT since instructions for payment through SWIFT will often initiate payment through CHAPS.

There is no "central" operation with CHAPS and full use is made of PSS. The integrity of the system is based in gateways implemented on a Tandem computer (a non-stop dual computer) system. Each message that is transmitted receives a logical acknowledgment via PSS back to the originating gateway. The gateways are able to provide time logs, sequence and totals for each transaction.

Like SWIFT the larger banks run payments on their mainframes and the smaller banks on a Tandem computer that holds the gateway.

The encryption mechanism is the DES algorithm which is provided in "black box" mode and is tamper resistant. Key management is integral to security since a master key is used to protect session keys which are transmitted over the network.

Confidentiality and main security is provided by the encryption of messages at the point of entry to PSS and de-cypherment at exit. Authentication is implemented in the bank's payment process with the aid of a hardware module. The two processes of generating and checking authenticators are carried out in physically secure modules and therefore, the ability to generate authenticators can be confined to the sender.

Within the banks a two stage password is used in exactly the same way as SWIFT with two people involved. Ideally, a third has a log book containing the next sequential number of transmission.

Automatic Teller Machines

Automatic Teller Machines (ATMs) are now used not only to obtain money but also the status of accounts, to effect transfers between customer accounts and to provide cheque book requests and account details. ATMs can now deliver travelers cheques and accept cash deposits.

ATMs are always connected to a central data base to prevent payments to stolen cards or people that have infringed the bank's rules of payment.

A Personal Identification Number or PIN is integral to security of the cards that are presented to initiate payment. The PIN is verified within the ATM to the card number by means of an algorithm. The algorithm has a secret key which is common to all ATMs in a bank and represents a danger since, if the key and the algorithm can be discovered then the fraudster can create his own cards with appropriate PINs. The weakness is the way in which the key is loaded into the ATM. The key can be the result of a complex calculation or the algorithm itself can be complex using several keys. In the latter case no one person is in a position to forge cards.

PINs appear in two places in the banking system; at the center of generation and at the ATMs. Security is generally such that only the individual, outside the bank, can be aware of his PIN. Since integral information is held on the magnetic stripe, for local off line cash dispensation, there has been a move towards the EMI watermark. This stores the number of the card in a way which cannot be altered or forged, even when copying a magnetic watermark from one card to another. The magnetic watermark contains a relationship between the watermark data and other data on the card itself. Any copied or forged card can thus be detected.

A mathematical relationship exists between the watermark number and the other identifying information. Conceptually it can be represented:

$$RN = Ek(I,W)$$

Where RN is a reference number calculated from a secret key k combined with a watermark number W and the identifying information on the card I. The notation (I,W) indicates a cryptographic chain and if either I or W is changed it is necessary to recompute RN in order to generate a valid card. If k is stored securely the computation remains secure.

There are three types of PIN:

1. Assigned derived PINs,
2. Assigned random PINs,
3. Customer selected PINs.

Assigned PINs are usually numeric and have four to six digits. Customer selected PINs must conform to a basic pre-programmed requirement.

Once a transaction is initiated, it is in the form of a request from the ATM to the center for authorization and a response from the center itself.

Contents may be:

1. To the centre
   ATM identity,
   Account number and card number,
   Watermark,
   PIN,
   Amount of cash,
   Sequence number of transaction,
   Authenticator for all other data.

Response:
   ATM identity
   Operating code for payment approval/denial/retention of card
   Sequence number
   Authenticator

Messages to and from the ATM must be authenticated and the PIN must be encrypted for transmission. As a further security measure a log of transactions is maintained at the ATM this reconciles payments and ensures that an account is not debited without payment being made, it also helps to resist employee forgery and theft.

Encryption of the PIN is carried out in local mode and is generally a two stage transposition supported by modulo 10. At the centre the calculation is decrypted. Besides decrypting the centre also holds the sequence count and keeps the counters synchronized.

Problems arrive with shared systems between banks and building societies. In this case a group of banks would appoint an authority to operate on their behalf for the interchange of messages for ATM payment approvals. This interchange is represented by a processor which acts as a node to which all the processors of the ATM system are connected. As a result verification of PINs and debiting accounts, whilst transparent to the user, is effected through a series of exchanges within the network. The agent bank becomes the payee who must recover his cash from the customers bank and this is also effected on the network as an extra function.

Messages on a shared ATM network

Several different keys are in use in this type of system, firstly from the ATM to the appropriate center and then between the bank processors. PINs are encrypted and decrypted before onward transmission and therefore, appear in plain text at various points becoming vulnerable to attack. To be secure all sensitive data must be within a physically secure module or participating banks must trust each others security, since problems also arise with authentication where the messages must be deciphered and appear in plain text for validation purposes.

Many of the problems associated with this type of system are overcome with Smart Cards that identify the user and can contain transaction information, including bank balances, limits of payments and payment frequencies.

Point of Sale Payments

This system allows the shopkeepers account to be credited with the transaction amount at the point and time of sale, and the customers account to be simultaneously debited. Thus the deduction of credit card percentages do not apply to the tradesman. The advantages to the card user may be in monthly, interest free debits from his account.

The EFT-POS system depends on the merchant installing a terminal which displays the agreed price of the goods. The customer then passes his card through the card reader at the point of sale, and enters his PIN. Before the transaction is accepted a validation request is made to the customers bank. If this is successful the accounts are debited and credited and a print out is produced at the terminal for the customers use.

The main security requirements are the verification of the PIN entered by the customer which must be carried out by his bankers' system. Clearly the PIN must be enciphered during transmission. Messages requesting authority for payment must be authenticated to prevent illegal alteration by line tap or in the processors through which they pass.

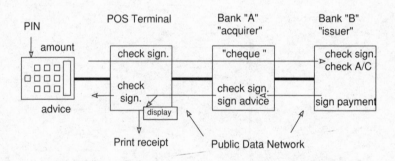

The advantages of the Smart Card or intelligent token especially come into their own with shared systems and POS. For example, the entry of a PIN does not have to be transmitted, which is expensive and can be dangerous, but is verified by accessing the micro chip in the card. Payments using this system have all the characteristics of an electronic cheque.

The Smart Card chip will also contain an authenticator which has the same value to the trader as a cheque and is accepted by the bank as an instruction to credit and debit. The authenticator for this type of message employs a key which is stored in the token and is known only to the card issuer, in this case the bank. This key is specific to the user and when payment is processed by the issuer, the customer identity in the message will allow his authentication key to be extracted from a table and used to check the authenticity of the entry.

The intelligent token is used to the advantage of both holder and issuer. The token checks the PIN to verify who is presenting, it then authenticates the message to the issuers computer. It also has the additional advantage of being able to hold a customer's public key which can be used in electronic cheques or for physical access rights.

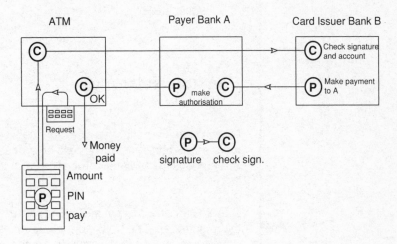

With electronic cheques the token provides the system with the customer identity, the expiry date and the public key. The bank provides its identity and its public key. If the keys are correct, encryption and decryption are possible and the token's signature is accepted. The input to the terminal will then be the amount, payee identity, date and time, currency and description of payment. The signature by the customer then makes use of the public key encryption system.

It is possible with this system to make off-line payments at the merchants terminal. The terminal collects the cheques, comparing them with a known black list, and then presents these to the merchant's bank in a convenient batch. The bank then sorts the entries and sends them to the appropriate bank for payment.

For on-line operation, the electronic cheque is transmitted at once to the card issuer bank where the signature is checked and the black list and the drawers account checked. A payment message signed by the issuer's bank is then sent to the acquirer's bank. When this has been checked a signed advice goes to the POS (Point Of Sale) terminal.

By the use of public key signatures, the security of each stage of payment process is dependent on the person who would lose by a fraud. Each party becomes responsible for his own secret key and its use.

Digital signatures have one weakness and that is signed documents can be copied and this requires the issuer bank to ensure that duplicated cheques are detected and eliminated. The cheque sequence number is administered by the intelligent token and is as secure as the holder's secret key.

In summary, the signature token stores a secret key and will reveal a public key. It is also able to write a cheque in the correct format and verify a cheque for refund updating balances as it goes.

One final advantage is that it can be used for physical access to buildings and to networks. In the case of physical entry to a building, the token would be presented to a terminal, which would give it a message to be signed. If the signature agrees with the stored public key the token and its holder are assumed to be legitimate.

Banking Networks

Modern banking systems work on networks with real time packages. This means that data does not have to be processed in batches and that all data that is entered is immediately processed and made available for output.

Current strategy is to put a Banking Network Computer (BNC) as a front-end to the mainframe. The BNC polls all terminals, in the branches and allows inter-branch communications. It will also perform protocol conversions, for example from X25/HDLC to the mainframes protocol. Thus the BNC or FEP becomes the point of network management and control and can utilize all the facilities of such a system, for example, down-line loading of software, workstation substitution etc., without there being need to invest in highly priced mainframe software and equipment.

Many packages are available to work with these systems. Most will handle all retail banking customer accounts, in sterling or other currencies. Once input has been made, the system will produce data on the following:

1. Base related accounts.

2. Advice notes and statements.

3. Daily interest accruals.

4. Stopped cheques, overdraft and loan limits.

The package will generate reports for use by management as follows:

1. Daily list of customer statements.

2. Monthly accrued interest.

3. Accounts in alphabetical, account number, general ledger control, currency and country order.

4. Overdrawn accounts.

5. Individual accounts.

This type of package will also permit portfolio management, maintaining all customer- and broker-accounts and will manage all purchase and sale of stock handled by the bank. in addition it will produce various analyses of customer and bank activities and generate contract notes etc.,

SWIFT modules usually come with the package covering all aspects of the bank's activities.

Modules exist for the wholesale banking market covering foreign exchange transactions and detailing spot and forward purchases and sales, take up options, extensions, counterparty compensations, loans and swaps and multiple dealing.

The dealer usually enters the first part of a deal which will up-date in real-time, the total overall position for each currency, short dated positions, the value dated balance in each currency and projected balances of nostro accounts in each currency.

The second part of the deal slip is passed to the back office where client account numbers are encoded, with currency accounts disposal instructions and so on. Generally all confirmations, advices, cheques and receipts are printed automatically.

Typical security on a Nixdorf 8864 network system

Digitized signatures are stored on a central main frame which can be called up by the teller on a vdu window, at the point where the transaction is taking place.

For EFT a system of finger print comparison of authorized staff is possible. The authorized staff member has his digitized index fingerprint stored in the memory of his own Smart Card. The card is placed in a reader whilst the actual fingerprint is scanned by the same device. A successful match will authorize the procedure.

To ensure the security of the network the following functions are used:

1. Network user management
2. Network wide access control
3. Encryption on data communication lines
4. Identification of users by RSA (public key)
5. Network management for key management
6. Central software administration
7. Central password administration.

Security Officer Requirements

It is anticipated that the Security Officer will work closely with the Network Controller to ensure the security of the company's networks. They must work together to ensure:

CONFIDENTIALITY: The protection of transmitted data from accidental or deliberate disclosure to unauthorised persons.

INTEGRITY: Ensuring data received is exactly as the data that was sent and contains no later additions, modifications or erasures.

ACCESS CONTROL: Limiting and controlling systems access to individuals and/or terminals.

AUTHENTICATION: The identification of a remote entity. The assurance that the source of data received is the one claimed.

TRAFFIC SECURITY: Disguising or hiding traffic patterns and volumes to prevent extrapolation by an intruder. The use of traffic padding and spurious message generation to disguise traffic flows from eavesdroppers.

DENIAL OF RECEIPT/DISPATCH: The prevention of recipients and senders later denying they have received or sent a message by logging.

ACTIVITY LOGS: The minimum activity data to be logged will include date and time, user identification, data identification and destination identification. Regular security audits to analyse breaches of security in order to identify unauthorised access.

PASSWORDS: The Security Officer will be concerned with the issue and use of passwords since these play a vital role in the authentication process. If encryption software exists then passwords should be encrypted in the data base to prevent browsers gaining illegal privileges. They can also be transmitted in encrypted form to remote sites. Security alarms that are activated by illegal password usage should be installed.

PHYSICAL SECURITY: The need for secure rooms, cabinets ,terminals and micros. Micros should be secured to desks and not moved without the Security Officers permission. Tokens should give access to computer areas and be part of the micro or terminal enabling procedure.

REGISTER: A register should be kept of all devices, users with their authority to access resources, terminals to be connected to the network, the clearance level allowed to each terminal, changes to hardware and software and any security modifications.

Communications can be a doorway into the business system to defraud, disclose, modify or destroy data. Communications have become a specialismwithin the overall field of information processing. The technical side will always need an expert who has been cleared to the highest level, however, the Security Officer, providing he is supported at Board level, can ensure that all basic and necessary security is in place to prevent computer misuse and abuse.

Questionnaire

1. Are all remote terminals uniquely identified?

2. Do your communications connect and disconnect procedures:
   a. specifically identify switches, panels, plugs and any other equipment that is used to control these interfaces?
   b. provide for the identification of personnel in remote areas?

3. Are all communications switch panels labelled in such a way as to aid authorised personnel and confuse intruders?

4. Are locked inspection panels used for physical access to lines?

5. Is encryption used?

6. What key management procedures exist?

7. Do modems have alternative voice capability for trouble shooting between sights?

8. Is the mean time between failure of communications equipment lower than other equipment on the system?

9. Where are back up modems located?

10. Do modems have automatic dial-up on leased lines?

11. Are line numbers changed regularly? Are they confidential?

12. Are modem telephone numbers visible to passers by and visitors? Does the central site call terminal users for connection to the system?

13. Does the remote site log all inbound messages?

14. Does a contingency plan exist?

15. When new equipment is added is the contingency plan updated?

16. Are regular tests of corporate contingency plans conducted?

17. Is a register kept of access privileges?

18. Do levels of security classification exist?

19. Are planned cable paths deviated from?

20. Who installed the network and cables?

21. Are there power control units on the network? Is the voltage constantly regulated?

22. Can nodes be by-passed?

23. What network diagnostics are available?

24. Who acts as network controller?

25. Who is responsible for software standards and release?

26. Who audits the software?

27. What audit and management controls are in place?

28. Are lines fitted with spare access points?

29. Is the cabling linking floors fiber optic?

30. Does full configuration management exist to prevent illegal joiners?

31. Are authorisation tables used?

32. Is an ACC unit with NIUs used? Do they:

      a. define and implement security compartments?

      b. prevent information flow between compartments?

      c. provide information flow between users with the same level of clearance?

      d. label outgoing data correctly?

      e. maintain the labeling of incoming data?

      f. verify the user is allowed to access at the desired level of security?

33. Have closed user groups been defined and documented?

Financial Security

SWIFT

1. Who is responsible for the physical security of the SID or DSL?

2. Who holds the documented procedures for messages?

3. Who is responsible for the authentication algorithm key?

4. Who assembles the message?

5. Who checks the message?

6. What stand-by arrangements are there for assembly and checking?

7. Who is responsible for the sequence of passwords?

CHAPS

1. Who is responsible for the security of gateways?

2. Who is responsible for the security of encryption keys?

3. Who assembles the message?

4. Who checks the message?

5. What contingency arrangements exist?

6. Who is responsible for the sequence of events?

BACS

1. Is an authentication algorithm used?

2. What controls are in place?

3. Is the feed back check sum information compared with the original?

ATMs

1. What management procedures are in place to load the ATM key? Who is responsible for loading?

2. Is an EMI watermark used?

3. What type of PIN is used? (Derived/Assigned/Selected)

4. Who verifies the transaction log at the ATM?

5. Does the PIN encryption have the support of a modulo?

6. If the system is shared what security is in place to protect the PIN when it appears in plain text?

7. Is a Smart Card used?

EFT-POS

1. How is the PIN verified? Locally? Remotely?

2. What form of authenticator is stored in the card? Public Key?

3. How are users identified?

4. What key management procedures are in place?

5. What password procedures exist?

Cryptology in Computer Systems

7

Cryptology has been in use in diplomatic and military circles for thousands of years but has only recently attracted commercial attention because of the growth of computerisation and computer networks. Satellites and telephone links are vulnerable to eavesdropping and wiretapping. The act becomes passive and almost undetectable. For example, it recently came to light that the antennae on Russian embassy and consulate roofs were used to listen to domestic telephone conversations in Washington.

If the data transmission is in English then the eavesdropper can sort messages on the basis of their content by "listening" for brand names or significant nouns. Once these targeted words are found the eavesdropper can home-in. While the information listened to may not in itself be significant, when it is combined with other information it takes on an order of sensitivity if not secrecy.

During World War II the Allies broke the German and Japanese codes and the Japanese broke the American codes. If military systems are insecure then a secure cryptological method becomes vital for commercial applications. Low cost electronic data processing has made this possible and it is doubtful if network systems would have been so successful had it not been for the availability of low cost cryptology.

Cryptographic algorithms are easy to develop but the level of security provided is difficult to measure. A good algorithm will have the following characteristics:

1. To authorised users encryption and decryption will be simple.

2. The decryption operation will be difficult and time consuming for non-authorised users.

3. The security of the data should not require that the algorithm should be kept secret, although a secret algorithm improves security.

4. The efficiency and security of the algorithm should not be data dependent.

Once the data base and programs have been classified it will be necessary to protect sensitive data by encryption. Of the types of data that might be encrypted the following are amongst the more obvious:

1. All financial data and related transactions.

2. Personnel and payroll data.

3. Proprietary data.

4. System control and audit data.

Of the various crypto products available the Data Encryption Standard (DES) is probably the most widely used. In hardware terms DES is available in chips, boards, sub-assemblies, hand held units, teletypewriter like devices, modem look-alikes and various other forms. It can be made available with tamper proof cabinets, locking panels and fail-safe key entry systems. Should it be decided to use DES as a software product, then the algorithm and key management system tends to use large amounts of memory and CPU time. As a result software encryption tends to be highly selective.

Keys

Cryptographic algorithms use a combination of functions operating on plain text under the control of a parameter known as a key, to transform the plain text into cipher text.

When the same key is used for enciphering and deciphering it is known as a secret key algorithm. If different keys are used for the two operations and one is secret it is known as a public key algorithm.

The secret key system uses the same key for enciphering and deciphering sessions, as for example DES. All communications points must posses the key and the whole is known as a "crypto-net".

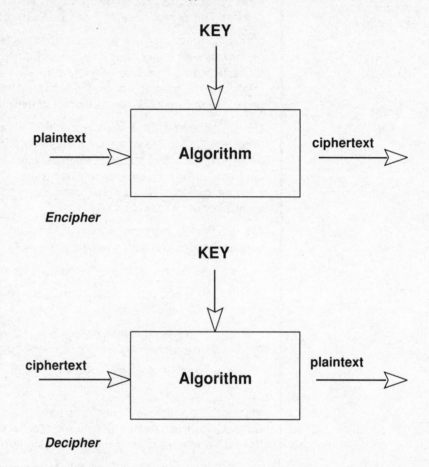

Encipher

Decipher

DES, the Data Encryption Standard, was published by the National Bureau of Standards for use by the US Federal Government. The standard is a mathematical description of an encryption algorithm and its inverse decryption algorithm. Both are based on a secret key.

The algorithm enciphers and deciphers blocks of data in 64 bit blocks under the control of a 64 bit key. 56 bits of the key are used by the algorithm and 8 bits for error detection during key management functions. Thus an algorithm using a 56 bit key has 2 raised to the 56 power or 72,057,594,037,927,936 possible keys to use. An attacker using a computer trying one key every micro second will take 2,700 years to try all the keys. All possible combinations of 64 bit inputs result in all possible combinations of output.

Additionally, the result of either encryption or decryption depends on every bit of input and every bit of the 56 bit effective key. Any change will cause the result to change with equal probability. Therefore, great care must be taken in generating keys, otherwise the enciphering and deciphering process can differ radically.

In a communication system, when an error occurs either at key generation time or during encipherment or decipherment, it can mean that some unauthorised person has interfered with the key.

Public Key cryptology is different. The user maintains two separate keys, one of which is the public key (encrypt only) and the other the secret key (decrypt only). The public key is known to everyone on the system and the secret key only to the authorised receiver.

In practical applications the sender who knows the receiver's public key enciphers the message in established public key code. The receiver uses the secret key to decrypt the message.

In principle the Public Key (RSA) scheme works as follows:

1. Two large prime numbers A and B each about 100 decimal digits long are to be coded. A is to be kept secret.

   Then let $n = AB$ and $x = (A-1)(B-1)$

   A random integer I is chosen between 3 and x which has no common factors with x. An integer C is found which is the inverse of I modulo x, that is C.I differs from 1 by a multiple of x.

2. Given a plain text message A which is an integer between 0 an n-1 and the public encryption number I, then the ciphertext integer is:

   $D = A^I \bmod n$

   That is, A is raised to the power I and divided by the result of n, and D is the remainder.

   To decrypt using the secret number C the plain text of A is found by:

   $A = D^A \bmod n$

To determine the secret decryption it is variously estimated that the task would take a million years with the best algorithm known today. The system is secure but there is a small disadvantage in that users of the public key system utilise the same encryption algorithm built into identical firmware.

Clearly, frequent key changes are desirable since this will increase the security of the system by making it more difficult for the potential attacker to learn the key. Secure key management is of paramount importance.

Key Management

For a cryptographic system to be strong, the key management system must be unimpeachable. Key management is the term used for the generation, distribution and use of key variables. Cryptographic algorithms use a combination of variables operating on plain text data under the control of a parameter known as a key. The key assigns the permutation used to transfer the data into ciphered text. The cryptographic key contains the parameters used for creating the enciphered message.

Key management in a secure network should be performed by two identical micro processor systems dedicated to the task of key management. The two Key Management Centres (KMC) are normally physically isolated and protected.

The centres appear to the system as two Network Interface Units (NIU) with rotary address sequences, i.e. if the first interface unit is busy a second is tried. Two units are normally used for reasons of security. If a single unit only is used and is then damaged the installation may very well be forced to suspend cryptography until the unit is repaired. Also, human error may cause the loss of a cryptographic key. If the lost key cannot be recovered the data that has been enciphered by the key can also never be recovered. To overcome this problem a duplicate set of keys is held by the second KMC.

NIUs are a basic tool of network security. Each terminal device in a secure network will have an interface connecting it to the network. Data travels through the network at the rate of one million bits per second and it travels in logical units called packets, which appear simultaneously at all NIUs.

Network security requires that only the intended NIU can read a a message that is intended for it. To ensure that this requirement is met every packet in the network has the same form. Each will have a destination address, a source address, a data field, an error field, together with control information.

A packet is assembled in the memory of the source NIU prior to transmission and then once the network is not busy begins its transmission. Should two units transmit simultaneously then provision is made for the re-transmission of one of the packets.

A secure NIU will have a network circuit board, a user circuit board, which a normal NIU will have, plus a security board. The network circuit board will implement the protocols of the network communication and the user board will control the functions of the NIU. The security board will contain the DES or similar device , together with the ROM memory chip holding the cryptographic key as well as the memory for the storage of session keys. Data that is to be encrypted is passed by the user board to the security board.

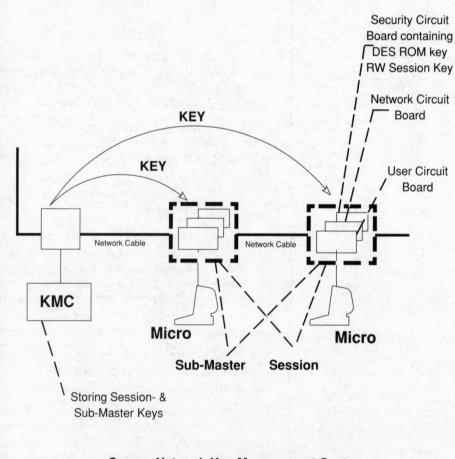

Secure Network Key Management System

In a secure network the key management system is based on a hierarchically structured set of cryptographic keys, the master key, sub-master keys and session keys. The master key is stored in secure memory within the cryptographic unit and is generally not vulnerable to unauthorised access. Sub-masters are enciphered under the masters and will themselves be used to encipher other keys. Session keys are generated by the KMCs and distributed to the security boards of NIUs taking part in a transmission.

Cryptographic keys are enciphered before they are passed outside the KMC and as a result never appear in plaintext in the operating environment. This enhances the security of the system.

Master keys generally have a lifetime of twelve months. This may be shortened if an attack on the system is suspected or if security merits it. Sub-masters have a lifetime determined by the user, based on a sound risk management methodology and session keys have a life equal to the length of the session.

When two users wish to exchange keys contact is made with the KMC which sends a sub-master and session key to one user in encrypted form. A second sub-master and session key is sent to the second user also in encrypted form. The KMC then withdraws, allowing both to exchange information. If multiple KMCs are used the security of the system is proportionately enhanced, since all the KMCs would have to be subverted to compromise the system.

All sub-master and session keys are stored in the KMC which are in turn encrypted, in storage, by the master key.

Security Considerations

There must always be full password control of the Master Key generation facility. This must be supported by a token of some kind and an additional form of identification, as for example, a short question and answer session to ensure only an authorised member of staff is accessing the utility.

As a main security principle the Master Key must be changed at least every twelve months and certainly if there is any suspicion of compromise.

When the key generation utility is in use the keys are in plaintext and vulnerable. Therefore, at that time no other users should be on the system.

If hard copies of plaintext keys are retained, for example if carelessness or inefficiency results in the loss of a key, then they should be held in a locked safe, possibly requiring two physical keys to unlock it.

Each invocation of utilities to develop Session and sub-master keys must be logged.

A log should be made when the KMC is put into key generation mode.

All unauthorised attempts to access the key generation utility must be logged and a central console alarmed.

A log should be made if an error message occurs after the key generation start command has been issued.

Block and Stream Ciphering

Messages to be encrypted are of varying length and the most convenient way of dealing with them is to break them up into short segments and then encrypt. There are two basic ways of ciphering:

>   a. Block cipher
>
>   b. Stream cipher.

Block Ciphering

The basic premise is that all ciphers are divided into blocks of fixed length and each block is encrypted separately. Each bit of the cipher text should be an involved function of all the bits in the plaintext. Once encrypted no item of plaintext should ever appear in plain. Also, any alteration to the plaintext should result in a large alteration to the cipher text.

DES is a block encryption algorithm requiring 64 bit blocks. Should the block size be less then it is padded out to make up the size. At decryption time the padding is discarded.

Stream Ciphering

Stream ciphering uses a continuous random data stream (key stream) and adds this to the plain text to yield the cipher text. When plaintext is not present a key stream alone is transmitted. The key stream is indistinguishable from the normal cipher text to any attacker. Consequently to decode the message the entire cipher text must be decrypted.

Link by Link/End to End Encryption

There are two forms for incorporating encryption techniques into communication systems:

>   1. Link by Link Encryption
>
>   2. End to End Encryption.

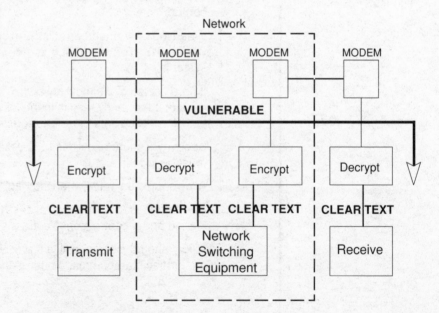

Link by link encryption

Link by Link Encryption is the technique most commonly used. Messages are encrypted for transmission over the communication links between network nodes. As already stated the network nodes use session keys to communicate with each other. Any translation from one key to the next must occur within the node.

End to End Encryption ensures that each end of the system holds a unique key. The processor communicates with both devices and generates a temporary session key. This is then encrypted under the sub-master key of the originator and the sub-master key of the recipient. The originator then decrypts the session key using the sub-master key as does the recipient.

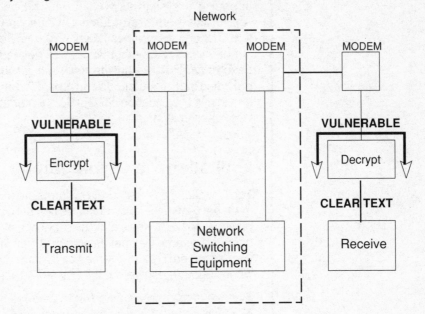

End to end encryption

Mainframe Cryptography

The techniques used on mainframes differs from that used in networks essentially in the duration of protection. In networks or in host to terminal or host to host protection, the duration of cryptology is short. In larger systems where files are encrypted for security reasons the duration is usually long.

Another difference is in key handling. In networks or communication systems the key is usually associated with the session. In file security the encryption key is associated with the file. However, as in networks, key handling has a major role to play in file security.

Mainframe systems usually have a PCF (Programmed CryptographicFacility) or similar unit within the host processor to encipher data before writing it to a file, another processor or terminal or decipher data after reading it from file, another processor or terminal.

Using either the PCF or a similar facility, personnel can allocate cryptographic keys in such a way that only specified, legitimate devices and programs can decipher data. To keep the value of keys secret the unit uses DES as a Master and Sub-Master encrypting key. Generally, only one key ever appears in clear within the facility. All other keys exist in encrypted form. In addition a key manager must be appointed to control the system.

On larger systems the cryptographic unit can be protected by RACF, ACF2 or other similar products.

Own Encryption

Installations often prefer to use their own system of encryption. In this situation the cost, as a security countermeasure, is in the measurement of the effectiveness of the algorithm rather than in the creation of the algorithm.

If the commercially available algorithms are ignored there is a danger of operating a system with unknown and potentially dangerous weaknesses. Against this there is an argument that a secret algorithm does not need repeated key changes to enhance its security. However, if a secret algorithm of good strength is used together with a well defined system of key management and generation, it follows that the security thresholds are significantly raised, always providing that monotonous and repetitive input produces random cipher output and that in this situation ciphers do not repeat themselves with a frequency that weakens the system.

Limitations in Cryptography

The limitations on most crypto systems are those of key management. Poor key management techniques or inattention or human carelessness can lead to files being exposed. Keys may also be destroyed or become unknown due to hardware or program malfunction or human error in handling. For example, the wrong data encryption key may be used or the key in use may be modified and, where files are encrypted, the key stored with the file may be destroyed.

Also, keys may become known to persons not authorised to know them. For example, an attacker may quickly guess a key if it is meaningful to the originator, for example the name of the programmers wife, or if an English word is used. In the latter case it may take only a minute to try every word in the English dictionary using a computer.

If pseudo random number generators are used for key generation purposes then care must be taken to ensure that there is no predictable pattern in their working. Organised and therefore, predictable ways of choosing keys must be avoided at all costs. A possible secure system with a 56 bit key is to toss a coin 56 times assigning the result of each toss to a bit in succession.

Questionnaire

1. Are cryptographic keys enciphered before passing outside the processor?

2. How is the master key held?

3. How many processors are used on the system's crypto function?

4. How is a lost key recorded?

5. How are keys stored?

6. What security keys exist for master key generation?

7. What procedures are in place to protect keys when the master is changed?

8. Are logs kept of sub-master and session keys?

9. Is a log kept of the time when the processor is put into key generation mode?

10. Are unauthorised attempts to access the key generation utility logged?

11. Are error messages logged when the key generation utility is active?

12. How are key generator utility program output listings protected when keys are printed in clear?

13. How are files and data sets protected where keys are written?

14. Are keys available in clear to any person or process other than those charged with setting, invoking and recording those keys?

15. Is it verified that each session partner possesses an identical data encryption key? By the exchange of a test message?

16. Is a test pattern stored with the enciphered data in files to establish that the correct key is in use?

Viruses

A virus may be defined as a program that can infect other programs by modifying them to hold a copy of itself. It is self replicating and attaches itself to a host in the form of a program or data object for the purpose of concealing and then transporting itself from one domain to another.

Viral attacks are relatively easy to develop and leave few traces in most systems; they tend to be effective against most security systems and require a minimum of expertise to implement. Once implemented they spread through systems at phenomenal speeds. Thus, they represent a major threat to all computer systems.

An erroneous impression is that viruses only affect micro computers, whereas the truth shows that many of the larger mainframes and minis have been successfully attacked and that viruses have been spread through their time sharing systems.

Micro computers are especially vulnerable because knowledge about the systems are wide spread. Once a virus has entered the system it usually has full access to everything on every disc that is used on the machine. The vulnerability of these systems, especially networked systems is further increased by the general absence of suspicion and precautions.

Minicomputers are also highly vulnerable because most users share software and can easily communicate the virus through the system. A further vulnerability is that of the "systems manager" who has all access rights to everything on the system. As soon as the Systems Manager tries an affected piece of software the virus is spread through the entire system. On the credit side the systems are small and users familiar with applications making detection more probable but by no means certain.

Mainframes are vulnerable in their test environment which can be the source of infection and once infected the virus can spread program by program to the production environment. Like minicomputers there may also be a System Manager function that becomes infected spreading the virus through the system. In general RACF, ACF2 and MULTICS are likely to be ineffectual in preventing virus attacks.

Every major manufacturer in the USA and Europe has been attacked by viruses. A sizable majority have publicly stated that the attacks have succeeded and that defense against attack is limited.

A virus is known to have damaged several hundred discs and crashed the hard disc micros in the Lehigh University Bethlehem, Pennsylvania. It is also known to have infected several hundred discs owned by students and faculty members. The virus was concealed within a COMMAND.COM within the Operating System. Once triggered it replicated itself on any other disc on the system that contained a COMMAND.COM. It then wrote zeros to the first fifty sectors of disc, removing the first critical 12 sectors and making the disc unusable.

More famous is the IBM Christmas Tree Virus. This first appeared in IBMs internal network in December 1987 as a drawing of a Christmas tree accompanied by a Christmas greeting. Every time a machine accessed the system it became infected as were all the discs used on the machine. The virus slowed the network system down and was detected and removed.

Executable programs are not transmitted over the IBM system and since the virus moved around the network it must be assumed that it had embedded itself in data files for transmission.

Viruses may :

      a)   destroy the file allocation table. This table keeps track of the specific locations on discs holding programs or data files. Logically, this causes the user to lose everything on the disc;

b)   alter the data in data files;

c)   erase programs or data files held on disc;

d)   change the disc assignments so that data are written to the wrong disc;

e)   suppress the execution of RAM resident programs;

f)   create bad sectors on discs;

g)   overwrite the discs directory;

h)   decrease the available free space by making extra copies of programs or data files without interfering with their working;

j)   format tracks on discs;

k)   increase the number of bad sectors on a disc;

l)   hang the system so it will not respond to keyboard entries.

The best line of defence against viruses is to limit their spread either through a no-share policy on stand alone micros, or by limiting the information flow so as to form a partitioned system in a network or minicomputer. In such a system a virus can only spread to those domains which are in the transitive flow path from its initial source.

In the main viruses can only enter through an entry port that will accept computer programs and cannot enter through ports limited to data (although the IBM Christmas Tree tends to disprove this theory). Thus systems which limit the number of programming ports are likely to be less prone to attack.

Many software packages are available that perform virus detection routines. Usually they apply all the programs to an authentication algorithm arriving at a check sum. This type of software might check a standard directory:

ASM	.COM	2670	6.10.87	14:47
EXCHANGE	.COM	5800	3.5.86	20:39
CONFIG	.COM	7829	12.23.85	18:26
ED	.COM	1298	8.6.87	14:32
FORMAT	.COM	5391	11.17.84	22:35
MAINT	.EXE	56111	4.13.86	18:41
MAINT	.DME	8342	6.10.87	12:11

If a virus is implanted the directory might read as follows:

ASM	.COM	2670	6.10.87	14:47
EXCHANGE	.COM	5800	3.5.86	20:39
CONFIG	.COM	7829	12.23.85	18:26
ED	.COM	2698	8.6.87	14:32
FORMAT	.COM	5391	11.17.84	22:35
MAINT	.EXE	56111	4.13.86	18:41
MAINT	.DME	8342	6.10.87	12:11

From this it will be clear that 1400 bytes have been added to ED.COM increasing its size to 2698 bytes. Each time the infected program is executed it spreads to other programs on the disc. After a very short period the directory could look like this:

ASM	.COM	3070	6.10.87	14:47
EXCHANGE	.COM	19800	3.5.86	20:39
CONFIG	.COM	7829	12.23.85	18:26
ED	.COM	12498	8.6.87	14:32
FORMAT	.COM	5811	11.17.84	22:35
MAINT	.EXE	112111	4.13.86	18:41
MAINT	.DME	8342	6.10.87	12:11

Within a short period of time most of the discs free space will have gone, the virus will be in other parts of the system and the attacker will have achieved his goals.

To protect the system, software can be bought that will form cryptographic check sums of files in a computer system in order to allow their integrity to be validated at will. The program will form cryptographic check sums of files and discs and verification of the cryptograhic check sums, particularly prior to the execution of the program. This will alarm at a central console should an erroneous comparison be made.

Other more practical steps can be taken which includes making employees aware of the potential damage that a virus might cause.

As a normal security feature employees should be prohibited from bringing into the work area outside programs for installation on the business system. This should especially apply to Bulletin Board Software.

Software that is bought from reputable suppliers should be tested by a central group who are skilled in machine architecture, operating systems and assembly language. Only when programs have passed this agency should they be used on the system.

Periodically comparisons should be made of known, clean software with existing software. This can be performed by the system that can be made to store a protected version of the program to be compared and to execute the comparison as required. All differences should be thoroughly investigated. Files kept on the system should be reviewed at regular intervals.

Similarly, the length of each clean program can be stored and kept for comparison at the time of execution. Differences in size will indicate program modification. If this is cumbersome a test can be made on part of the program.

Electronic mail can present problems. Ideally electronic mail should be received on a stand alone micro. Programs that are downloaded or received by electronic mail should be sent for testing before use.

If source coding of software can be obtained it should be both for comparative purposes and to compile the programs in house for ultimate security. If the source documentation is impossible to follow specialist help should be obtained.

Should there be any doubt of the veracity of any program and a virus attack is suspected it will be essential to reduce the spread of infection by creating separate libraries with separate authorities and completely superheating and isolating development and production runs from each other.

There can be no doubt that all present computer installation are vulnerable to attack. The situation can be improved by implementing strong personnel procedures coupled with programming and operating procedures. These latter procedures must include software development and release standards, which take into account a central testing group for bought-in software. This will allow better routines for entering software into the system to be developed. Which will be especially significant on networks.

Copies of original sanitised programs should be retained and when a virus attack is possible cryptographic check sums should be applied to all programs. By discipline and alertness it will be possible for most installations to protect themselves against this type of attack.

Passwords and System Controls

A password on a computer system is exactly the same as a password given at a secure army camp. It identifies a friend and allows him to pass into the camp as a trusted member of the community. An enemy armed with the same password would also get access to the camp and would be able to cause havoc. The same applies to the computer system. If the correct person has the right password he can gain access to the data base and information. If an unauthorised and ill-disposed person also has that password he gains access and obtains the same privileges which he can then use for illicit purposes.

The Security Manager or Officer can play a vital role in preventing misuse by the proper control of passwords and access. But to prevent fraud, malpractice or accidental access to sensitive files there must be an initial level of protection. The first stage must be user identification and authentication. Firstly the user must identify himself to the system. This could be by his name or number. The computer will then check which files he may access and will generally ask for some other means of authentication. This is usually the presentation of privately held information to verify the claimed identity. Each individual is assigned a unique identifier or "user name" by which they will be known to the system. This name will generally remain the same as long as the employee works for the company. For example, it could be his own name or an employee number. The privately held information used to verify an individual's claimed identity may take the form of:

a. something KNOWN to the individual,

b. something POSSESSED by the individual,

c. something CHARACTERISTIC of the individual.

Something KNOWN to the individual can be a password or a set of facts from his background. Something POSSESSED by the individual can be an object such as a token or access card. Something CHARACTERISTIC of the individual can be fingerprints, voice signature dynamics or other personal attributes.

Passwords are the most widely used means of controlling access to computers and computer networks. In practice a user will log on to the computer system through his visual display unit by giving his name or number. The computer will then ask for his password and possibly ask him to insert his badge or token in a device associated with the terminal to verify its location and that he is in fact who he claims to be. Passwords should be comprised of a sufficient number of characters and generated in such a manner as to ensure a degree of protection commensurate with the value of the resources to which access is being controlled.

For example, using a five letter password, there will be 26 to the 5th power of possible combinations, which is equal to 11,881,376. If a noun or proper noun is chosen, it is well recognised that the complete English dictionary can be mounted on a micro computer and then run against the table of passwords to gain illegal access. Finding such passwords by this method can be achieved in a minute and a half. Consequently, a password should be comprised of easily remembered combinations of letters together with groups of numerals.

Some systems allow the user to generate his own password. This should never be allowed since control passes to the individual who usually chooses a word that has some significance to him. It is well known that crossword addicts, after talking to programmers or analysts who have determined a password, can quickly conclude what that password is. It follows that the security of self generated passwords, which are rarely changed, is very low indeed.

Special computer programs are available to generate arbitrary passwords which are pronounceable and, therefore, capable of being memorised. These should be under the control of the Security Manager or Security Officer. It should be his responsibility to allocate unique passwords to each employee.

Often it is policy for a group accessing the same resources or data to have a common password. This is clearly bad policy since it prevents any audit of personal actions and makes it impossible to hold any particular user accountable for illicit use of the system.

Provision should be made to prevent passwords being seen when being entered. If the system displays the password on the screen, the Security Officer should arrange for software to suppress the image so that there is no printing of this information at terminals. In systems where it is not possible to suppress the display of the password it may be possible to mask the password with several sets of arbitrary characters without printing it, or underprinting the area where it is to appear. When the password appears in clear on the visual display unit it follows that a browser can read the word, remember it and later use it at his convenience.

Password Management

Since passwords are the initial step in access control it is important that they are managed correctly. In this area the Security Officer comes into his own.

All passwords should be machine generated and be in alpha numeric form. Ideally, they should be of sufficient length to preclude an exhaustion attack. This is where every possible combination is tried by electronic means until the correct combination is found. Thus using the twenty six letters of the English alphabet in any arbitrary arrangement, the number of passwords that can be generated using "n" letters is 26 to the power of "n". Clearly security can be further increased by making numerical substitutions instead of letters.

Password security can be further enhanced by the use of punctuation marks. Thus a typical password might be MFK/26!T. Generally, seven letters or character combinations will be the maximum recall. As an aide memoir the password should be restricted to arrangements of letters that are pronounceable even if nonsense in meaning. Interestingly programs have been devised and are available which generate arbitrary passwords which are pronounceable.

If the Security Officer decides to follow this course of action he should ensure that the algorithm that generates the passwords will be difficult to break by Cryptoanalysis and in this respect he would need to take advice.

Unique Passwords

Ideally unique passwords should be assigned to each user. This will enhance security for the following reasons:

    i.   Records can be kept of each access by a specific password and the purpose for which the access was made;

    ii   Users can be made accountable for the illegal use of passwords;

    iii An audit trail can be maintained of accesses and resource usage.

Other types of passwords exist and they are as follows:

    a.   Once-only codes

    b.   Event restricted passwords

    c.   Responses sequences

d.   Mathlock.

"Once-only" codes are essentially passwords but they become invalid once they are used.. Consequently, the casual browser seeing a password entered into the system will not gain access when he tries the same password at a later date. The advantage of this type of password is that it does not have to be written down.   Modern systems give the user the opportunity to change a password once it has been used. The danger with this system is that the user will have to write down the password each time or use words that are very familiar to him, for example, his wife's name, his father's name, etc.. This in turn makes the system vulnerable . If there limited opportunities to enter the password and a mistake has been made, then it is almost certain that the efficiency of the system will be undermined whilst master tables are accessed to find exactly what the password was.

"Event restricted" passwords may be associated with expiry dates or a maximum number of uses for the password. For example, the password may expire on a given date during the month or after it has been used twelve times. This has some of the advantages of the "once only" code but without the need for many changes. Also, if the usage count is staggered and dates are randomly changed, it follows that new passwords do not have to be distributed to all the users at the same time with the possible compromise to the system security.

Personnel Security

10

Sir John Hoskyns of the Institute of Directors referred to data processing staff as nomadic mercenaries. This is caused by the highly technical nature of the work which they perform and the total dependence on them of the employing companies. As a result they become a sealed off enclave within the company, usually earning more than equivalent management staff in other departments and often with no structured career path within the company. This is particularly so in the medium and small computer systems where the data processing manager has reached his total level of advancement, the likelihood of a board position being remote. As a result staff change jobs continually to achieve greater financial rewards. The average within the data processing industry is something less than two years with each company. Skills are developed to run a particular manufacturer's machine and therefore the individual moves from company to company which has that machine. As a result loyalties go first to the individual, secondly to his skills, thirdly to the manufacturer's equipment and lastly to the company he works for. It is imperative, therefore, that data processing staff are selected with discretion, paid correctly and integrated into the company itself. In short the first aim of control must be the staff themselves.

The Stanford Research Institute maintains that computer fraud grows at 500% per annum. It grows because of the level of trust that is placed in computer personnel.

Unlike the USA, official statistics relating to electronic crime are non existent and an authoritative picture cannot therefore be obtained in the United Kingdom. For this reason we have to look to America where there is a legal requirement to report fraud. Needless to say there is a tendency to veil computer fraud and risk in secrecy on the other side of the Atlantic as well as here in the United Kingdom. As stated in Chapter 1 The American Law Association surveyed 1,000 companies and found 480 had experienced fraud. The losses ranged from $2 million to $10 million. Automatic Teller Machines frauds in the USA are estimated to be in excess of $1 billion per annum. In the UK The Daily Telegraph estimated that the four main UK clearing banks had made £98 million provision for computer related fraud using bank cards. It has been variously estimated that the average computer fraud in the UK runs at £650,000. The fraud itself continues for 3 years as a general rule and then stops.

Of all frauds perpetrated only some 1% are found in time to take some form of legal action, according to the FBI. Of those discovered only 20% are prosecuted and of those prosecuted only 5% are convicted, according to the Stanford Research Institute. In other words the odds are 10,000 to 1 in favour of the fraudster not going to prison.

Fraud is always complicated. For example, the Roskill Committee recently recommended that two experts should be used with a presiding judge in all fraud cases rather than the conventional jury system, because of the complications of fraud trials. This has been rejected by government. However, if conventional fraud is regarded as too sophisticated for the average man in the street to form an unbiased judgement then how much more so with computer fraud where besides the complication of the fraud itself, the whole computing process may have to be explained to a jury.

The first effort at reducing computer related crimes, either fraud, espionage or destruction of information, must come in the selection of people.

It has been variously estimated that 25% of the general public are rarely honest, 50% are honest only if there is a likelihood of being caught (in other words controls exist that might lead to detection) and 25% are always honest no matter what occurs.

For example, shoplifting is now a fact of life and is allowed for in the pricing of retail stores. Low margin stores might very well double their profits if the 25% group could be identified. The main bulk of the 50% group can be defined as those that would commit a crime if they thought the odds of being caught were very much in their favour. For example, most people will exceed the speed limit on a long car journey, but will observe the speed limit if a police car is about or there is a suspected police radar trap. Thus, the police control is effective in reducing crime.

Who then embezzles? Dishonest tendencies cut across all socio- economic groups. From figures produced by the United States Fidelity and Guarantee Company, which compiles statistics on embezzlement throughout the USA and Canada, the following figures came to light:

Occupation	% of Cases
Men	
Branch Manager	18.3
Salesman	17.4
Driver/Deliveryman	6.3
Union Official	5.6
Clerk	5.1
Book keeper	5.0
Executive	4.1
Women	
Store Clerk	21.8
Cashier	19.9
Book keeper	16.0
Branch Manager	7.7
Office Clerk	6.4
Union Official	5.1
Department Manager	4.5

The above table represents an analysis of some 845 men and 156 women who were known to have embezzled or compiled frauds of some magnitude. Over 80% of the embezzlers were employed five years or less. 33% of the men were 29 or younger and 33% were in the age range 29 to 39. Of the women some 50% were in the 29 or younger group with 25% in the 30 to 39 years range.

Of computer frauds it is estimated that some 20% of all incidents are perpetrated by top executives of companies whilst computer staff account for almost 35% of all computer frauds and are responsible for 25% of all incidents. As we have seen fraud, which would once happily run at £10,000 per incident, now runs somewhere at around £650,000 or even higher, making the situation serious. If the 25% who would commit a crime regardless, are employed in sensitive positions then computer fraud will happen. However, it is to be hoped that the broad spectrum of the honest and those who are compelled to be honest through controls will be those individuals that are employed in sensitive job locations.

Management Policies

This is one of the most important factors in controlling honesty of employees. A company which expects every employee to act, in every instance, according to the highest standards must make these standards known. Also, it must not accept any compromise standards.

The very enactment of management policy should refer very clearly to such matters as:

> Protection of assets
>
> Moonlighting
>
> Questionable payments
>
> Vested interests
>
> Gifts and entertainment
>
> Accurate expense reports
>
> Accurate test reports.

Management should also clearly define what they expect in terms of performance objectives. This must not be seen as overriding ethical behaviour so that employees can conclude that providing they are meeting sales or profits then behaviour is unimportant.

Detailed policies should exist for all sensitive and potentially fraudulent situations. The following are given as examples:

> Stock adjustments that are manually inserted to agree with the physical count, where a discrepancy exists between the computer printout and the actual count.
>
> Large exception items such as manually prepared cheques.
>
> Vendor and customer complaints where reported errors or discrepancies could be symptoms of a continuing fraud.
>
> Indiscriminate use of variance allowance which would cover up routine fraudulent activity, say in scrap or trade-in values.

The above are generalisations, but are illustrative of the areas where policy should be defined and inflexible. The intention being to deter the potential embezzler before he or she tries their hand. As an example, a periodic review of complaints from vendors reporting late or missing payments can be made a part of routine operation.

In an analysis of the largest frauds that have occurred both in Europe and America, it has been found that stock and payroll account for just 14% of all losses and 15% of all incidents. Disbursements account for 63% of all losses and receipts some 15% of losses. This will illustrate the areas of greatest vulnerability. In tracing a fraud auditors usually have to "follow the cash" which can be time consuming and often lead to nothing more than the identification of an area of weakness. Ideally, the auditors should be able to evaluate and identify opportunities for fraud or embezzlement and be able to implement controls that will strengthen the company's planning and administration. The keys to effective data processing auditing are:

> **Independence**
>
> **Competence**
>
> **Management commitment.**

The above are all aspects of implementing control which will be considered in greater depth in later sections. All controls should deter the vast bulk of employees from committing a fraud and should raise the threshold of time and money necessary to effect an embezzlement such that the top 25% of dishonest people are also deterred.

Motive sufficient to commit a fraud may develop suddenly or take a period of years to grow. There may be a critical combination of motives or a single motive that actually triggers the fraudulent act. It also appears that motives have a way of developing strength in direct proportion to the size of the fraud that is taking place and the time that it has been continuing. Thus, during the period of the fraud, the motive itself may be small whilst the size of the fraud is small, but once this grows to large proportions then the motive can become almost a dogma.

The categories of motives that appear most frequently in terms of computer fraud are:

Greed

A desire for material possessions

Financial problems

The challenge of the fraud

Revenge

Criminal coercion.

In the analysis completed by the US Fidelity & Guarantee Company the following motives were identified:

Men
Living beyond his means	24.8%
Criminal character	13.5%
Gambling	13 %
Alcoholism	10.1%
Influence by a woman who benefited	6.6%
Irresponsibility	4 %
Extravagance of spouse or children	3.9%
Bad business management	2.9%
Family illness	2.8%
Accumulation of debts	2.8%
Bad associates	2.8%
A grudge against employer	2.7%
Other causes	10.1%
TOTAL	100 %

Women
Living beyond her means	19.8%
Family expenses	11.5%
Extravagance of spouse or children	10.3%
Criminal character	10.3%
Influence by men who benefited	9 %

Desire for a new start elsewhere	5.1%
Family illness	5.1%
Alcoholism	4.5%
Own illness	3.8%
Bad associates	3.2%
Mental problems	2.7%
A grudge against employer	1.9%
Other causes	12.8%
TOTAL	100 %

The key to dealing with motives is to make sure that supervisors are alert to indications that employees are having problems similar to those described above. This aspect of the supervisor's job should be emphasised in training programmes.

Embezzler's Profile

The majority of computer frauds are committed by people who have no criminal record. They are white collar employees from respectable backgrounds and generally in some position of trust.

Interestingly, the US Fidelity & Guarantee Company described the typical embezzler of Depression times as:

> White collar male, 36 years old with a wife and two children. Of good education, he had no criminal character and lived in a respectable area. He owned a medium priced car, took occasional weekend holidays and had a two week vacation in the summer. He had an occasional drink, was regarded as sociable and participated in community and civic functions. The embezzler's friends and wife concluded that he was earning twice the actual amount of his salary, which was always in the middle range. His length of service was just over five years and he was regarded as competent and hard working with above average business reputation and future.

In contrast to this the modern embezzler is:

> About 26 years old, earns more money, is rarely married and has fewer dependents. His character and past record of employment is not favourable. He has worked for shorter periods for an employer and has changed jobs several times. He lives a faster paced existence and is rarely classified as "a normal middle class person". He is still a white collar worker, falls prey to the same temptations and fails his employer's trust in the same general way that the embezzler of Depression times failed. He is much less likely to confess voluntarily to the crime he has committed and even less likely to commit suicide than his predecessor of the Depression period. His hobbies usually include jogging or other solitary occupations.

The Stanford Research Institute describe the individuals as:

> Average age 29.
>
> Management and professional skills predominant.
>
> Violation of occupational trust evident in 65% of all cases.

Always viewed as a highly desirable employee.

Greatest fear was detection and the disgrace that would come from prosecution.

In modern times fraud may be 150 times greater than in pre-computer days, essentially because the information is compressed into a small area by the computer. The media tend to increase people's desires for the good life and make them aware of all kinds of luxuries that would otherwise be outside their ken. Computer fraud may be the only way to make dreams come true.

Inflation also makes its contribution by steadily robbing employees of the value of their earnings since earned income often does not keep pace with the rising costs.

It is also fashionable these days to talk scathingly about Government, the effects of commercial bribery, illegal or questionable payments by companies, Social Security cheats and tax haven companies etc. These all tend to fan the motivation of the average embezzler.

Personnel in Frauds

Wherever possible, controls will exist to discourage either accidental or malevolent behaviour. However, as has already been seen, motives can play a very high part and therefore it is important to employ only the right people and once they have been employed to keep them. To begin at the the beginning, the most important aspect of employee relations will be the hiring procedures.

Hiring Procedures

These are intended to identify competent and honest applicants. The functions might be broken down as follows:

a. A detailed job description which the applicant is to meet

b. A job application form

c. Matching applicants

d. Interviews

e. Verification of the applicants' background and qualifications

f. Testing

g. A probationary period.

Job Descriptions

Often job descriptions are produced on a random basis. However, from a security standpoint it is imperative that all members of the computer department and associate departments have a specific job description. This should be used as part of the interviewing technique and in the first stage the application form must be compared with the requirements of the job description itself.

The document must specify the following:

The title of the job

Position to whom the job holder reports

Which jobs report to the job holder

Educational requirements

Experience requirements

Qualifications and skills

Duties and responsibilities together with a definite limitation of authority, especially since individuals often assume other employees are handling a specific function when in fact they are not

Information to which the incumbent is entitled to have access

Information to which the incumbent may not have access

Physical areas to which the incumbent may not have access

Details of leaving procedures:

Non management employees should know from their job descriptions exactly what activity will result in instant dismissal. If, for example, dismissal is for a breach of security, then if the breach is casual or pernicious, the individual should be dismissed immediately. In this respect the possible effect of an Industrial Tribunal should be ignored.

Similarly, the job description should contain a copy of   the leaving document which the individual will be expected to sign, stating that secret information gained whilst working in the building will remain secret and that he has returned all copies of manuals, documentation, program listings, etc.

The salary range.

The job description should be prepared in advance of a hiring activity. If this is not a new position and an old job description exists then this should be updated before any hiring steps are undertaken.

The Job Application Form

All applicants must fill in this form prior to being interviewed; with the form, all applicants should be asked to supply their birth certificate and a photograph. They should be informed that a thorough background, reference and qualification check will be performed and that they themselves may be required to submit to personality testing prior to being offered employment. Having made this statement then the individual should be advised of the sources from which this information will be obtained together with the nature of any testing to be performed. The applicant should then sign a statement to the effect that he has understood that checks will be carried out and that he agrees to them being carried out. If this is not signed then it should be taken as immediate disqualification of the job applicant.

The application form should contain as a minimum the following information:

1. Names.
    a. Maiden name if applicable.
    b. The name previously held if there has been a legal change and when the name was changed.
    c. Date and place of Birth.
    d. Current address.
    e. Telephone numbers, both business and home.

2. **Employment.**
    a. Company names and addresses that have employed the applicant since leaving school.
    b. Hiring and termination dates with months.
    c. Job title and description of the job.
    d. Salary of the job.
    e. Name and title of immediate supervisor.

   f. Reason for leaving job.

   g. A referee from each job or location.

 3. **Details of military service.**

 4. **Education.**

   a. School/college/university name and address.

   b. Dates of attendance.

   c. Principle fields of study.

   d. Degree qualification obtained and date.

 5. **Professional bodies.**

 6. **Personal referees** (at least three).

 7. **Specialised skills.**

 8. **Leisure interests.**

 9. **Union membership.**

 10. **Health.**

 11. **Driving convictions.**

Matching Applicants

From the employment application it is now possible to match the job description to qualifying individuals. If an individual does not compare with the description, then no further action should be taken except to send a "regret" letter.

Under-qualified and over-qualified employees can represent significant risks. The over-qualified individual must be regarded with suspicion and the under-qualified may affect morale. Consequently, unless there are exceptional circumstances neither should be considered.

Interviews

If funds permit the interview should be conducted in at least of two stages, the more stages the better. The first stage should be with the personnel department who will screen out the totally unacceptable individuals.

The second stage should be with the applicant's future supervisor. Since both will have the same disciplines this is the ideal time to check the applicant's suitability in terms of experience and skills. As both have an understanding of data processing this is the time to pay attention to the applicant's reasons for leaving previous jobs. Clearly any hostility to a previous employer should be regarded with deep suspicion, since if there has been one abrasive situation it may very well follow that the individual will become hostile to your organisation. If there have been frequent changes of residence this should also be checked out. He should be encouraged to talk about his education and employment history, his interests and hobbies. A man who has no outside interests or hobbies and is totally dedicated to his job will eventually drive you mad. The ideal personality will not only have exterior interests, but will have made some achievement in these areas, for example as secretary of a tennis club.

He should be sounded out about any arrests, convictions or participation in illegal activity, especially when a student. If the individual has a number of driving offences to his record it could be a clear indication of his ability to disregard controls unless supervised.

Also at the interview it is important to assess exactly what the applicant needs in terms of salary. The amount of mortgage repayments and hire purchase debts should be assessed. If the individual has maintenance payments to make to ex wives or to his children this should also be assessed and compared with the applicant's apparent need for the job's salary. If the salary, for example, does not equate to his total needs, in other words it approximates to his total outgoings, then the man will have to make money from other sources which will breed disloyalty or he will have to set up a fraud.

Additionally, if he has outside sources of income he should be evaluated for possible conflicts of interest or performance which could impinge on his efficiency. The axiom that "no man can serve two masters lest he will love one and hate the other" is all too frequently proved in practice. Also, he will find one job accommodating and the other irritating. Rather than be the job that provides the irritation it is better not to employ the applicant.

Having selected the "probables" it is now a good time to check them out with a credit agency. Every person who has a court order against them or who is on the electoral register will have a record of some kind. This is an opportunity to check that the man is really what and who he says he is.

The final interview should be held with two members of staff skilled in interviewing techniques. A short list should be drawn up of, say, two or three. These interviews must be carefully structured and the questions to be asked should be planned and listed in advance of the interview. One person should ask the questions and the other take notes. Careful attention should be given to body language which will tell the interviewer more about the interviewee than, perhaps, his replies.

Plan to discuss the candidates early work history first. Activity in the past is easier to discuss than work done yesterday. This will put the applicant at ease and let him talk more confidently about his current work once he is lead forward in time.

Do not answer the candidates questions during the interview but promise to answer them at the end when you will "sell" the company. Candidates that suddenly find questions are usually avoiding a question that they do not want to answer.

The interview should last at least an hour and a half and becarefully structured. The 90 minutes time limit is not an arbitrary choice, but is the usual time it takes an individual to exhaust a predetermined and rehearsed role. When all of us are interviewed we more or less decide what we are going to say beforehand and will discreetly manoeuvre the questioner in the direction that we want. Consequently, in the first 90 minutes of an interview the image of the individual rather than the actual person is projected; therefore, importantly, take the man through the 90 minutes and then begin the real interview after this period has elapsed.

Now is the time to interview to maximum advantage. All impressions of the applicant's suitability should be carefully and completely recorded by the interviewers and any weaknesses should be discussed in depth and probed as far as is practicable and polite so to do.

Verifying an Applicant's Background and Qualifications

Now that you are in a position to offer the job to the applicant it is important to verify that everything that has been said and stated is correct.

The applicant's career history should be carefully checked. All time periods must be accounted for because gaps of even a month may very well indicate that that the individual was in jail or had specific reasons for covering up the time. It is the easiest thing in the world to extend periods of employment to cover such gaps and it is important that telephone calls to other personnel departments specifically verify exact times and dates of employment.

A further way around this problem of unemployment or being in jail is to list oneself as being self employed. This is more difficult to verify, but even an individual who has employed himself must have had agencies with known firms which can also be verified.

Most organisations will conduct their reference checking over the telephone. If the man or woman to be employed will be working in a sensitive area then it is very well worth while taking the trouble to talk to a previous employer face to face and by appointment. In this situation it is possible to verify the exact specifications of the job that the applicant held down. His level of competence, the relationship he had with other employees and those to whom he reported, whether he had habits that were detrimental to his employment, his political or union affiliations, his state of medical health and, above all, his honesty.

If the individual has committed a fraud and has been dismissed for this reason, even in a face to face interview, it may be very difficult to elucidate this information. Though a fraud has taken place often companies want to hush the matter up. The effect of a scandal on the share quotation of an organisation can be dramatic and companies would rather write off #40,000 or #50,000 than lose millions on the Stock Exchange. To uncover this situation the investigator must be experienced and be able to evaluate evasive responses and the individual to whom he is talking.

Personal references should always be taken up and should be with at least three people. Everyone can provide two references, but if they have recently moved to an area or have something to hide then three or four referees will prove difficult to provide. The referees should be asked to give information on the individual's family background, his habits, his hobbies and interests, his educational record and the length of time that the individual has been known to them. It is expected that these will always be glowing, but they might very well reveal a discrepancy, either in terms of recreational habits or family details which bear further investigation.

All qualifications should be verified. Degrees can be quickly verified with the university recorder or chancellery. Professional qualifications can be verified with similar ease. Military records, if applicable, should be checked since this will tell you more about the individuals background and are freely available. If any discrepancies are discovered between what the individual has written about himself or said about himself and background information being sought by the company, these should be exploited in depth. Any applicant who has deliberately mis stated facts should not be considered for employment; if the individual has already begun employment when this is discovered then his conditions of contract should be such that he can be dismissed should a discrepancy be found.

Testing

Numerous tests to assess basic intelligence, aptitude, attitude and personality and also to predict weakness in character, are available to screen prospective employees.

In America the Polygraph test is now playing an important role since it works as a lie detector. Questions are asked the prospective employee about his job application form and his responses are monitored. The acceptance of this test in this country will be met with resistance from unions except for very senior posts. It should only be conducted by a very experienced interviewer and certainly under the supervision of the personnel department.

Honesty tests, on the other hand, can be conducted as a pencil and paper exercise and can often be filled in by the individual in the privacy of his own home and posted back to the organisation. Such tests will tell whether the individual is honest and exactly what his personality represents. This can then be compared with the impressions of the interviewers received during discussions.

Handwriting tests may also be used and apparently are extremely effective.

From experience most prospective employees will submit to the tests providing they know what the results are. There should generally be no reason not to make known to the individual how he scored in such tests.

Probationary Period

It is best that the individual should then be employed for an initial period of three months which gives time for detailed checking and, since it is a probationary period, it allows the firm to dismiss an employee without fear of legal action. This is a time when information on bonding, health, military records etc. becomes available. During this time he should have access only to those areas which are imperative for him to perform his job and sensitive files should be well out of reach. The probationary period gives the management the opportunity to complete its studies of the individual and its information gathering. It also provides the opportunity of verifying that the individual has the skills he has claimed and to make quite sure that he is of honest background.

Even at this time the individual should sign a copyright document. This might state:

> "The information contained herein is proprietary and is the copyright property of .... The holder of this document may not divulge any of its contents to an outside party without prior permission. The document must be surrendered if the holders employment is terminated for any reason.
>
> The computer personnel advise that all computer programs and associated material prepared by .... is the property of .... Without the written consent of .... , given by contract or otherwise, no document or associated material concerned with the design, development or implementation of the computer programs may be copied, reprinted or reproduced in any material form, either wholly or in part, or may its contents or any method or technique available therefrom, be disclosed, either wholly or in part, to any person whatsoever.
>
> The computer programs and associated material available to .... but not prepared by them may, nontheless, be the property of .... who may also have control of the copyright, and personnel are advised to ensure that the above regulations apply to such programs and materials."

A derivative of the above document should be signed as a condition of contract, but in any event all documents should bear this frontispiece to highlight the importance of confidentiality and copyright. Whilst it would not stop the individual bent on stealing or copying documents, it will serve to underline that copying is unlawful. It should also be stated that the following are confidential and may not be disclosed:

      a.   Customers' names, addresses, sales data etc.,

b. Supplier names and prices

c. Product cost, discounts, profitability

d. Computer systems software, application program, intrinsic software and security features and plans

e. Any business plans

f. Trade secrets, formulas and research findings

g. Financial information

h. Collective bargaining strategies

j. Shareholder names, addresses and holdings

k. All personnel data.

One of the largest crimes existing in the computer department after fraud is espionage and this is almost always carried out by data processing personnel. Proprietary software which has been developed over a period of years is always a marketable commodity. It should be remembered that the theft of reservation systems software from BOAC cost that company about £7.5million. If software is not marketable then it will ease the life of the analyst or programmer when he moves jobs to copy software, either tape to tape, disc to disc or document to document.

It will be readily appreciated that removal of disc or tape volumes should be prohibited except for authorised personnel and then only with accurate records to support such a movement and signed permission by the individual's superior. Also, access to the photocopier should be restricted to one or two members of junior personnel, who log all documents that are copied.

Keeping the Honest Employee

Having selected and employed the right man for the right job it is now important to keep him and the way to do that is by keeping him contented.

The first part of contentment must be salary which should be pitched at the right level. A man who is disgruntled over his earnings will become disaffected and turn against the company. This could then result in malicious damage or fraud to supplement his earnings. It is possible to get comparative salary analysis from readily available sources and to ensure that the equivalent grades in your organisation earn the correct salaries.

Inadequate salary is one of the root causes of staff moving from job to job.

Grievances

Grievances will occur and resentment will be felt from time to time by most employees against the company. This will be regardless of whether the resentment is justified or not. There must be a safety valve in the formal procedures that an employee can follow to have grievances redressed. These procedures must be structured in such a way that the employee does not lose his job or status should he give voice to his frustrations under correct procedures.

Grievances come in many types. These can be from performance evaluations that have gone against the individual, a promotion that has been given to someone else, unwanted extra duties, boredom, personality clashes within a department or with supervisors, poor working conditions etc.

Individuals should discuss grievances with their supervisor first under an "open door" policy. If the discussion with the supervisor fails to find a solution then the employee should be entitled, with the supervisors knowledge, to go one stage up the ladder and air his problem there.

The existence of these procedures does not ensure that the grievance will be resolved in a way that is acceptable to the employee. However, it does ensure that the man is able to discuss his problems confidentially and that if his grievance is valid to know that some action will be taken.

Personnel Review

Effective hiring procedure has been discussed. If a man continues in employment then periodic rechecking is valuable from the company's point of view and also from that of the individual. It will give the supervisor and personnel department the opportunity to discuss progress and, if necessary, structure training courses so that the individual's goals can be fulfilled. It will also make management aware of an individuals changed goals, since very few people maintain the same targets throughout their employment with a company.

Reviews allow the employee to be acknowledged and to be applauded for contributions that he has made towards the well-being of his fellow employees or the company. It gives employees an understanding of their weaknesses and areas where improvement is needed.

The employer has a moral obligation to ensure that morale is high amongst those whom he employs. By conducting personnel reviews and performance evaluations he should be able to ensure that as far as is practicable he can meet these goals. Additionally, management will be able to identify the capabilities of its employees and determine the direction in which employees should be guided to enrich their careers. In their turn, employees are reassured of management's concern for their well-being.

Finance must be built into their performance evaluations. The existence of standard evaluation form, and weighting factors will aid management to perform this function objectively. Employees should have the opportunity to challenge evaluations.

The evaluation should include a review of the job description and how the employee measures up to it, the duties that he has actually been assigned and how he performed in them. The attitude of the employee, his aptitude, productivity, learning ability, maturity etc. should all be covered.

The regularity of these reviews should be a discipline within the organisation so that at least on a six monthly basis the employee knows how he is performing against the company's requirements for him.

Job Termination

When a job is terminated either by the employee or the employer, several things should be taken into consideration. The first and most important is whether the period of notice should be worked out.

In all, or even one, of the following cases, he should be compelled to leave the company that day:

     a.   If he has access to sensitive files.

     b.   If he is being employed by a competitor.

     c.   If he is disaffected and holds a grievance against the company.

d.   If he refuses to state to which company he is going.

e.   If he has committed a security breach.

f.   It he has recently joined the company.

If for any reason an individual is to be dismissed then it is important that the employee be removed from the data processing computer areas prior to being given notice of termination. If this is not complied with then the individual may take his revenge on the company by wiping files or destroying discs.

Whenever an employee terminates or is terminated the following steps and procedures should be taken:

a.   All company identification, including badges, identification cards, business cards etc. should be collected.

b.   All keys, magnetic stripe cards, etc. should be collected, and all sources of authority should be revoked.

c.   All relevant locks or codes, passwords and access codes should be changed.

d.   All outstanding accounts should be settled including loans and expenses.

e.   Accounts over which the employee had control, should now be reconciled.

f.   The leaver should sign documents stating that he has no Company property, such as computer files, programs, flow charts and reports.

g.   Other members of staff should be promptly informed of the termination.

Defence Against Fraud

Formal Standards

It is imperative that formal standards should be documented with regard to:

Payments or benefits from other business contacts.

Expense accounts.

As part of the contract of employment, statements should be made that no employee may accept gratuitous payments, services, gifts, entertainment from business contacts in any form whatsoever. Exception to this can only be those things of normal value such as a business lunch or calendars. Difficulties may arise in distinguishing between bribery and the desire to promote goodwill. A strict and disciplinarian approach in this case is the only one that can possibly yield dividends.

Expense Accounts

These have to exist in order that business can continue. However, it is the interpretation of what constitutes a legitimate expense that is the key to control. The amount of interpretation that is possible by the individual should be very restricted and narrow. Even the area where the individual uses discretion should be subject to accounting policy and strict scrutiny.

It should constantly be brought to the employee's attention that inaccurate expense reporting is illegal. The individual should list on his expense account everything that he has paid for which he believes the company in turn is required to reimburse him for. This figure should neither be more nor less.

The documentation covering expenses should define limits of payments for unreceipted lunches or breakfasts when the individual works away from home, the levels of transportation he is entitled to and the limits to which he can entertain the customers.

By the same token, having defined what the employee may or may not do, management must also conform to similar standards. If top management appears hypocritical then employees will quickly discount any standards and procedures they are required to conform to.

Since Egyptian times there has been a pyramid structure in all organisations. It follows that individuals at the apex of the pyramid have less opportunity for contact with those at the base. Therefore, unethical practices by those in the middle may be unnoticed by top management and become bad examples to those at grass root level.

Therefore, any method which will ensure that top management is aware of conditions and attitudes that prevail amongst staff is to be recommended. The following are useful suggestions:

a. An open door policy that encourages feedback from the base of the pyramid.

b. Observations of attitudes displayed by employees. An encouragement of middle management to analyse things being said or done at informal meetings or associations.

c. Questioning of the means used to achieve any given result whether advantageous or not.

d. Being alert to office politics where competitiveness becomes a contention.

e. The grapevine: Always listen to office gossip.

Where policies exist to enhance the ethics of business conduct then there should be demonstration of management's concern for compliance with these standards and corresponding disciplinary action for lack of compliance.

Summary

In terms of personnel security an ounce of prevention is worth many pounds of cure. Basic precautions will ensure that the 25% of people who are congenitally dishonest are never employed. Adequate controls within the working environment will guarantee that the 50% of the population that are honest, because they have to be, will stay honest and loyal. The key to security in data processing is ensuring that leavers (for whatever reason) leave at once. There is always a temptation to hold people for the period of their notice. Almost invariably this is a false economy. A resignee never works at his best because he knows he is going and will not be called upon to answer for his mistakes or indifference. A thief will use the time to set up a fraud or to remove data that might compromise him if he has been defrauding the company. Resignees and dismissed staff should be escorted to their desks which should be cleared out there and then and all confidential information taken back immediately. If everyone is aware that this is a routine procedure ill feeling is avoided. Leaving parties can always take place later, but always outside the company premises.

For some unaccountable reason references are rarely taken up within the computing department. The computing manager assumes that the personnel manager has taken up references and vice versa. The security officer or manager should monitor what has taken place and implement security with a minimum of ill feeling.

When a man is hired for a computing position it is important to check, double check and then check again to make sure he is exactly who he says he is and what he says he is.

To ensure that security precautions are correctly implemented and that no aspect is overlooked it is imperative to work from Questionnaires. Questionnaires will allow a disciplined approach to the subject of security and should be worked through systematically, irrespective of the possible irritation of the interviewee and the obviousness of the question. The findings should be noted carefully and the conclusions drawn logically. Each section will now be followed by questions which are intended for use in the field.

When a candidate is to be employed with sensitive, Level 1 data or critical programs he should be screened by an outside professional company. The cost justification for this action is clear when the damage the dishonest can do to a company when they are trusted with this type of information and code is properly assessed.

Personnel Questionnaire

Candidate Screening

1. Do employment application forms require that three references be submitted?

2. How are the references taken up?

    a. By telephone,

    b. By written request,

    c. By face to face interview with the candidates employer.

3. Are relatives, friends or partners in positions where collusive penetration of the systems security might occur?

4. Are the candidate's work and academic history checked to determine past levels of responsibility and performance, and indication of work attitude?

5. Is the candidate's length of residence and financial stability checked with a Credit Rating Agency in the area of the candidates residence?

6. Is the candidates medical record checked?

7. Is the candidates background checked for the possibility of a criminal record?

8. Are the gaps in employment thoroughly checked?

9. If the candidate is a non-citizen, are alien registration papers or valid working papers required? Are they in order?

10. Is a photograph of the job candidate taken immediately to be placed in the files upon employment? .

11. Are skill tests given to candidates to determine their basic technical competence?

New Employees

1. Are all personnel, including contractors who have access to the classified processing system or data, properly cleared for the highest level and category of classified information processing?

2. Is there a policy for periodic screening of employees in sensitive positions or having access to sensitive information?

3. Unless job requirements call for new employees to be given confidential or classified work, is this work withheld until they are proven trustworthy?

4. Are there screening procedures for maintenance workers, other than consultants and contractors?

5. Do contracts and terms of employment clearly and adequately define codes of behaviour, responsibilities, obligations and liabilities with respect to security matters for:

    a. Permanent staff?

    b. Temporary or contract staff?

    c. Consultants?

6. Do such contracts adequately cover liability for disclosure of informa-

tion, both during and after the periods of employment?

7. Can employees take part-time work without the company's approval?

8. Must employees disclose interest in other companies?

9. Are staff encouraged to introduce new employees and are records kept of these introductions?

10. What relatives of DP staff work in other departments?

11. Are employment contracts, and in particular definitions of dismissible offences, agreed with unions and staff associations?

12. Do you have a viable security education programme?

13. Are appropriate records maintained to identify the security training provided to each person within the organisation?

14. Do you interview all contract workers before offering them a place in your organisation? Do you make them sign a declaration of confidentiality and copyright of documents, programs, systems and flow charts?

15. Are contractors' security agencies legally liable for unsatisfactory performance or behaviour of their personnel, in respect of:

   a. transportation of property,

   b. disclosure of information,

   c. onsite protection,

   d. offsite protection,

   e. indemnity by insurance?

16. Do detailed job descriptions exist for sub contracted employees which:

   a. define limits of authority?

   b. define emergency responsibilities?

   c. define security requirements and reasons for dismissal?

   d. define activities expected of the employee?

17. Does a document exist and is it signed as part of the contract of employment declaring company copyright of documents, programs, systems and flow charts?

18. At interview time is it policy to match the completed application form to the job description?

19. Is the interview criteria based?

20. Do you check reasons for leaving previous employers?

21. Do you check salary levels of previous employers?

22. Do you include personality tests?

Employee Practices

1. Is the employer conscious of employee morale?

2. Are supervisors and management close enough to personnel to detect changes in living and personal habits?

3. Are personnel fully cognisant of their individual security responsibilities in the organisation?

4. Are they provided with an open channel for the expression of their fears, concerns and observations concerning security matters?

5. Does each employee have a copy of the security procedures and controls applicable to his set of responsibilities and activities?

6. Are employees given education and training in the execution of these procedures?

7. Are employees cross trained or rotated to minimise the dependence on key personnel?

8. Are self-employed contract personnel required to adhere to company security regulations?

9. Is the execution of security responsibilities by employees included in the job performance evaluations?

10. Are personnel required to wear identification badges?

11. Are contract personnel required to wear identification badges? Are these of a different colour to differentiate them from regular personnel?

12. Does an open door policy exist?

13. Are personnel appropriately debriefed before they leave the organisation?

14. Are all security positions adequately deputised?

Are staff subject to spot searches including personal, vehicle, and desk searches?

15. Are personnel briefed on how to react to:

  a. physical threats,

  b. hostage taking,

  c. blackmail attempts,

  d. bribery attempts?

16. Do dismissed employees or resignees work their notice?

17. Are holidays compulsory?

18. Has any member of staff had an extended illness?

19. Are salary reviews regularly conducted?

Employee Termination

1. Are all keys, cards, and other sensitive items taken back upon resignation or dismissal? Are the passwords then deleted from the computer control list?

2. Is a check made for all ID badges, program documentation, operating manuals, library books etc.?

Physical Security

11

One of the most important resources that a company can have is its' computer. Not so long ago, proud company directors would site their computer on the ground floor where passers-by could see it in all its' expensive splendour. Fortunately those days are gone and with the advent of networks, computer hardware has vanished into the body of the company.

The threat of malicious damage or accidental destruction through fire, flood or explosion is now recognised as a significant risk. Statistics show that only one in four companies that sustain a major processing loss remains in business three years after the disaster. Physical security, therefore, is of considerable importance.

Terrorist Attacks

In Europe bomb scares are now a fact of life and we can be certain that terrorism will continue to play a role for the rest of this century. Publicity dividends play a part in this as does unemployment and the growing number of young people who find that life's opportunities do not meet their expectations.

Terrorism is no longer confined to communist or nationalist movements but has spread to animal and ecological groups. It is no longer limited by ethnic or educational backgrounds but has become the universal weapon of protest. Added to this, terrorist groups exchange information across a wide front making protection extremely difficult and expensive.

Historically bank raids have been the source of revenue for most terrorist organisations but during the 1980's kidnap and ransom have held the main ground. Technology has reduced the prize in the average bank hold-up and the kidnapping of politicians and captains of industry is far more lucrative for no significantly greater risk. As a result computer fraud and extortion are becoming a new and accepted way of raising terrorist funds. This is underlined by statistics which show that the average successful bank hold-up yields the equivalent of £20,000 and the average computer fraud yields £500,000.

Most terrorist organisations have members with University backgrounds who will know how to use a computer and where it's vulnerabilities are to be found. In the UK. the IRA have not attacked computer systems by choice, whereas the Red Army Faction, Red Brigades, PLO, Direct Action and the Japanese Red Army have all physically attacked computer systems.

However, all the organisations will use a computer to raise money. For example, in Belfast a company supplied a customer with goods at a 99% discount, the goods being quickly sold to inflate party funds. The fraud was achieved by coercing the Sales Manager and Computer Manager. The Sales Manager authorised the discount and the Computer Manager altered the records to allow the discount and to suppress interrogation by auditors who might look for abnormal discount structures. The low value invoices were paid on time completing the audit trail.

This is typical of low technology attack but the real threat lies in the area of criminal cooperation and the growth of apparently respectable businesses owned by terrorist organisations.

Every state has its own sophisticated criminal gangs, most of whom have regular international contacts. They are generally headed by respected members of the community with contacts in finance, industry and politics, as for example the Mafia.

Political groups degenerate into criminal gangs, using the facade of political cause and allegiance to a party as a method of holding their membership together. Generally, disillusionment has set in and individuals have become greedy. Usually, they are on police wanted lists and have very little opportunity other than to live as criminals. Many IRA gangs have degenerated to this level and only offer lip service to their brigade headquarters. As a result they come into contact with professional criminals whose professionalism and experience enable them to carry out the most elaborate of attacks.

Professional criminals have much to offer the political groups and the political groups, being well financed are known to hire the criminal gangs on a specialised basis. As such the future is not bright in terms of computer security. Indeed, experienced, educated and very professional criminals may carry out an act and be totally unaware of the political group that is financing their operation. Thus terrorists can set up frauds and use their party funds to increase capital.

Terrorists share information. The IRA have close contacts with the Red Army Faction, ETA, PLO and the Basque Separatists. The dissemination of information is rapid and effective. The article written by Robert Moss of the Institute of the Study of Conflict entitled "Computer Sabotage, The New Target for Terrorism" and published by the Daily Telegraph gives some alarming statistics.

He stated that in Italy over the past five years there have been 25 well led commando style attacks by terrorists on computer installations and the average damage was over £500,000 in each instance.

The victims included:

> 5 manufacturing companies,
>
> 4 service bureaux,
>
> 3 chemical and pharmaceutical companies,
>
> 4 central government agencies,
>
> 4 banks,
>
> 2 local government installations,
>
> 2 universities,
>
> 1 oil company.

In one attack on a Honeywell Bureau Facility, four separate systems were knocked out and losses were in excess of £2,000,000.

The Red Brigades also mount commando type raids on computer installations and the Montedison Works is a typical example. Well dressed and apparently respectable young men brought a package to the works reception and said they wanted to leave it as a birthday present for a colleague. Once admitted they tied up the guards and entered the computer centre where, knowing precisely what was critical to the operation and what was not, they blew up the front end processor which put the system out of action for four months.

The Red Brigades manifesto the "Resolution of the Strategic Directorate" asserts:

> "Increasingly computerization is part of a sinister plot to maximise social controls and implant espionage sections within every fundamental institution."
>
> "Computer staff represent a repressive ideology."
>
> "Computers represent the domination of US multinational companies and the control structure of a capitalist system."
>
> "The objectives of terrorism are to dismember and unravel these networks."

From these statements it will be seen that computers have a symbolic importance for any terrorist group. As has already been stated the exchange of information between terrorist groups is highly organised and the lessons learnt in Italy will be applied elsewhere.

In Italy the situation is very acute. At the Fiat works in Turin, for example, between 50 and 70 active terrorists work with 350 supporters on just one shift! In another company it was discovered that the wife of a convicted terrorist worked in the personnel department with free access to sensitive files.

In the UK, Sir Robert Mark, formerly the Metropolitan Police Commissioner, publicly stated that the police could not deal with commercial crime; that the public must assume responsibility for protecting its' own property and that for the first time the State cannot effectively protect people from burglary and theft. It follows that crime against property will continue to increase and especially against computer centres.

A truly determined attack by terrorists will succeed in penetrating all but military and government installations. All that can be achieved is to delay entry until help can be summoned.

The Security Officer should find out how long it will take the local police to arrive following an emergency call-out and especially at weekends, when most attacks are to be expected. Thus if the response time is twenty minutes, the security measures employed on the premises should be sufficient to delay attackers in reaching sensitive areas by at least that time.

It should also be possible to monitor intruders by closed circuit television. Thus it will be possible to tell the police exactly where the intruders are and in what strength.

Turn to **Appendix C** for Tables showing typical time penalties which can be incurred by various barriers, methods of construction and associated counter-measures.

For most installations it is possible to time an attack and to raise the threshold of security. Lorries present the most successful terrorist weapon since they can strap telegraph poles on the back and reverse at high speed into walls. Afterwards the lorry can be used as a climbing frame and initial get away vehicle. It follows that there should be no areas where lorries can get up to speed; access roads should have gates and sleeping policemen, as well as many turnings to prevent unwelcome visitors getting up speed.

Car parks, which offer cover for intruders, should also be sited away from the computer building. Closed circuit televisions should have good views of car parks, main entrances, roofs and the sides of the building.

Postal Bombs

Another form of attack much favored by the terrorist community is the postal bomb. This is usually a device that maims or blinds and is used as a means of attacking a specific individual. If an X-Ray device is not available to test that the contents of letters are as they are supposed to be, then office and especially postal staff should trained to look for suspicious packages.

Group 4, the UK security company, advise their staff to take special care with the following packages and letters:

Restrictive markings such as "confidential"or "personal"

Foreign mail, air mail and special deliveries

Excessive postage

Hand written or poorly typed addresses

Incorrect titles

Titles but no names

Misspellings of common words

Oily stains or discolorations

No return address

Excessive weight

Rigid envelope

Lopsided or uneven envelope

Protruding wires or tinfoil

Excessive securing materials

Visual distractions

Their advice is exceptionally good and the organisations for which they are responsible for have never been victims of letter bombs.

Locating Computer Rooms

To prevent illegal penetration the computer should not be located in an obvious area. In the City of London a prominent bank has its main computer room on the ground floor adjacent to the staff car park. The rationale was that heavy equipment could be easily off loaded in the car park prior to lifting into the computer room. The disadvantage is that visitors arriving with staff can look in through the computer room windows at the bank's main resource. Another financial institute has moved its computer resource to a nondescript warehouse, well away from the financial sector. With strong security measures at a remote location, this is the most satisfactory of the two installations.

A computer department sited on the ground floor, should without question, be moved either to the basement or to another floor well above ground. If moving the system is impossible the windows should be fitted with reflective glass supported by venetian or other blinds. At night reflective glass becomes transparent and the blinds would then be used to hide the installation from passers by.

Within the complex all corridors should be straight with no alcoves to hide intruders. The installation, within its protective shell, should be open plan so that management have full visibility of all activities. If two computers are used, to provide full systems resilience, then it should be divided over two levels. The advantage of dividing the installation is because a fire or an attack will generally be on one level leaving the second level unharmed.

Access points on the roof should be as secure as access points from the road. Closed circuit television should be used to monitor all roof top doorways and entrances. At night the roof area should be illuminated.

Lift shaft mechanisms should be similarly protected and air conditioning intakes, especially where these are mounted on the roof. If the building adjoins another care should be taken to restrict access. Often the other roof is used as a fire escape area. Alternatives should be sought and the roof isolated.

End of day searches should be conducted by Security to ensure no one has hidden in toilets or other areas during the day, to attack the system at night.

Access to any building should be via locks accepting tokens and in sensitive areas the tokens should be supported by identity numbers and passwords. The various access controls that are available are discussed below.

Access Controls

Identification Tokens

Photo Identity Badge

This is the most common credential and is usually a colour photograph mounted on an ID badge and is worn by an employee or visitor. The visitor will usually wear a colour coded badge to differentiate him from an employee.

Clearly, an impostor who has found a lost ID card can make himself look like the photograph on the lost card in order to gain illegal access to a restricted location.

To improve the system the photo identity badge could be held by Security who will compare and issue the card to each arriving employee. As an additional security measure the employee might carry a numbered card which he exchanges for the ID badge. If the badge and face do not match then the ID is not issued. The ID card should only be worn on site. If it is lost it has been lost in a secure area.

Optical Coded Badge

This badge contains an array of printed spots within an opaque laminate. The badge is inserted in a reader that has a photodetector which reads the code. Optically coded cards offer a fairly high level of security.

Electric Circuit-Coded Badge

This badge has an electric circuit on one of its laminate edges which, when it is inserted into a reader completes an electric circuit. The badge can be decoded with a simple electrical continuity tester and counterfeit badges made.

Magnetic Stripe Coded Badge

This badge contains a sheet of flexible magnetic material on which an array of spots has been permanently magnetized. The code is determined by the polarity of the magnetic spots. the badge reader has sensors which read the spots and if acceptable pass the badge. This type of card will hold about 60 bits of information which can be sensed and duplicated on a counterfeit badge.

Magnetic Stripe Coded Badge

This is identical to the stripe held on credit cards. At creation the stripe is coded and the code read by a magnetic reading head. Some cards can have up to 90 alphanumeric characters on their stripes, which can include the holders name and number. The card can be swept through a reader making for speed of recognition but it has the disadvantage that it can be decoded and counterfeited.

Passive Electronic Coded Badge

The Passive Electronic Badge has electrically tuned circuits in its laminates. To read the badge a radio frequency field is generated and at the correct frequency, the frequency of the tuned circuits, the code can be read. An advantage is that the badge does not have to be placed in the reading mechanism but only in close proximity. The badge can be counterfeited by the use of common radio frequency test instruments.

Capacitance Coded Badge

The Capacity Coded Badge has an array of small conducting plates that are laminated into its body. Selected plates are connected and the code is read from the badge by an electronic reader which measures the capacitance of the badge and then distinguishes which plates are connected and which are not, this connection and absence of connection makes up the code. In a similar way that the badge is read it can be counterfeited, however, it must be regarded as reasonably secure.

Metallic Strip Coded Badge

This uses rows of metallic strips embedded in the laminate. the presence or absence of the strips determines the code as it is passed through an eddy-current sensor. Each badge can hold about 40 data bits and is reasonably reliable. Again, however, duplication is a real possibility.

Active Electronic Badge

This badge is amongst the most secure. The sensor unit supplies power to the badge by magnetic induction and receives and decodes the credential number transmitted by the badge.

The Smart Card

The Smart Card has a micro chip embedded in its' laminate. When presented to a reader the chip is read in exactly the same way as any micro circuit is accessed by a computer. The card contains sufficient memory to hold information on the carrier as well as a Personal Identification Number (PIN). Thus once the card is presented to the reader and the PIN input, the card can pass information to the reader, such as the holders' name, address and various personal characteristics, which can then be requested of the card's holder before access is granted. The card can also hold information on the gates that the holder has passed through which can be verified at a later date.

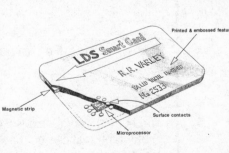

Smart Cards are expensive to produce and difficult to counterfeit and with the additional information that they can hold must be regarded as the most successful and secure of entry tokens.

Coded-Credential Systems

Multi Level Access

This system has a computer as its central control. Access areas are designated and input to the processor together with individual authorisations. Thus when an individual presents his card to a reader, access rights are verified by the computer and if the individual is allowed to enter the area the card holder is logged together with the time and access is granted. The reverse procedure applies when leaving an area.

Since the system is computer controlled access can be changed and might even be altered through the working day, especially if sensitive files are being processed.

Occupant List

The control processor can be made to hold a list of occupants by area. In the event of an emergency a muster list can be printed of individuals in the area just prior to evacuation.

An additional advantage is that anyone slipping back into an area during a contrived emergency can be identified and tracked. Also, Security can verify that the occupant list is empty prior to shutting down an area.

Anti Pass-Back

This feature prevents an entrant passing his badge back to a second person so that he or she can use it to gain illegal access.

Instant Access Change

This feature allows Security to re-program the system if a badge is lost. It is therefore, possible to issue a new badge immediately and program the rights of the new badge into the system and at the same time delete all the rights accorded the lost badge.

Performance Features

Badge Size

The normal badge size is 54mm by 86 mm which is probably too small for a photograph that can be read by a guard. This is slightly smaller than a normal credit card and should be regarded as an absolute minimum. If this size is used it should be worn with the large access vertical providing a more readable photograph.

Badge Preparation

Ideally this should be done on site and the photograph embedded in the laminate by a responsible member of staff. Users should ensure that an automatic voltage supply is available and especially if all badges have to be re-enrolled when the power fails. Most, but not all, systems obviate this necessity since it represents an obvious security weakness.

Durability

Cards cost between £3 and £7 to fabricate, depending on their design. Ideally cards should withstand daily use for a minimum period of five years. They are expensive to remake and re-enroll.

Decoding and counterfeiting

Generally it is not necessary to decode a badge in order to counterfeit it. If a PIN is encrypted it is only necessary to copy the encrypted code and present it to the reader for it to be accepted. For this reason a further action should be required by the holder to ensure identification is complete.

The order of security for identification tokens is as follows, beginning with the most secure token:

1. **Smart Cards,**
2. **Active Electronic Code,**
3. **Passive Electronic Code,**
4. **Capacitance Code,**
5. **Optical Code,**
6. **Metallic Strip Code,**
7. **Magnetic Code,**
8. **Magnetic Stripe Code,**
9. **Electric Circuit Code.**

Badge Readers

These should always be provided with tamper alarms, which trigger an alarm at the Security Lodge or Computer allowing Security to rapidly respond. Similarly, readers should fail safe.

Fire

Fire is one of the greatest threats to a computer installation. Adequate fire detection and fighting equipment must be available.

Automatic Sprinklers

Sprinkler protection prevents a fire from going out of control and becoming a major disaster involving the total destruction of all records, equipment and software in the fire area. The sprinklers will back up any other equipment being used. Back up in this sense is because cable fires will produce dense acrid smoke which will exclude firefighters.

It should be borne in mind that the older electronic systems are more susceptible to water damage than those manufactured with the newer plastic technology. In the situation where there are cotton braid covered wires, for example, special consideration should be given to on/off sprinklers.

Automatic Smoke Detection Equipment

The smoke detection equipment has a threefold purpose:

1. To alert operations staff so they can use fire extinguishers prior to the use of the automatic extinguisher system.

2. Automatically call the fire brigade.

3. Initiate controls for the automatic extinguishers and for the shut down of air-conditioning units etc.

Portable Fire Extinguishers

Extinguishers are provided for the control of small localised fires. Carbon dioxide extinguishers must be used on electrical fires. Extinguishers using water should not be used on electrical equipment but on ordinary combustibles only, such as paper, wood, cloth etc.

Halon Systems

These are used when there is a desire to reduce damage caused by sprinklers, or when there is a need to protect void spaces not suited for sprinklers. When halon is installed there must be sufficient ventilation to remove the gas after a fire.

For safety reasons there must be a delay from the alarm being sounded, to the halon being released, to allow staff to evacuate the premises. A manual override should be in full view so that it can be activated if staff cannot escape.

Power

In the natural course of events power supplies can be interrupted and voltages fluctuate. Either can be expensive and time consuming. Fluctuations in voltage can be overcome by constant voltage units which ensure that the mains power is "ironed out" to a constant level.

If a data base is in use power failure can be very serious since recovery may take half a day and reinstatement of data a further day. Ideally an Uninterrupted Power Supply (UPS) should be available. This offers the best power protection. It supplies clean power by rectifying commercial power to produce DC which operated a DC/AC inverter. Operation during power outage is by means of a battery reserve with about 15 minutes capacity, designed to cover the period before emergency generators take over.

Air Conditioning

Adequate back-up of the air conditioning system is essential. Thus if two units are required to control the atmosphere in the computer centre a third should be available to act as back-up in the event of failure of a single unit. Increases in temperature can quickly cause chaos because of the fine sensitive adjustment on critical parts of the electronic equipment.

A register should be maintained of filter changes in the air-conditioning equipment and an individual made responsible for checking that there is no ingress of molds or rodents or fibres.

The air intake units should be located where they cannot be sabotaged or interfered with. An ideal location is the roof of the building with a protective wire mesh surround. If CCTV is used on the roof it should scan this area.

Housekeeping

Good housekeeping is a central element in the protection of the computer room. Piles of boxes in the computer room, over-filled waste paper bins and smoking are indicative of poor management and high risk.

If the room is orderly and clean it indicates that the thought processes of those in control are also orderly and audit trails and controls, which are supported by good documentation, will also be present.

Other items that play their part in housekeeping are as follows:

Electricity

Water mixed with electricity spells disaster. A raised floor in a computer room is a potential water trap either from condensation or water leaks. A humidity detector placed under the floor and connected to an alarm is one protective threshold an industrial vacuum cleaner, that will pick up water, is another.

Accidental electrocution is another problem in computer rooms. Individuals carrying out fault finding run the risk of electrocution. If they should receive a shock it will be necessary to pull them from the equipment without imperiling another persons life. The ideal solution is a wooden walking stick which should be mounted in full view of the computer room. This is good safety practice and it will also have a prophylactic effect.

Emergency Lighting

Emergency lighting in the computer room is highly desirable as in the event of a general power failure, there may not be sufficient light to enable staff to move without a high risk of injury.

Failing this provision, it is advisableto have adequate flash lights located at a convenient places in the computer room and allocate a member of staff to replace all batteries on a bi-monthly basis.

Fire

A cable fire in the computer room will result in heavy smoke. This in turn will force staff to the floor and oblige them to crawl to safety. They will not be able to see the exit signs and will almost certainly lose their sense of direction. To avoid this the floor should be marked with iridescent tape that points the way to safety.

Flood

A burst pipe on another floor might flood the computer room. To protect against this have a large sheet of transparent plastic available to throw over immovable equipment. A hair dryer may also prove useful for drying out damp circuitry prior to starting up.

First Aid

Victims of heart attack, seizure or electrocution require immediate assistance whilst awaiting the arrival of an ambulance and professional help.

Industrial First Aid courses are available through the Red Cross or the St. John's Ambulance Brigade.

> A bottle of oxygen.
> A stretcher.
> A walking stick.
> Some rope.
> A gas mask.
> Flashlight.

A periodic check should be undertaken to ensure that each is present and usable. None of the items is very glamorous but their use could mean the difference between life and death.

Questionnaire

1. Is the installation a target for political sabotage or vandalism or commercial espionage?

2. Are security guards provided:
      a. on a 24 hour basis?
      b. at all street level entrances?
      c. at entrances to terminal areas?
      d. at car park entrances?

3. Are guards or CCTV available to monitor:
      a. roof levels?
      b. car park areas?
      c. loading and unloading bays?
      d. all exits including fire exits?

4. Is night time illumination provided for:
      a. all entrances?
      b. all exits including fire exits?
      c. all open spaces within the perimeter?
      d. roof areas?

5. Are all entrances alarmed to notify security personnel of entrances or departure:
      a. during working hours?
      b. after working hours?

6. Is the status of each emergency exit monitored?

7. Do you utilize badges, tokens, keys or other access control tokens?

8. Are key combination and control procedures in use:
      a. to ensure accountability?
      b. to regularly change keys and codes?

9. Is a photo ID used to identify employees, contractors etc.?

10. Is a visitor badge system and control procedure employed in the centre and terminal areas to:
      a. identify visitors?
      b. escort all visitors?
      c. maintain a log of all visitors with access to restricted areas?

11. Are staff made aware of their responsibilities before escorting visitors?

12. When employees are dismissed or transferred are:

    a. security personnel immediately advised?

    b. all badges and tokens retrieved from the individual?

    c. they escorted from the computer environment?

    d. door codes automatically changed?

    e. password, libraries etc. up-dated?

13. Is partitioning within the computer area adequate with respect to:

    a. visibility of vdu screens and listings?

    b. access to supervisory terminals?

    c. access to the hardware, switches and cables?

    d. access to telephone frame rooms and switch panels?

    e. access to documentation?

    f. access to libraries or storage media?

14. Are security personal provided with a list of employees who are authorised "after hours" access to the facility?

15. If security guards are not employed to restrict after hours access to personnel:

    a. are personnel trained to challenge unidentified visitors?

    b. must visitors wear identification tags or cards?

    c. are cleaning and maintenance personnel monitored whilst they are in the computer area?

16. What procedures are in place to monitor public services (fire, police, medical representatives) whilst they are in the area for inspections, drills, actual emergencies?

17. Are maintenance staff cleared at the highest level of category of classified data processed in the system?

18. Are all windows at or near street level covered with protective grills or fitted with unbreakable glass?

19. Are terminal areas monitored for access? Are terminals immobilised at the end of each session?

20. Is the computer overlooked?

21. Are areas which contain telephones, circuit junction boxes, manholes etc. locked to preclude tapping or monitoring?

Terminal Security

1. During non-working hours are the remote terminals secured by:

    a. 24 hour security?

    b. a suitable secured cabinet or protected room?

    c. terminal and circuit disconnection?

    d. intruder alarms?

    e. terminal and circuit protection?

2. Does the terminal security during working hours satisfy the classification and category of data being processed?

Fire Exposure

1. Are combustible supplies such as paper, cleaning fluids etc. stored outside the computer area?

2. Are old tapes and disc packs stored outside the computer area?

3. Are files stored in reinforced fire proof containers when not in use?

4. Is smoking prohibited in the computer area?

5. Are operators trained in fire fighting techniques and assigned specific responsibilities in the event of fire?

6. Are raised floors, curtains, rugs and furnishings non-inflammable?

7. Is there an evacuation plan?

8. Are fire drills conducted? When?

9. Have procedures been published and tested for securing data, hardware and software in the case of fire?

10. Can floor sections be removed easily to allow exposure of fire or smoke sources?

11. Are appropriate fire extinguishers located in the computer room? Are they clearly visible?

12. Are smoke detectors fitted beneath the floor, in the ceiling or in air-ducts?

13. Does the system automatically shut down air conditioning?

14. Does the frame room have detectors?

15. Are emergency power switches fitted adjacent to doors?

Water Damage

1. If the computer is below ground are there adequate flood pumps available?

2. Is there floor drainage?

3. Is a moisture detector fitted beneath the false floor?

4. Is there a history of flooding?

5. Is there provision for water accumulating on the roof?

6. Are large plastic sheets available?

Air Conditioning Systems

1. Are filters changed regularly? Are they non-combustible? Are duct linings non-combustible?

2. Is the back up system tested on a regular basis?

3. Does the back-up include stored water and emergency power supply?

4. Are air intakes at street level? Are they protected?

5. Are emergency controls and recorders available?

6. Are there audible alarms?

Electrical Systems

1. Is there a UPS?(Uninterruptible Power Supply)

2. Can power be led through alternative switch boards and distribution units?

3. Is the back up tested? When?

4. Is the fuel supply protected?

5. Is the power unit protected?

6. Is emergency lighting available?

7. Does the back-up supply allow for the operation of fire alarms, access locks and air conditioning?

8. Are the transformers adequately protected?

Physical Security Case Study

Overview

You are the Security Consultant to Joseph Bloggs & Son Plc. (JBS) a large group of international companies with interests in pharmaceuticals, industrial chemicals and fertilizers. They have considerable trade interests with Africa.

JBS conduct experiments and trials of drugs, pharmaceuticals and chemicals on animals, at a special establishment remote from their main offices. they have always been aware of the need for physical security because of the threat posed by extremist elements in the "prevention of cruelty to animals" lobby , who do not hesitate to use arson and destruction in their campaigns. There is concern that there might be a backlash against *ANY* JBS location because of this, a threat which is heightened by their South African connections. It is important, therefore, that the company's vital computer installation is adequately protected.

As a security measure, the computer department is to be relocated in a country town. A site has been bought on a trading estate and a new building erected under the guidance of the company's architect. No one from the computer department has been consulted during the design or building period and it is only now, just prior to occupation, that you are being consulted.

The Group Board has instructed you to examine security requirements on the site. You are to asses the risk in the light of the current situation, and to prepare a report on the recommended measures to be taken.

Terms of Reference

Security defences are to be provided that will ensure,as far as is reasonably predictable, that unlawful entry to the site and access to sensitive areas of the site is prohibited for a minimum period of 15 minutes.

Reliable systems are to be provided for the detection of an intruder and the observation of his progress and activities so that up to the minute information is available to the security officers, the police and to management.

For political reasons the Chairman would prefer that guard dogs are only used as a last resort and then only in such a way that the public is not aware of their use.

A budget already exists for five security men and these are being supplied on a contract basis.

No budget exists for physical security. JBS will pay whatever is cost justified to protect their installation.

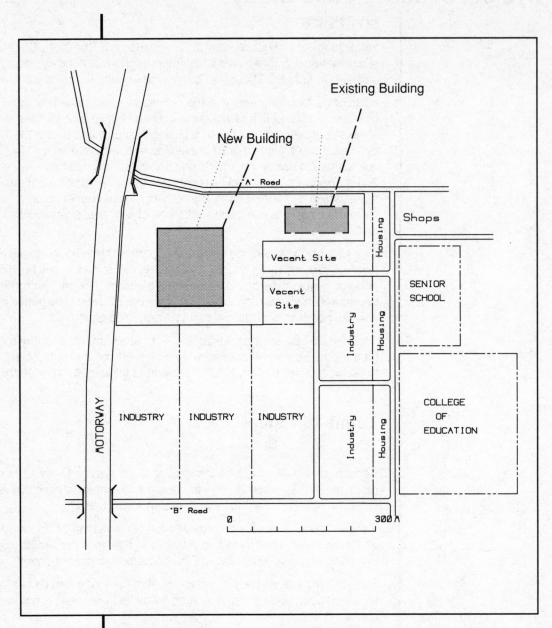

Site of JBS Plc

Case Study

What would be your programme of activity to research the background and financial requirements of the project?

What can JBS expect to loose in the event of a fire or an act of sabotage which prevents them from using their computer system?

What would your recommendations be to the Directors in terms of physical security? How will you justify your recommendations?

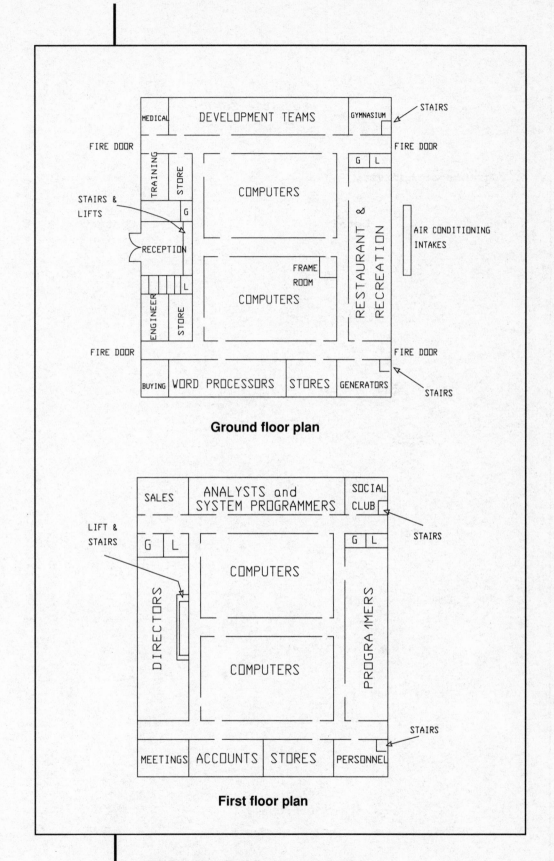

Ground floor plan

First floor plan

JBS Plc. New Building as surveyed.

Possible Solution

Programme of Activity

Item	Detail	Contact
1	Arrange Site Visit	Site Administrator
2	Arrange meeting with local police	Chief Supt.
3	Visit Site, Dates.	Guide
4	Inspection. Drawings .	Architect
6	Evaluate Current Loss.	Insurance Manager Insurance Broker Computer Manager Financial and Managing Director
7	Determine Risk	
8	Evaluate Loss. Consequential.	
9	Write Report.	
10	Prepare Presentation. Drawings - Overlays.	
11	Write Investment Proposal.	

Survey Details

The survey revealed the following facts and proposals:

A. **Access Control.**

Gate security contacts reception by telephone when a visitor arrives. Sometimes security will telephone direct to an individual if the receptionist is busy.
No visitors badges are worn and visitors walk unescorted to the main building.

Admin. Bldg.

Reinforced concrete post and beam. Concrete floors, all accept required load.

Walls - 11" cavity brick and block .

Roof - Reinforced concrete frame, metal clad bitumenised.
Interior - all partitioned.

Single plate glass windows.

Doors, external - hardwood in hardwood frames
Doors, internal- single offices - softwood in softwood frames, open plan - glazed with centre bar.

C. **Communications.** Telephone. Dedicated telephone lines for computer systems.

Computer. Mini Vax Computer System. Communicates with 10 remote locations.
All systems are duplicated. There are 2 CPUs , 2 complete backing stores systems and dedicated printers

There are two front end processors and 31 micro computers, 30 of which interact with the mini and also 25 ``stand alone'' word processors.

No provision has been made for fire proof safes. Storage of back up copies is generally on site.

D. **Development.**

Cavity walls - brick exterior - block interior - 11".
Single plate glass windows and glazed doors.

Softwood doors in frames - 2M X 1M with centre bar.

Roof - flat - aluminum - bitumenised.

Interior partitioning. Mainly top glassed with glass plate and wired for intruders.

Doors and frames solid - softwood.

E. Environment.

Busy road. Students in area during term. Crime rate; 40 minor incidents and 4 major incidents over past five years.

Demonstration; anti-nuclear,1 in previous year.

Society; mixed but including affluent farmers and commuters. Most local work is in farming, the remaining employment is light industrial, with some office and shop work.

Fairly active site and area. Railway nearby.

Easy access to site.

F. Fire.

Good protection system; modern main panel in the Security Gatehouse with satellites in buildings.

Own well trained Fire Team.

Fire protection No.1 priority.

Fence.

Chain link with cantilevered 3 strand barbed wire. Total height 2 meters and the condition is fair to good .

G. Glazing

Windows and doors as as stated above except fire doors which are wired glass.

Sizes; windows 1M X 1M , 1M X 2M and 1M X 3M

L. Lighting.

Adequate for normal use - no black spots

Locks.

External; 5 lever mortice

Internal; nil.

S. Site Security.

Working hours - Commissionaire plus Receptionist. At all other times - 2 Security Guards. Holiday relief etc. provided by contractors.

Little or no supervision from Contract Company.

Security Costs. Contract - £4.50 per man hour

V. **Value of**

  Equipment.

The mini computers represent a capital investment of £1.2 million.

The micro computers represent an investment of £120,000.

The Mini Computer Software cost £400,000.

Micro computer software value £30,000

Company Information

Annual Return

Annual Turnover.....................................£285 million

Dividend Profit....................................£27.7 million

Annual Debt Funding...............................£22 million

Assets..£190 million

Borrowing...£120 million

Interest on loans 12% fixed.

Share prices last year: high.....590p

                                    low......180p

Capitalisation ''high''   £885 million

Computer Staff Payroll

4 Managers	£120,000 p.a.
4 Analysts	£100,000 p.a.
1 Systems Programmer	£40,000 p.a.
5 Programmer Analysts	£80,000 p.a.
12 Operators etc.	£120,000 p.a.
8 Clerical/typing support	£50,000 p.a.
6 Contract Programmers	£180,000 p.a.

Contingency Arrangements

If the machines are destroyed, back up will be on equivalent machines owned by a bureau located one hundred miles away. There is no direct communications link. Cost of machines £500 per hour.

Agency and Contract staff could be brought in from previous city location which is outside daily commuting distance. Agency and Contract staff will cost 250 % of company staff.

Software and Data

Destruction of the building would mean partial software recreation etc. Extra working would be required estimated at 120 computer days of three shifts.

History of Consequential Loss

A Bomb was detonated in the company's headquarters, three years ago. There were no deaths or injuries. Last year a demonstration of socialists, animal freedom groups and students caused £5,600 worth of structural damage to the buildings. A guard needed hospital treatment. On the basis of the latter event it was decided to move the computers, which are key to the company's well being , to a country area.

When the bomb exploded property damage valued at £84,200 occurred but there was no attack on the computer or its ancillary equipment.

However, the cost to the company after 18 months was much higher:-

44 employees left JBS , they had an average service of 5.5 years.

Cost of recruiting replacements proved to be.......£52,000

Production down-time cost £90,000

Overtime to meet the production schedule...........£51,100

Executive time directly related...................£96,200

Temporary agency personnel.........................£78,500

Union contract : Salary/wage issue at
next balancing period (estimate).................£100,000

Increased security costs (one year)................£69,000

Property damage (not covered by insurance)........£22,480

Employee time lost day after blast.................£77,300

Reports : Police, Insurance........................£8,800

Training costs (for replacements) £75,000

Scrap and rework, new employee errors.............£40,000

The total cost of the incident was found to be £760,380 and this unlike the £84,200 bomb damage payment was not covered by insurance. After this an Insurance Manager was recruited.

Examples of Costs

CCTV Cameras and Console...................£1,700 per camera

Harden Fencing............................£15,000

Gate House................................£19,200

Gates, electrically controlled............£10,000

I.D.Cards with magnetic stripe............£10 each

Fire Proof Safe £5,000

Guards' radios............................£2,400

Computerised Access Control...............£15,000

Sleeping Policemen........................£1,500

Possible Costs caused by Fire or Third Party Attack

The building and office equipment, including the computer hardware,software and ancillaries are covered by insurance.

It is recognised that a total disaster, such as an aeroplane crashing on the building will cause four months extra work. Since the company is totally computer dependent there is no possible reversion to a manual system. Processing will have to continue on the stand-by bureau.

Bureau Costs: £500x24hoursx120days   £1,440,000

                1st & 2nd shift maintenance   £25,000

Staff: Based on history of previous disaster.

         25% staff loss, recruitment costs £1,200

         per person   £12,000

         Training costs at £1,700 per person   £17,000

         Bonus to be paid to all workers at £500

         per person, external staff and employees   £60,000

         Executive time   £100,000

         Increased security costs   £70,000

         Reports-police/insurance etc.   £9,000

External Staff: 40 Contract staff for four months

         will cost 250% of employee rates   £575,000

         Auditors to monitor work   £50,000

         Consultants   £50,000

         P.R.   £100,000

Accommodation: Own staff half board 40x£50x120days   £240,000

         Contractor staff 40x£50x120   £240,000

         Others   £60,000

         Temporary Offices at 45 square foot per

         employee, 40x45x£50 per square foot   £90,000

Transport: Taxi runs from office areas to bureau   £60,000

         Miscellaneous travel costs,staff   £10,000

                      Total   £3,208,000

Additional: The loss on share capitalisation if their value reaches a new low, due to sensational press comment could be as high as £615,000,000 making JBS vulnerable to a take over bid.

There might be problems with debt funding perhaps even an increase in interest rates

Security of Premises

The area does not have a history of militant activity, especially as most of the local income is generated from the land.

There is a high density of students fairly near the area but without a high record of militancy. However, it is recognised that rabble-rousers travel around the country and that other militant students and trade unionists can be shipped in to beef-up the locals. The main threats might lie with animal rights and anti-vivisectionists but not the hard core terrorist organisations. Even so, adequate precautions must be taken.

Adjacent Vacant Lots:

> Buy and use for staff cars
>
> keeping area inside perimeter fence
>
> clear.................................£120,000

Perimeter:

> Harden fencing with concertina coils....£15,000
> Ensure no gaps under fence.

Gates:

> Locate two gates one at entry to campus
>
> the other by the Gate House at the NE
>
> corner of the newly purchased lot.......£10,000
>
> Secure Gate House with CCTV Monitors....£19,200
>
> Two sleeping policemen between gates.....£3,000
>
> Brick wall after campus gate to force
>
> lorries to turn and not get a speed run
>
> at the building.........................£1,500

Reorganisation: Move the Social Club, Gymnasium and Restaurant to the other building. The Sales Office should also be moved because of the high incidence of employees and visitors entering and leaving the building. One CPU. and F.E.P. would be located on each floor. Cost of this exercise would be less than £2,000.

The Air Conditioner intakes to be moved to roof level at a cost of £5,000

All main doors within the computer building to have magnetic card locks. These would include:

> Door from reception to main building.
>
> Doors to Directors' Suite.
>
> Doors to Development, Analysts' and Programmers' Areas.

A second level of security (privileged passes only) would give entry to:

Both Computer Rooms.

Word Processor Areas.

Media Stores.

The access would be computerised so that the Gate House had a print out of all exits and entrances, with times and individual names.

The cost of this system will be £15,000 or £350 per month rental over five years.

CCTV cameras would scan all sides of the building, with a fifth covering reception and a sixth and seventh the computer room entrances. Total cost £12,000.

Windows on the ground floor would be protected by 1/2" m.s. bar and the glass would be changed to reflective to prevent passers-by seeing what occurs within the building. Reflective glass would also be fitted to the first floor windows. All glass would be reinforced. Cost £17,600.

A fire proof safe would be installed in the adjacent building. Cost £5,000.

The entry doors to the building, computer rooms, media stores and word processor areas to be hardened with mild steel. Cost £3,200.

Personnel. All staff to wear I.D. Cards which will duplicate as entry tokens. Cost £500. Guards to have radios at a cost of £2,400.

The total cost of the security requirements is £111,400 excluding the land purchase which will become a capital asset.

The presentation to The Board would take the form of a comparison of Single Loss Expectancy, in this case of £3,208,000, to an expenditure of £111,400. The purchase of the adjacent sites for £120,000 would also be compared to the loss of share capitalisation if the worst happened. This purchase would have the additional benefit of increasing the company's asset value besides increasing security.

In an actual presentation all costs would be annualised.

Documentation and Libraries

12

Everyone dislikes documentation or procedures. Like security in a data processing environment, documentation is seen as a need that does not contribute to deadlines. However, good documentation is necessary for two reasons:

    a. In the event of absence of key personnel to follow the work that has been done;

    b. To re-create the computer system after a disaster.

Therefore documentation becomes a part of information processing that should always be in the care of the Security Officer, who in turn, must ensure that the documentation is up to date, readable and useful.

Documentation Overview

It is imperative that documentation should be as simple as possible. During the 1960s, the New York banks spent a great deal of time and money to produce operations manuals. Only one bank, in the end, actually used the manual, and this was because the author had tested the draft manuals on his teenage daughters.

The girls had been required to read them and then explain the contents back to him. When they could do this successfully, he allowed the drafts to become firm documents. This approach was successful because it was designed for the needs of the users and matched their ability.

The objective of simple manuals should be that they are so clear and complete that the user needs absolutely no additional help whatsoever. The author must assume nothing and take care to explain everything.

For example, a page in a manual headed "Use of 2 initiator key" is describing the system in a way which can mean nothing to the user. The page should in fact be headed "How to initiate data" which is the function of the 2 key.

Detailed instructions should be separated from general descriptions. It goes without saying that if the user cannot carry out instructions as he reads them, the newness of the system or its complexity will cause him to forget them. For this reason all operations should be described in the order in which they are to occur. Axiomatically if an operation is to be carried out several different times, then the instructions should be repeated as many times as is necessary to complete the sequence of events.

It is always important to use visual information. A good pictorial introduction to a section would have 66% more effect than any amount of verbiage. This could apply to information flow, the way data is organised and decision processes. Also, a multiplicity of type faces could be used to accentuate points and also colours would be helpful. Something that is visually interesting is one which people find easy to use. If they do not find it easy, it will not be used, as the New York banks found.

Good documentation will always turn expenditure on hardware and software into results. Conversely, poor documentation gives poor results. It goes without saying that the proportion of total cost should be kept as low as possible, but if a firm's documentation cost is less than 5% of the systems development cost, then it will certainly be economic.

Types of Documentation

The following are the basic documentation requirements for almost every computer installation:

    a. The old manual system or fall back system,

    b. Operations documentation,

    c. Software development and release documentation,

    d. Security manual and strategy,

    e. Personnel controls, clearances and procedures,

    f. The contingency plan.

The Old Manual System

When a computer is acquired the old systems are phased out. As time passes the individuals who were aware of the method of operation also tend to either retire or leave the company. As a result after two or three years of processing the method of operation of the old manual system is forgotten. This does not mean that the overlying principles are obscure, but rather the underlying detail is missing.

For recent users of computers it is therefore vitally important that the old manual system should be documented whilst everyone remembers exactly how it works. Samples of stationery should be kept and a detailed method of operation should be written down and stored in a remote location.

This document should never need updating in the accepted sense of the word but should be checked from time to time to ensure that the manuscript does not deteriorate. In a disaster situation, if the computer is put out of action, or the computer room destroyed the old manual system may have to be used on a temporary basis.

Operations Documentation

Operations documentation is almost invariably provided by the manufacturers of the mainframe, communications equipment and micros. This can rarely be improved upon but copies should be kept by the Security Officer.

Software Documentation

This should include all programs and systems documentation taking into account algorithms, the objectives of the system, programming details, programming modules that are interdependent, data file manuals, etc. These should always be kept under lock and key and at least one copy which must be a complete printout of all programs be held in a remote location. If possible the remote location should be another division of the company quite separate from the user or in the company's bank. This form of storage and detail of documentation is essential should a disaster occur in the computer room. It will then be possible to compare salvaged media with printouts and recreate missing data.

Software release procedures should also be documented and should be a separate document from the overall software documentation. Thus every individual will know how program modifications are requested and authorised and how programs will be developed and later catalogued.

The documentation of security related code is also a factor that will fall under software documentation. Security related modules or sections of code must be clearly identified and completely documented. These will include:

      a. Code that implements security controls

      b. Code that performs critical processing

      c. Code that has access to critical sensitive data in its execution.

Security Strategy Manual

Ideally, security strategy should be defined and documented. Realistically, this is rarely the case but most certainly a security manual is absolutely essential.

The purpose of the security manual will be to document computer security controls, procedures and standards within the company.

The manual will be used by the Security Officer and the management services department. It should describe how security and contingency development and implementation fit into the life cycle of the company's information system. The "system life cycle" is defined as being all stages during the life of a system from user requirement specification through implementation until the system ceases to be operational. System controls and procedures should be described as well as manual controls and procedures. If applicable a risk analysis methodology that is used by the company should also be documented in the security manual. The threats dealt with would include the following:

      a. Environmental hazards

      b. Hardware and equipment failure

      c. Software failure

      d. Errors and omissions

      e. Personnel policy.

Whilst program development has been described under Software documentation it will be necessary to include program development, program changes and program libraries within this document.

Besides dealing with the mainframe it should also deal with any micro computers, terminals and word processors.

The Security Manual should reference the Contingency Plan or include the essential security sections.

Personnel Controls, Clearances and Procedures

Any clearances that have been obtained should be retained by the Security Officer and any documents such as copies of signed Official Secrets Acts should be in his custody.

The personnel policies should be held by the personnel department and the Security Officer.

Disaster Plans

The prime aim of a contingency plan is to ensure that user departments can perform an adequate work load in the aftermath of a disaster. It will identify critical functions, alternate site operations, the key processing requirements, the recovery of data and the restoration of the facility.

The contingency plan should not just deal with the total disaster when the entire installation is lost but with action to be taken in the event of say an air conditioning failure, or an electricity failure, industrial action, a lock out or local disaster denying access to the computer room.

Of all documentation this is the one item that the Security Officer should test and know completely. In disaster the role of coordinator will certainly fall to the Security Officer.

Physical Security of Documentation and Media

This is a procedural control of data related to data classification rather than the preserving of vital documentation.

Having classified the the data within the data base and having determined the type of controls that are necessary to secure the input of data, by classification, it is of equal importance that the security of media and output documentation should be maintained.

To this end it is vital that all magnetic tapes, cartridges, discs, discs and hard copy, draft copy, printer ribbons etc., are clearly identified with their classification level and that their storage and disposal is appropriate. Markings should be identified by word or colour coding.

Identification

A typical identification system might be:

Level	Subject Matter	Classification	Colour
1	Highly secret data for top management e.g. strategy	Secret	Red
2	Medium sensitive data for limited circulation.	Confidential	Blue
3	Low sensitive data for company eyes only.	Restricted	Yellow
4	Non sensitive data requiring no protection.	Unclassified	Green

The classification should be printed prominently on all paper work from manuscript draft to hard copy print out. The colour code should be indicated by adhesive coloured tabs on magnetic media and placed so that it is readily visible.

It is important that both the classification and the colour coding should be at the highest level of classification of data contained in the document or media device

Records

Records should be maintained of the status, location and disposal of all Level 1 material and a system of periodic checks of the accuracy of the record should be made, requiring the physical production of the material or certificates of its destruction.

Storage

All magnetic discs and cartridges containing level 1 and 2 material should be kept in lockable containers and preferably in a secure store. During the working day it is vital that micro computers or terminals accessing level 1 and 2 type data are automatically disenabled after a period of non-use and that they never face walkways when in use. A "clear desk" policy should exist at the close of the working day.

A "Responsible Person" should be nominated for each area, where highly sensitive data is in use, who will be responsible for local security. Amongst the responsibilities of this person will be the implementation of local security measures, recording breaches of security, ensuring used media is degaussed prior to release or reassignment and that all media movements are logged.

Centres using discs and tapes with red or blue markings will take special measures to ensure that the media is secure. Media usage must be logged, monitored and regularly audited by Security. Media with red or blue labels must be degaussed before reassignment or release to other areas. In the event of a non-removable disc being damaged that contains level 1 or 2 data consideration must be given to dismantling the housing so that the disc may be degaussed prior to dispatch to the manufacturer for repair. When non-removable discs are due to be upgraded the discs should be zeroised so that no data can be read.

Disposal

Drafts of level 1 material and unwanted print-outs should be destroyed by shredding. Shredding machines must be of a gauge fine enough to defeat recomposition. Consideration should be given to destroying level 2 and 3 data in the same manner. However, if this should be impractical then all print-outs and drafts etc. should be burnt having been first gathered to a secure store area in clearly marked bags.

Media should be erased under control and destroyed by pulverising. Ribbons should be destroyed in the same way as the data that they have printed.

Transportation and Transmission

Media and documents must be transported in a secure fashion and records kept of their movements.

Level 1 data will never be transmitted in clear and consideration should be given to encrypting Level2 and 3 data following a detailed security risk management study.

Level 1 and 2 documents should not be transmitted by facsimile.

Security Instructions

Details of the classification system and the instructions regarding the security of the media should be included included in the Security Manual and also in a Handbook for release to all employees.

Every employee should be instructed in security at a local level and also be required to sign a declaration saying that he has read the local Handbook. Regular briefings on security should be given by the local Responsible Person.

Libraries and Archives

Organising for Security

In the event of a major disaster it will be the organisation of the library and archives that will either save or lose the day. If a fire for example, destroys a computer installation, it will generally destroy the operating systems software and all the backing store of data and information since these will be held in the computer room. Literally, the companies eggs will all have been in one basket. Yet data storage is rarely a problem if well thought out. In the normal tape orientated office environment, secret information is usually stored in company cellars. Other information is in filing cabinets in the offices where it is needed on a daily basis and other files are in the archives. The information they contain may not be required until sometime in the future. Computers follow this pattern exactly in the way that information is securely stored.

Secure Utilities

Secret information and utilities that bypass all security arrangements should be in the custody of the Security Officer and normally stored away from the computer room. Other files, for example directors payroll or similar confidential information, would be stored in the accounts department, presumably separately from the computer department. Back up copies of the operating software utilities and key information should be made on a regular basis and the copies stored either with the companies bank or in a remote subsidiary or associated company. Working copies would be kept in the computer library, if the installation is big enough, or in a fire proof safe adjacent to the library for a small installation.

In either event an inventory of all discs, tapes and cartridges should be maintained. By reference to this inventory or register it should be possible for the Security Officer to know exactly which tapes are where and in what state. He should ensure that all storage devices, discs, tapes or cartridges are marked with the date of creation, the classification of data that they contain and an identifier and control number. To facilitate storage discs, tapes and cartridges should then be filed in an orderly and secure manner.

Ideally the library should be located in area secure not only from fire but from explosion or unauthorised access. It is only a matter of a few minutes work to copy an existing tape, put the new copy in a brief case and walk from the building.

Logging Media

Tapes, discs or cartridges removed from the library, even if they are going to the bank or the archives should be properly logged out. Tapes in transit should be protected from magnetic emanations, such as sparking on underground railways, etc. Grommets should be used to prevent tapes unwinding whilst in transit and afterwards when archived or put into storage.

Security Officers should ensure that there is a documented procedure in place covering the receipt and logging of new tapes, discs, and cartridges. This should include labeling procedures for new media and for media being reassigned from the scratch pool of working media.

Cleaning Magnetic Media

Cleaning of tapes, discs and cartridges is an important function since it prolongs the life of this media. However media sent for cleaning should be overwritten to ensure that sensitive information does not become available to the public. Similarly, any tape clippings which cannot be degaussed should be destroyed as classified waste, i.e., shredded. Similarly, if a degaussing unit has been bought then scratch tapes (or tapes that are used for casual work rather like a scribble pad) should be degaussed before being returned to the pool.

The Librarian and Security Officer should have lists of authorised users of tapes, discs and cartridges and the permissions that are allowed for their files, that is whether they they can read them only, write to them, or read and write to them.

Micro computer disc security represents a specific problem in its own right since units often have access to mainframe information, or secret information. Disc security in this instance is discussed in the chapter which covers micro computers in more depth.

A further consideration in terms of making the library secure is to encrypt information being stored. Encryption on daily communications has already been discussed but it is possible to encrypt data on tapes and other off line storage media to protect the confidentiality of the data whilst it is in libraries.

The value of encryption is that the thief stealing a tape or disc or copying a disc will find the information that he has stolen totally unintelligible. Normally, the computer would encrypt all data and decrypt it once it is re input. The primary problem in this respect is to ensure that the correct key will be available to decrypt the data when it is needed and that it will not be known to anyone else.

In general, the keys should not be stored in the computer since they would be subject to all the hazards applicable to computer data. Thus encryption whilst an adequate security arrangement might present all manner of problems to users. And whilst encryption protects the data if the physical media is lost or stolen it will not protect the data from unauthorised use through the computer system. Also, the data may be decrypted whenever it is to be used and the encryption will not protect the data from anyone who can masquerade as a legitimate user. Since encryption is extremely expensive in financial and memory terms it should only be used with highly sensitive files.

The storage of all media should come under the personal supervision of the

Security Officer. The inspection of registers recording the receipt of new tapes or the use of existing tapes should be performed on a team basis to ensure the necessary disciplines are applied.

Questionnaire

Documentation

1. Are programs and documents stored in a library so that they are inaccessible to those who have no reason to need them?

2. Are special programs copyright?

3. Does a contingency plan exist? Does it respond to different levels of interruption?

4. Are there arrangements for the call out of key personnel out of office hours?

5. Which files and which programs are critical to restarting the system on a limited basis?

6. Are the following documented and stored off site:
      a. Systems?
      b. Programs?
      c. Operations?
      d. Contingency Plans?
      e. Old Manual System?

7. Who is responsible for re-starting system?

8. Is the operating software standard?

9. In an emergency, can the manufacturers applications programs be used?

10. Have up to date records been kept of hardware specifications, and do they match with the backup machine? Has the match been verified regularly?

11. Where will emergency personnel come from?

12. Where will emergency stationery come from? How long will it take to be supplied?

13. Have you planned for minor disruptions?

14. Have you "dry run" these plans?

15. Do you have a security manual? Does this have clear, concise procedures which define in detail the steps and processes required to accomplish specific security related activities?

16. Does the security manual include detailed procedures for:

     a. Systems start up?

     b. System operation?

     c. System shut down?

     d. System maintenance?

     e. Access control mechanisms?

     f. System and operating configuration control?

     g. Personnel controls and clearances?

17.   Is the responsibility and procedure for updating the   documentation and ensuring its completeness defined and implemented?

Security Documentation

1.Is there a document classification system in use?

2.How are documents identified?

3.Is Level 1 and 2 documentation:

     a) Printed in secure areas?

     b) Delivered in a secure manner requiring recipients signature?

     c) Destroyed by shredding or burning?

     d) Is usage by others logged?

     e) Are on-line controls in place to prevent printing more than once?

     f) Are production logs monitored to control reruns and restarts that may generate extra copies?

     g) What authorisation is required for changes to circulation of sensitive data?

4. How are secure documents destroyed?

5. How is secure media stored?

6. Are there written procedures for the handling and storage of secure documents and media?

7. Do audit trails and checkpoints exist which cover all handling of sensitive data?

8. Is access to sensitive data restricted and authorised in a manner appropriate to the medium?

9. Is transportation of sensitive data by locked truck or container, or by

authorised couriers?

10. Is adequate back up provided for sensitive data based on recovery requirements?

11. Is the use of sensitive media logged and monitored?

12. Is a media inventory, including discs, performed at irregular intervals?

13. Is all media degaussed prior to reassignment?

14. If a non removable disc is damaged or sold is it first degaussed.

15. Are micros or terminals handling highly sensitive data disenabled after a specific time period? Do they face away from walkways?

16. Are microfiche copies of level1 documents stored in a secure place? Is a log maintained of fiche use? Is the use restricted to an area under observation by the fiche librarian?

17.Are level 1 documents transmitted by fax?

18.Are photocopiers locked when not in use?

19.Has a Handbook of local security measures been produced?

Libraries

1. Is an inventory of all ADP storage devices maintained?

2. Are all storage devices marked with:

> a.   The date of creation?
>
> b.   The classification of data contained on the tape?
>
> c.   User identification?
>
> d. A permanently assigned identification or control number?
>
> e.   Special access restriction?

3. Are storage devices filed in an orderly and proper manner?

4. Are tapes, discs and cartridges cleaned on a scheduled basis? Are tape heads cleaned regularly?

5. Are tapes, discs and cartridges kept in their containers when not in use?

6. Are periodic but irregular tests conducted to determine the general condition of the tape library?

7. Is the library located in an area secure from explosion or other dangers?

8. Do you use storage archives specifically designed for magnetic media or critical file storage?

9. Do you use grommets to prevent tapes unwinding whilst in transit or in storage?

10. Are tapes, discs and cartridges which are removed from the library properly logged out and accounted for?

11. Is access to the tape library restricted to authorised personnel only?

12. Do library procedures cover:

        a.   initial receipt and logging of new tapes, discs or cartridges?

        b.   labelling of new tapes, discs and cartridges?

        c.   assigning of tapes, discs and cartridges from the scratch pool?

        d. degaussing of sensitive tapes, discs and cartridges?

        e.   cleaning of tapes, discs and cartridges?

        f. over writing of tapes, discs and cartridges to de-classify them?

        g. transmitting and recording tapes, discs and cartridges from archives?

        h.   receiving, logging and controlling of discs, tapes, discs and cartridges?

13. Are tapes, discs and cartridges over written or degaussed before they are sent out for cleaning?

14. Is the librarian or Security Officer provided with lists of authorised users and permissions allowed for their files?

15. Is an access list maintained by the Security Officer for each tape, disc or cartridge in the library, and is it used to verify each request for access to the media?

Contingency Planning

13

Total destruction of a computer facility is rarely effected by accident, for example, fire or a Boeing aeroplane crashing on the complex. More often it is caused by attack from clandestine terrorist organisations or by politically motivated employees. Whilst some organisations could stand a prolonged interruption, perhaps even reverting to a manual system, it is unlikely that organisations who have been computerised for a period in excess of three years, and have made full and efficient use of their computer system could be totally interrupted, even for a short period and survive. Contingency planning is therefore a priority and is a requirement of senior management who bear a responsibility to their staff and shareholders to ensure that the business will survive a computer disruption.

User departments and groups must determine how long they can survive without their systems. Some may be able to continue for two or three days others for weeks. Armed with this information senior management can begin to determine the level of response that will be required to meet user needs.

What threats then present themselves? Generally the following pie diagram is the accepted norm:

Fire and Explosion 50%

Water 15%

Power 15%

Employee 10%

Terrorist and other 15%

Fire threats are seen as a remote possibility in the modern computer room. In the UK in 1987, 46 computer installations suffered fire damage. Roughly one third of these were started by employees. Where there was a major computer room fire and no contingency plan existed nearly 90% of those afflicted ceased trading.

The risks of an unexpected incident bringing some form of disruption are, therefore, real and must be catered for with a detailed disaster plan. Senior management can determine the effect of a computer disaster on its business, for example the loss of revenue, erosion of customer base, increased advertising costs, higher interest rates etc. Once a value is put on the impact of the disruption, users and computer professionals can determine who the facility will continue to be provided should the worst happen.

Their first step is to calculate the recovery time scale. For an installation with a mini or mainframe computer it will take at least three weeks to acquire replacement equipment from suppliers, and a further three weeks for full installation and commissioning before processing can recommence.

In the mean time a back log of work has been building up requiring extensive weekend and overtime working. This work may take anything up to 18 weeks to complete. However, other functions interface with the computer facility and it may take anything up to nine or ten months for business to be fully restored. These statements presuppose the existence of a contingency plan that has been thoroughly tested. Without a plan the situation is further exacerbated.

No single individual can hope to document a disaster plan on his own. Different skills and knowledge will be required to ensure the success of any plan. A Disaster Recovery Co-ordinator should be appointed who will co-opt other skills on to a Planning Team. The following might be a typical structure:

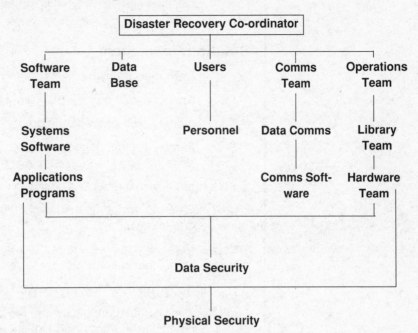

All will be able to contribute in a structured form. Generally, the disaster recovery review has three distinct phases:

> **Requirements Analysis and Research**
>
> **Solution Definition**
>
> **Solution Refinement**

Management approval will be necessary at the end of each phase to authorise progress to the next.

Requirements Analysis and Research

- Define the link persons of the various business units who will be expected to contribute to the project.

- Review disaster recovery costs, practices and procedures and identify shortcomings.

- Assess the implementation options for disaster recovery which will sustain current policy, with reference to planned and new systems.

- Assess the potential to resolve contention which may exist between the need for data availability for operational contingency and the requirements of disaster recovery.

- Identify trends in costs.

Solution Definition

- Develop a cost effective solution in line with agreed policies and requirements.

- Review the management process for maintaining the solution.

- Review all supporting documentation and standards to identify changes needed to provide consistency with the solution.

- Develop and agree a basis for the implementation of the solution.

Solution Refinement

- Determine recovery time scales.
- Assess the cost of the provision of the service.
- Identify problems with the proposed recovery plan.
- Identify system dependencies to ensure that inter - dependent systems will have the same level of recovery service.
- Identify cost reduction opportunities.
- Rationalise potential conflicts between different business area requirements.
- Present to management the refined plan together with alternative scenarios and cost profiles.
- Apportion business area responsibilities.
- It will be noted that activity in the business area begins and ends the planning. A successful Contingency Plan is heavily vested in the business.

Documenting the Disaster

The plan should begin with a list of the names, addresses and telephone numbers of all key personnel. It should detail in a quick and easy to read form who should be called out and under what circumstances. For example, a small fire brought under control quickly in the computer room may necessitate only calling out the computer operations manager. A major fire causing limited disruption will necessitate calling out the management services manager, the computer operations manager and other operations shift leaders.

The back up site, of what ever form this may take, should be listed and described together with the home telephone numbers of key personnel.

The home telephone numbers and day time telephone numbers of key personnel within the computer suppliers organisation should also be listed.

It should be clearly specified that the Disaster Co-ordinator becomes Master Controller for the disaster situation. It will be his responsibility to ensure that the necessary personnel are transported to the stand-by site and that accommodation is available to house them in local hotels or guest houses. Discs, tapes, cartridges and backup copies will also be transported and arrangements should be made for cars or taxis to provide this service. Taxis or cars will also be needed to transport printout back to the home location.

With distributed processing within a company, the computer department should define a plan to establish communications facilities with a stand by location. Again, it will be necessary to put priorities on the work to be performed. It will then become the Disaster Co-ordinator's function to liaise with manufacturers and the PTT to establish communication links.

The stand by operation procedures should be carefully documented and must include a method of restoring the backing store system which integrates individual jobs descriptions. It will also be necessary to define the overall network and outline the objectives of the various action plans that become subsets of the overall disaster plan and to have the necessary budget allocations available.

Individual action plans should also be drawn up so that no one is in any doubt as to the activity that he must follow. This will clearly speed up the recovery process.

Back-up Options

Various back-up site options have to be considered. In general these are:

> **Reciprocal agreement,**
>
> **Cold start,**
>
> **Non-stop,**
>
> **Flying start,**
>
> **Hot start.**
>
> **Reciprocal agreement**

This is a mutual back up facility offered by another user of the same equipment. With small batch machines, or even small mini computers working single shifts, the back-up arrangement could be successfully implemented for a short period. Reciprocal agreements induce very good feelings of security but are, with large minis and mainframes, almost completely unworkable.

Cold start

Cold starts are generally empty rooms or cabins in which the stricken user must acquire and install equipment. The waiting period, especially for mainframe equipment can be protracted. It has the advantage of offering a low cost solution, however, this must be traded against the loss of business during the waiting period.

Non-stop

This is an in-house solution using parallel computing. If the parallel machine is suitably located it will provide an expensive form of back-up. The disadvadvantage is the machines are generally close together and in the event of a terrorist attack or aeroplane disaster would almost certainly be simultaneously destroyed.

Flying start

Again an in-house solution that offers parallel updating at separate locations. It is a solution that requires dedicated equipment and a very high investment in software, hardware and ancillary services.

Hot start

This offers the best of all possible solutions and is usually cost effective and certain.

To illustrate this statement a study was made of a typical Hot Start centre, that of Sherwood Locum of Salisbury in Wiltshire. The site offered back up for ICL and Prime users of various configurations.

Unlike the Cold Start facility, the Hot Start site has computers available at three hours notice. Full air-conditioning and back-up power facilities are available as well as office accommodation, telephones, telexes, faxs, hardware and software manuals (which may be destroyed at the home base), sophisticated fire protection equipment and library facilities.

Numbers of subscribers are strictly controlled and allocated to a machine. Subscribers normally do not come from areas served by the same flight paths or from within the same buildings or potential disaster areas.

The beauty of this system is that the stricken organisation's team take over the Hot Start offices and system as if it was their own, even taking over the physical security for the duration of their stay. The user is therefore, fully able to control their own services and link into a sophisticated communications network to provide full, remote terminal usage.

Sherwood Locum strongly recommend that their clients test their facilities prior to commencement of the service by declaring a simulated disaster and moving processing facilities for a single day to their Salisbury Centre. This permits a full rehearsal of stand-by facilities and allows the user to refine his Disaster Plan in the light of mishaps and slippages.

One final advantage with a Hot start site is that if it should ever be necessary to move a mainframe, the processing can be moved to the site in a fully simulated disaster situation whilst the new site is made ready.

Command and Control

It is vital that a Command and Control Centre should be located and earmarked for future use. In the example of Sherwood Locum described above this facility is automatically provided. Others may have to find one for themselves.

The Centre should be an area where the Disaster Co-ordinator establishes his Head Quarters for the duration of the contingency. It should accommodate staff and serve as a meeting area for designated staff. It must be equipped with telephones, power, water, sanitation, status media boards, telexes, faxs, micro computers and radio telephones.

Networks

Networks present their own problems in terms of crisis management but by their nature they are not as sensitive to major disruption. However, the principles that govern the selection and documentation of stand-by for larger machines still apply.

In this instance the team should determine what data is carried, its value to the organisation and what the effects would be on business if this data were disclosed to the unauthorised or if it were modified illegally. Generally, in a network disaster situation, well established security mechanisms are abandoned and a previously secure network becomes vulnerable.

Data sensitivity and critical programs that interface with sensitive data will have to be protected. If before, encryption and authentication were primary defences it may now be necessary to isolate these programs and continue to use encryption on a localised basis perhaps even reverting to manual transmission of output on a security basis. If this is part of the contingency decision then it must be documented and tested.

The listing of all terminals and microcomputers by location, which would be a normal security measure now comes into its own. This will allow the contingency team to prioritise applications and allocate these to stand alone units or local networks that continue to function. Consideration will have to be given to the level of terminal clearance and if this is low, what can be done in an emergency to enhance security.

Local area networks which are linked to each other by the PTT system should have triangulation as a backbone. In this case full consideration should be given, on a risk management basis, to linking into a secondary system, for example PSS. Alternatively the problem might be handed to a third party, IBM Network System or other commercial carriers.

During a disaster all abnormal job terminations, illegal access attempts and password failures should be logged and investigated. Crisis situations present excellent opportunities for the dishonest to penetrate systems.

Testing

After the contingency plans have been drawn up and a back-up system has been selected, there is no guarantee that it will work in a disaster. It is essential that it should be realistically tested.

The objectives of the test should be:

to ensure the type of stand-by site chosen is the right one;

to verify that the plan is largely correct;

toverify the recovery time scales;

to rehearse all personnel;

to review errors and omissions.

The London based clearing banks have contingency plans where computers of similar size act as stand by for the members. To test the system out a bank is declared "stricken" and ceases to process its cheques. These are then taken to the stand by organisation to be run on their cheque reading machines and processed at their Clearing Computer Centres. This would be an ideal state of affairs except the stricken bank knows in advance that it is to be stricken and prepares dummy cheques as they do not want the stand by bank to know their business arrangements. Since they have to generate these themselves it follows that the volumes are not realistic. The test is therefore incomplete.

A commercial test should use a full day's data, which should be live data. There should be no notice, except in very special circumstances, that the computer installation is to be designated as stricken. Adequate resources and budgets should be allocated to this very essential testing. Afterwards the plan should be updated in the light of the test. The Disaster Co-ordinator should be allocated the responsibility of planning and conducting tests to exercise the various action plans at agreed intervals.

At its very lowest level the action plan should include checks on the contents held at off site storage. Periodically the stand by system should be run with the contents of the off site storage. At least once a year a full test should be conducted without notice to other users or DP department.

All tests must be monitored and all post mortem findings incorporated into the disaster plan. Since the up-dating of the disaster or contingency plan can be extremely time consuming it is essential that the Disaster Co-ordinator allocates sufficient time for this function. As time passes there will be changes in stand by hardware and software and also in the in house hardware and software and this must be taken into account. New systems will be implemented, people will join and leave, the work load will alter and all this will affect the business impact.

In any event the test will give the Disaster co-ordinator a unique opportunity to evaluate, at first hand:

staff maturity and real experience,

the efficacy of transportation,

the use of the command and control centre,

supplier and user support,

data and document storage facilities,

communications links,

hardware registers,

security procedures.

No matter how irksome the task of re-writing large parts of the plan might be, it is essential that the task should be completed as soon as possible after the test. Another opportunity may never arise before the plan is required to keep the facility running and the organisation trading.

The Computer Disaster Recovery Process

The disaster recovery process is summarised, in the broadest terms, with the following diagram:

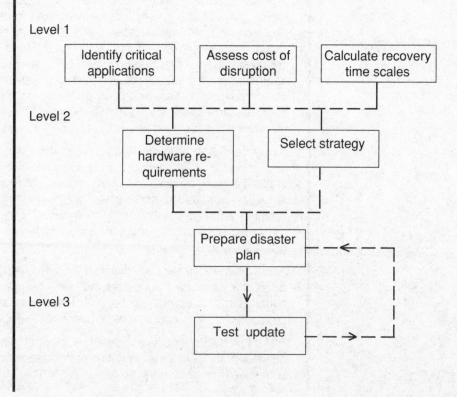

Questionnaire

Administration

1. Who has been designated disaster co-ordinator?

2. Does his team include:

   a. Systems/software expert?

   b. Programming expert?

   c. Operations expert?

   d. Internal audit?

   e. Security expert?

3. Has a command and control centre been specified?

   a. Is the accommodation close to or part of the Back-up site?

   b. Does it offer power, sanitation, telephones,P.C.s, Radio contact?

   c. Is it equipped with media boards, safes,cabinets stationery, storage facilities etc?

4. Have critical applications been defined and costed for impact?

5. What organisational functions are assigned to support these critical applications?

6. Who is responsible for declaring a disaster situation and implementing the contingency plan?

7. Who has immediate responsibility for press and television releases?

Mainframe Back-up

1. Has a choice been made of back-up/ support site:

   a. Hot-start?

   b. Cold-start?

   c. Flying-start?

   d. Non-stop?

   e. Back-up with a separate organisation?

2. Has the minimum acceptable level of operation been defined?

3. Have the levels of resources been defined for different levels of disaster?

4. Has the back up facility been tested and have plans been amended in the light of the test?

5. If a back-up with another organisation's computer is being used:

   a. Can it handle the company work load?

   b. Is it in a separate location?

   c. Is there a back-up agreement which is renewed

   annually? Is the insurer agreeable?

   d. Does a policy exist to advise each other of any changes to configurations or software?

   e. When was the back-up tested?

f. Does an implementation plan for the use of the back-up machine exist?

g. Is processing batch orientated?

Communications and Networks

1. Has an assessment been made of the front end requirements to support communications?

2. Can front end equipment use dial-up or leased lines, including kilostream or X25 packet switched services to link with a hot start site?

3. Where multi-minis are networked has triangulation been considered?

4. Has an evaluation been made of data that is being carried?

5. Has an assessment been made of the risks of disclosure, integrity and confidentiality of data, user accountability, system availability and resilience?

6. Has triangulation been considered? With what effect?

7. Has consideration been given to linking into a secondary system like the packet switching stream?

8. Has consideration been given to using a third party network like the IBM Network System?

9. Is a register maintained of all equipment by location?

10. Have priorities been allocated to applications? Can non-prioritised applications revert to manual or other systems?

11. Does a disaster plan exist? Has it been tested?

Disaster Plans

1. Does a written contingency plan exist that covers:

a. the designation of overall responsibility during a disaster situation?

b. Detailed notification procedures specifying names and telephone numbers of:

· Emergency staff

· Back-up site

· Users

· Suppliers

· Insurers

· Hotels/restaurants near back-up

· Chosen Command Centre

· Personnel

· Public relations

· Taxis and goods vehicles

c. the transportation of sensitive material and its secure storage?

d. security measures during the disaster?

e. the collection point and method of distribution of output?

f.list operator schedules for critical and sensitive jobs?

g.additional magnetic and output media?

h. the use of outside contractors and consultants and the procedures associated with their hiring?

j. procedures for the eventual restoration of service to the prime site?

7. Have all staff been trained in the contingency plan?

8. Has it been tested? And refined in the light of the test?

Investigating Computer Misuse

14

The Security Officer must take responsibility for the investigation of suspected computer misuse. Usually when an unlawful attack on the computer is suspected the Board think first of the external auditor and then of a computer expert to help them discover the truth. Auditors cannot drop everything and come and investigate every time the Board is uneasy nor are they trained fraud investigators. The computer expert from inside the company may be the very man who has perpetrated the crime, a gamekeeper turned poacher and asked to be gamekeeper again! In all investigations of this type action must be taken swiftly and efficiently.

The Security Officer is the ideal person to take over the role of investigator for the following reasons:

> a. He has experience of security matters.
>
> b. He is able to respond immediately to the situation.
>
> c. He is able to marshal and coordinate the skills he requires to aid him with the investigation.
>
> d. He knows everyone in the Computer and User Departments.
>
> e. He will have familiarised himself with the major ledger systems such as:
>
>> - Sales Ledger
>>
>> - Purchase Ledger
>>
>> - Nominal Ledger
>>
>> - Stock Control
>>
>> - Payroll.

The last point may not seem directly relevant but a knowledge of these systems in conventional ledger terms will pay dividends. Commercial computer systems are almost invariably mirror images of previous manual ledger systems and computer frauds are almost invariably the electronic equivalent of classic manual frauds.

Basic Problems

A number of problems exist common to all electronic frauds:

> a. The competence of the Investigator
>
> b. The complexity of the investigation
>
> c. Legal complexities.

The competency of the Investigator is the first problem that is surmounted by the Security Officer if only because the DP world is a mixture of hundreds of makes of computers, hundreds of operating systems, scores of program languages and thousands of packages. No one person can know it all, which emphasises the usefulness of the Security Officer who can co-ordinate the investigation and marshal the expertise specific to the problem.

The complexity of investigating a computer fraud, especially a high value one, is very great indeed. The numbers of terminals accessing a suspected data base may run into thousands and speed is of the essence since the very nature of computer transactions is that they are transient. If there is a poor audit trail, which is the norm, the chain of computer events may well have vanished before the investigation gets under way. Clearly, a team will be needed and should be listed well before any event occurs in the Security Officer's own contingency plan.

Legal complexities are myriad. Will computer print outs be accepted by a court? Will investigations of individuals result in counter actions for defamation? Has the fraud crossed national boundaries? Is it possible to specifically and legally determine computer crime? Irrespective of the difficulties, the fraud or attack must be investigated, the *modus operandi* discovered (if it exists) and further damage prevented.

Preparing for Computer Crime Investigation

Questions to be immediately resolved

The Security Officer must first determine if a fraud has actually taken place and whether the company will prosecute or not. If the directors are confident that a computer fraud has occurred then an investigation must be put in hand. However, if it is the Board's intention not to prosecute but only dismiss the persons responsible with a minimum of scandal, then the investigation in all its phases will be more discreet than if the police are to be called in.

Fraud is defined as **an intentional deception or willful misrepresentation of a material fact to gain undue financial, social or political advantage over another**. The corporate fraud will involve financial embezzlement with or without third party help.

The Investigator must now satisfy himself on the following questions:

> a. How credible is the source of information?
>
> > i)   How was it obtained?
> >
> > ii) Is the information first hand?
> >
> > iii) What evidence supports the allegation?
>
> b. What was the motive in reporting the fraud?
>
> c. Will the source provide a sworn statement?
>
> d. Will the source testify as a witness?
>
> e. Will the source make a credible witness?
>
> f. How, when and where was the fraud committed?
>
> g. What is the extent of the loss?
>
> h. What was the perpetrators motive?

Unsatisfactory answers to these questions will suggest caution but providing the answers are satisfactory then the Investigator can proceed with confidence to the next stage.

To understand the nature of the fraud the Investigator must have an appreciation of how the crime was conceived. A good knowledge of the business function will be invaluable.

The Scenario

The Investigator must have an approximate understanding of how the crime was possible, what vulnerabilities were exploited and who was aware of them. The logic of a fraud scenario is never structured but always intuitive and depends on being able to imagine the setting up of the fraud and then the concealment of evidence after the fraud has been committed.

In order to determine the systems weaknesses and vulnerabilities it will be useful to ask the following questions:

a) What weaknesses are there on internal controls?

b) Have the controls been compromised before?

c) Who is aware of these weaknesses?

d) What is the simplest way to exploit these weaknesses?

e) What is the most likely outcome?

f) How can unauthorised access be effected?

The Investigator will need to determine what factors exist which enhance the possibility of fraud or embezzlement. These will provide good guidelines leading to the culprit(s). The factors might be:

1. Inadequate financial rewards for employees

2. Poor management controls and employee accountability

3. Lack of employee recognition and related rewards

4. Lack of resources to meet corporate objectives

5. Poor inspection, auditing or monitoring

6. Poor recruitment standards

7. Lack of Security Strategy.

Having covered this ground the Investigator should have a good "feel" for what has occurred and will be ready to move to the next stage.

Audit Plan

Reviewing exceptions and oddities is an important part of fraud investigation. All normal computer and business transactions have a logical sequence and timing. Events that occur out of sequence or at strange times and places or with illogical repetitiveness will ring "alarm bells".

In general the investigation or audit plan will be based around the fraud scenario and the areas to be examined will conform to the way that the fraud was probably executed.

The Investigator must determine:

a) What accounts are to be examined,

b) Which procedures will be tested,

c) Specific transactions to be analysed,

d) Specific policies to be reviewed,

e) Documents to be evaluated and analysed,

f) Employees to be interviewed and questions to be asked.

All this information will be gathered without alarming members of staff and with as much secrecy as it is possible to attain. It is vital not to alarm the culprit so that he wipes files or destroy vital evidence.

It is assumed that the Security Officer has an inquiring mind otherwise he would not have the job. Without this attribute few Investigators will succeed. He must be capable of marshalling and organising a team without necessarily following the total logic of the computer system. He must be able to analyse results to build up a case.

Use of Outside Professionals

He has three groups of people to bring in from outside:

    a. Computer specialists

    b. Auditors

    c. Police.

The latter will of course only be involved towards the end of the investigation, unless specialised skills are available from within the local force. The necessary skills of the three groupings are required in three areas. These are shown below as approximate percentages of total effort.

Group	Computer	Audit	Investigative
Specialists	70%	15%	15%
Auditors	10%	75%	15%
Police	10%	10%	80%

Clearly the computer specialist will need training in auditing and investigation to be effective. Auditors will need training in computing and investigation. It is therefore most effective to use the division of labour by employing specialist skills where they are most effective and coordinating results. It is possible that one of the reasons for the poor ratio of computer fraud convictions to computer frauds is because of the disorganised way in which they are investigated.

Investigating the Computer Fraud

The first and most essential activity, when a fraud is suspected, is to try to determine what has happened and its extent. This is the same as a doctor visually examining his patient before touching!

Secondly, the relevant outside expertise should be assembled and the bureau or other outside computer installation to be used should be notified.

The next and equally important activity is to copy immediately all media and remove the originals, duly identified as such, from the site. Similarly, all activity and access logs together with magnetic media records should be obtained and removed to the investigative site. If possible this should be done without arousing interest, for example, under the guise of a contingency exercise. Leaving the copies on site will allow business processing to continue and may even prompt the guilty party to try and correct the records. A comparison between the media being audited and that in use may yield dividends.

Jobs must be allocated and care taken not to destroy the chain of evidence. A second security copy of tapes and discs should be made. However, if the Security Officer has to fall back on these during the investigation the guilty party will argue that they were not originals and may have been tampered with.

The Security Officer should now begin a discreet investigation into backgrounds of staff members. The thief will almost certainly have been honest to the point in time when the crime was initiated. He will have had:

    a. Sufficient knowledge

    b. Sufficient resources

    c. Access to sufficient financial return.

It will be necessary to find the person with the changed life style and not necessarily for richer since a wife's extravagance or drug taking may have been the cause of the crime. Investigate staff motives, so that they can be matched to staff, saving time and effort. Use a matrix to match people to motives.

Use the full psychological pressure that an investigation brings by maintaining an open door policy. Allow and even encourage staff to offer their opinions, views and information.

Secrecy must be observed at all times and especially the result of analyses. As the modus operandi is discovered make sure that nothing is communicated to anyone else since the culprit may very well slip up in general conversation and drop hints on an activity that only he could know about. This is especially relevant where the attack has been made out of vanity or from a sense of revenge.

The Investigator will need help from other members of the company, for example directors, user managers, computer managers and auditors. None, however, are above suspicion, and none should be privy to any part of the investigation. At this time the Investigator should be aware that the fraudster is on home territory and should be on his guard for the member of staff with a heightened appreciation of what is going on.

Exercise great care in confronting the suspect. A professional thief may very well hide behind threats of slander and defamation of character which may force the company to back off. Also ensure that the team are covered by professional indemnity insurance for the period of the investigation.

General Investigations

The detection of computer crime is extremely difficult. The Board or Chief Accountant may not be certain that a fraud is taking place but may have an uneasy feeling of general business malaise. This feeling needs to be investigated, especially since it is estimated that a third of American bankruptcies may be as a result of fraud.

Altman carried out an investigation into Predictive Bankruptcy which, whilst hypothetical, is none the less a good tool for the Security Officer to use before beginning an investigation. There are five key ratios he maintained:

  a. Working Capital to Total Assets   (.012)

  b. Retained Earnings to Total Assets (.014)

  c. Earnings before tax to Total Assets (.033)

  d. Market Value of Equity to Book Value Debt (.006)

  e. Sales to Total Assets   (.010)

The procedure is as follows:

  a. Calculate the ratios as percentages

  b. Multiply by their respective coefficients

  c. Add the products

  d. Compare the total of the products with 1.8

If the value is below 1.8 then bankruptcy is highly likely and fraud as a cause must be regarded as a 1 in 3 chance. Between 1.8 and 3 fraud is possible and above 3 highly unlikely. This then becomes a rule of thumb to be applied to an otherwise healthy company to determine if fraud is occurring.

A further test that the Senior Director could apply would be to compare the ratios with similar companies in the same industries. If there are variations to the disadvantage of your company or if a comparison within your own group by company shows a variance then investigation is worthwhile.

Some Legal Requirements

If a prosecution is brought it will be necessary to show in court by clear and decisive proof that:

1. The alleged fraudster or embezzler made a representation in regard to a material fact,

2. That such a representation was false,

3. That such a representation was not believed to be true by the defendant,

4. That it was made with intent to be acted on,

5. That the complainant acted on the misrepresentation to his damage,

6. The complainant was ignorant of the falsity of the representation.

Method

Having amassed and analysed the information available it is essential that the investigator should fully understand the mechanics of the fraud. Often it will be necessary to draw on the available expert opinions since the most usual mistake in this type of investigation is to begin interviewing too early with too little supportive evidence. As a result it becomes impossible to place prime suspects under any sort of stress.

Before the interviewing begins the investigator will have a very good idea of who is guilty and will have a clear set of objectives.

The Interview

Once the interviewer has identified his suspect, he should at the very start of the interview make it clear to the interviewee that he is the suspect. This allows stress levels to be pre-set and with a quiet, structured and relentless approach confessions may be obtained.

The guilty party will confess if he believes that his guilt is proven and that confession will minimise his punishment. The computer criminal may be different from the general run of thieves in that he may often admit his guilt and defy the investigator to prove it. This type of gauntlet will be thrown down when the crime has been an intellectual challenge. The investigator may be sure that his path will not be a straight one nor the evidence all that it appears. The investigator will use his accounting and computer experts to the maximum to have any hope of breaking the case.

The general run of computer frauds will not be initiated because of the challenge; they will have been implemented by the greedy who are intent on covering their tracks and surviving to spend their gain.

Where an immediate admission of guilt is not obtained it will always be necessary to test individuals in the computer and user departments to establish guilt or innocence.

The Interview Room

The room chosen should not be one where any of the interviewees can feel at home. Ideally a single table should be used with chairs arranged along the same side of the table. There should be no distractive focal points such as;

> a) clocks
>
> b) telephones
>
> c) pictures
>
> d) windows with views.

If there are key documents in the case then these should be enlarged and pinned to the wall as focal points.

All interviews should be on a one to one basis but where, for what ever reason, a second person is used, then he should be out of the interviewees line of vision and should not take part in the dialogue.

The second person will normally only be present for the purposes of providing a witness. When this is not possible the interview should be recorded or a statement drawn up at the end of the interview and the interviewee asked to sign it.

Observation

Body language will play a significant role in identifying the guilty. Police watch for a suspect touching his ears or covering his mouth as a sign of guilt. All language plays a role.

A guilty party left to his own devices will examine what ever papers have been left in a room to try to find what might be used to incriminate him. Similarly, on entering the room the guilty party will examine the documents pinned to the wall and ask questions. Innocent parties will have no reason to be curious.

The next stage of the investigation is to ask the interviewee to explain everything that he knows about the crime in his own words. He should never be interrupted and everything he says should be written down. He should be asked to produce all supportive or relevant documentation in his possession. At the end of this stage the interviewer will have a very good idea of his guilt or innocence. Confirmation can be obtained by the use of simple questions , for example:

How would you have committed the crime?

The guilty party may describe in detail the steps in the fraud and reveal information only the thief could know.

Have you ever thought of committing a crime like the one under investigation?

The guilty will always admit they have but with qualifications.

Should the police be called in?

The guilty will respond in the negative.

What do you think should happen to the guilty party?

The guilty will deprecate the value of the crime and the words "thief" "theft" etc., will be avoided.

The guiltless will take a hard line.

As the evidence mounts the suspect may very well become aggressive. This is to deter the investigator who may be intimidated with threats of violence or legal action. The demand that a solicitor should be present is typical of the beginning of this type of aggression.

A solicitor at this stage would be counterproductive but certainly within the suspect's rights. To counter this the investigator might suggest that as a solicitor would be present it is possibly the ideal time to involve the police.

The Guilty

The guilty will generally fall into three categories:

> 1. The repentant.
>
> 2. The controlled.
>
> 3. the political.

The **repentant** will always co-operate with a view to reducing the penalty. He will always minimise the seriousness of his actions and will not blame anyone that he knows to be innocent. He will also accept accusations of guilt with resignation.

The **controlled** criminal will have rationalised his situation and in his own eyes will not be guilty of any serious crime. he will regard all that he has done as meeting a natural requirement and all that he has received as deserved.

The **political** thief will never feel remorse and if the crime is proven he will see it as an act of defiance. He will attribute blame to the innocent to draw away the hunt and will accept no accusations of guilt.

All three criminal types will have an ambivalent attitude to moral ethics.

Summary

The Security Officer should not under any circumstances back away from this role of investigator. Who better to perform it? Who could co-ordinate an outside team? Who has the investigative skills?

All that is necessary is a knowledge of computer basics and security coupled with an understanding of ledger systems. A knowledge of computer programming may be useful but is unlikely to equal that of the outside professional. Interestingly the FBI run a programming course as do the Royal Canadian Mounted Police. The British police are perhaps more realistic using a team approach and buying in outside skills.

Questionnaire

QUESTION	GUILTY	INNOCENT
1. If you were the fraudster how would you justify this action?	Attempt to justify	Not justify
2. When is it justified to steal from the company?	Will explain	Never
3. What would be the easiest way to steal from the company?	Knows	No idea
4. Are most people dishonest?	Yes	No
5. Most people are honest because they fear punishment?	True	False
6. Why couldn't it be you that committed this fraud?	Explains	Not dishonest
7. Why do you think the evidence points towards you?	Explains	No idea
8. Should this investigation be handled by the police?	No	Yes
9. People think you are the the fraudster.	Passive	Angry
10. If you had to steal money how would you feel?	Explains	No idea
11. The computer fraudster is cleverer than the police?	Agrees	Disagrees

Check List

General

1. Check the backgrounds of all employees through credit agencies and voters lists.

2. The past and present addresses and telephone numbers of all past and present employees and compare them with suppliers addresses and telephone numbers.

3. Check all suppliers and customers for accommodation addresses, post office box numbers etc.

4. List all abbreviated supplier and customer names.

5. List the authority levels of employees to approve purchase orders, and purchase invoices.

6. Print out the highest discounts, lowest prices, balances in excess of agreed credit limits, accounts with credit balances, ratio of credit adjustments, Y.T.D. sales against last Y.T.D.   sales.

7. List all processes that by-pass the computer.

8. Evaluate customer complaint files.

Payroll
9. Print out details of all employees that have joined since the suspected fraud began.

10.List all cash payments to temporary or contract labour.

11.List all salaries greater than a specific figure.

12.List all increases greater than an accepted value.

13.List employees who do not take holidays.

14.Ratio of income tax, NI. etc. to total salaries.

Sales Ledger
15.Analyse customers to find:

       a) Customers without telephone numbers.

       b) Customers that do not pay VAT.

       c) Customers with post office box numbers.

16.List all highest discount customers.

17.List all customers with highest value free samples.

18.Evaluate altered names and addresses on delivery notes.

19.List written-off goods and free issues.

20.Compare ratio of cash received to credits by branches.

21.Compare bad debts to sales by branches.

22.Analyse salesman's calls to sales.

Purchase Ledger

23.Analyse cheques paid through Building Societies or that have been endorsed to someone else.

24.List abbreviated business names.

25. Compare purchases Y.T.D. with previous Y.T.D. by suppliers and analyse large increases.

26. Print out all new accounts in the period under consideration.

27. Print out goods described by product number only.

28. During stock taking print out and analyse:

        a) Stock transfers between company locations,

        b) Credit notes issued during this period.

        c) Drivers activities during this period.

29. print out credit notes issued immediately after the year end.

Electronic Fund Transfer

30. Establish the initiating instruction.

31. Establish if information is missing or whether there were deviations from normal procedures.

32. Establish if any employees are absent.

33. Who was aware that sufficient funds were in the account that has been embezzled?

34. Why were funds available in that account?

35. Did the format and test key verification correspond with that received by the bank?

36. Are all records of message sending complete and in proper form?

37. What methods are used to prevent substitution and deletion of messages?

38. If information is buffered on tape or disc how is this protected?

39. Did delays exist in transmission and receipt of the message?

Case Studies:

In addition to the following Case Studies, the reader should also turn to Appendix A **"Typical Overview Report"**

Case Study One

Stock Losses at JBS Plc.

The Crime

JBS decided in 1985 to use an external stock taking firm for the first time in its history, instead of responsible warehouse staff. The company found that there were stock shortages amounting to £850,000. The auditors compared their findings with the computer data base which indicated conclusively that there were no discrepancies.

It was concluded that the Data Processing Department had been helping to conceal these losses by:

> a) downgrading stock levels;
>
> b) inflating stock despatches.

The "Edit" program was available to all programmers and analysts employed on development work. Edit allows the deletion, alteration and modification of data and is almost as powerful as a Superzap. The use of Edit was not recorded in either the computer log or the audit trail system.

The Computer Manager considered his security measures adequate and was hostile to any questioning regarding his department.

Incoming freight was verified by comparing the delivery note with the purchase order. Carton count procedure assumed a given number of cartons per pallet. Cartons were not inspected, it was claimed, for unit count of contents, nor were they weighed. Truck drivers had free access to the receiving area. They often lingered after unloading and socialised with the company employees. They also helped employees make delivery counts.

Action

Only the Audit Team and Board of Directors are aware of the discrepancy at the point in time when you are called in to investigate.

Having been provided with this information:

> 1. How would you set about the investigation?
>
> 2. Detail the avoidable mistakes present in this case?
>
> 3. Suggest measures to reduce the risk of similar occurrences?

Possible action on the theft of stock

1. Theft and computer aided embezzlement were assumed to be present and the evidence of fraud was accepted as impeccable. The Board intended to prosecute and it was important to have evidence that would be acceptable in court.

The company business was increasing and profitability was good.

The scenario was that collusion existed between persons in warehousing and data processing. The lax procedures at " goods inwards" would give adequate opportunity for the theft of goods. If the computer records were altered it was unlikely that anyone in authority would be concerned enough to investigate stock situations. The use of "Edit" was unlimited and the lack of controls and procedures in the computer department meant that anyone in the department could falsify stock records.

A bureau was booked through a friendly third party organisation to avoid the possibility of information filtering back to the culprit. It was booked a considerable period in advance. Simultaneously, media that was compatible with the existing system was ordered, an external computer expert was retained and the Account Executive of the company's auditors agreed to make himself available on the date that copies would be taken of existing media.

The second step, but really the first positive step, was to investigate very discreetly:

>   a) Personal relationships existing between warehouse staff and data processing staff.

>   b) Changed personal circumstances within the data processing staff. (Salary structures had previously been provided by the Personnel Department.)

>   c) The existence of any gamblers, drug abusers or alcoholics in either of the two relevant departments. This investigation covered marriage partners and boy/girl friends.

>   d) Middle aged employees among the warehouse or associated staff of lengthy and stable employment in a position of trust, with knowledge of procedures and controls who might feel abused, exploited, neglected or resentful to the company.

When this phase was completed copies of all media were taken at 4.00 a.m. Four independent witnesses were present to testify that media was not interfered with and at 9.00 a.m. two further independent witnesses were present when copies of the copies were made. The original copies were lodged with the bureau manager and stored off-site.

An analysis was begun immediately of the data and programs. This covered:

>   a) Stock requisition procedures including requisition, storage, maintenance and physical control.

>   b) Stock withdrawal procedures including re-ordering levels and procedures, when and how stock-outs had occurred and the procedures and controls in position to ensure the system was not abused.

c) The system was audited by following a series of transactions through the computer. Computer audit trails and controls were all in place.

d) The computer log was analysed and it was found that the use of "Edit" was not recorded in the log.

2. a) Local staff should not be relied upon to carry out stock-taking roles.

b) Programmers,analysts or maintenance engineers should not be allowed unimpeded access to live company data. Where this is allowed then accesses must be accurately monitored and controlled and their activities must be fully recorded.

3. "Edit" facilities exist in all systems. They will edit, amend, delete or insert information held on computer files. It is also possible to delete illegal activity from the central log by the use of Edit.

The use of this facility needs to be carefully controlled and all activities with it logged and reviewed at day end. Programmers who have normal access should never work on live data. Development work should be monitored. Peer audits must always be used when programs are patched.

4. All 'goods received' procedures to be documented and to be incorporated into job descriptions, which would be signed by the employee as part of his/her contract. This would define methods of counting and receiving deliveries and procedures for visiting drivers.

Case Study Two

Hacking into Joseph Bloggs & Son PLC

JBS using the latest VAX machines found evidence of illegal entry into the computer system and hacking was suspected.

Two VAX machines were in use one linked to the other so that having gained access to one system it was possible to move to the other. The second system contained company secret information on take- over models for an existing bid which was managed by a merchant bank for JBS. This was protected by multi-level access control mechanisms. The activity log indicated these had not been breached.

However, the first system spooled some word processing information. This detailed, in plain text, all the external correspondence and memos on the bid, making penetration of the second system a waste of time. Yet the hacker persisted and, it was discovered, made his initial access because he had obtained the privileged access code of a computer maintenance engineer. This access code should not have existed since the bank had stopped remote diagnostics.

A board room panic began because of the recent Guinness scandal. This was exacerbated because one of the directors had read a press account of electronic eavesdropping and was convinced that passwords were being obtained in this way. All the evidence suggested this was not true but panic begat panic and action had to be seen to be taken.

Action

1. What security lessons can be learnt from this case study?

2. What measures could you implement to overcome the concern over possible electronic eavesdropping?

Solutions to the Hacking Case Study

Computer manufacturers offer remote diagnostics by their engineers as a benefit to the user. The access privilege of an engineer are of a very powerful kind so that they may explore various parts of the system unimpeded by normal user constraints. The engineers port (or point of access) is usually an open connection on the communications equipment.

The computer manufacturers user manuals contained a number of privileged user identification codes and passwords. It is necessary for the user to disable these facilities to prevent illegal access.

JBS had opted out of the diagnostic arrangement but the engineer had not closed off his access port. A second port existed for remote software maintenance and this was thought to be in good order and suitably protected and was not used by the hacker.

The computer department, largely through ignorance, had failed to take action on the above elements of risk.

A 'gateway' had not been set up between the two VAX machines which would have checked users and controlled individuals moving from one system to another.

The hacker was never caught! However, in addition to the above measures the following steps were taken:

a)   All line numbers were reallocated by B.T.

b)   Line numbers were not displayed on modems.

c) Pseudo dial-back facilities were instituted on all top secret files following a data classification study that hardened up password procedures.

d) Encryption was used on all stored documents that were marked 'confidential'.

e)   The manufacturer closed off the   port and gave a written undertaking that it had accomplished the work. The Zone Engineering Manager also agreed to randomly inspect the site and ensure that the port remained closed.

f) Despite recommendations to close the software port this was not done, perhaps because of management omission or more probably because the Board lost interest in the subject.

2. The installation of 'Tempest' shielding proved too expensive for the Board. The alternatives open to them were:

a) Buying-in shielded terminals, printers and communication cabling.

b) Submerge signals from existing equipment in electromagnetic noise.

c) Screen encryption, transparent to the eye, but randomised to prevent fine tuning by eavesdroppers.

d) Clustering vdu's to prevent accurate tuning from a distance.

e) Photographing all television aerials in the vicinity and comparing photographs for new aerials, from time to time, to ensure new units on the skyline were not pointing at existing vdu's.

Insurance and Single Loss Expectancy

15

Insurance provides the last line of defence against unexpected loss or damage. Since premiums are based on an equation in part made up of the value of the probable loss and its frequency of occurrence, it follows that costing possible failures and assessing their frequency of occurrence can have a very significant role, not only in insurance but also in security risk management.

Nowadays package policies give the widest cover available in one document. It is possible to cover:

a. Hardware

b. Software

c. Consequential loss

d. Recreation costs

e. Computer misuse

f. Professional indemnity insurance.

Hardware

It is important that the sum insured should be as accurate as possible. For hardware if the user is under-insured and at the time of disaster the figure for which he has a quotation is 85% or less of the replacement value, then averaging will apply. Averaging is where the insurer is only liable for a proportional amount where an inaccurate statement has been made. Thus for a piece of equipment costing £100,000 to replace, where the user has insured for only £50,000 then the insurer need only pay £25,000.

In view of inflation it is important to constantly review policies to make sure that this parity is not applied. If the policy allows for "escalation of sum insured" then there is protection against inflation. Similarly if it has "a new for old" clause then it is also likely that the user is protected.

Software

Often software is not updated on insurance policies. Software brought in five years ago at £300,000 is in all probability still insured for £300,000 even though inflation and modern salaries might very well treble or quadruple the value if it had to be replaced.

Additionally work carried out by in-house analysts and programmers on program amendments should be added into the software figures so that the insured amount is exactly equal to the cost of replacement at the moment in time the premium is paid. Again, because of inflation, this figure should be reviewed on a quarterly basis.

Consequential Loss

These are the losses a firm might expect in consequence of computer disruption. Policies are becoming more available covering this exposure but they usually are preceded by a detailed systems survey for the underwriter.

Consequential loss in this respect is every cost that will be incurred as a direct loss of the facility but excluding values already covered by other policies, for example, hardware, software, recreation of data etc. Contributors to computer related consequential loss will include:

a) loss of sales through computer failure,

b) cost of resecuring market share,

c) loss of return on investments,

d) increased bank interest,

e) losses incurred through reduced market capitalisation,

f) legal costs attributable to the failure etc.

It is vital to assess these figures accurately since the effect of averaging if a mistake is made can be punitive. This is a figure almost always underinsured because of the inexact knowledge on the part of senior management of what would be involved in a computer department.

Re-Creation Cost

Re-creation costs are almost always wrongly assessed. These are the costs that would be incurred in recreating and reinstating the system in the event of a disaster. Invariably too much emphasis is put on the loyalty of employees who, at the best, might find the unsociable hours they have to work in the event of a disaster putting strains on their marriage, and are therefore tempted to find other work. At worst computer staff may be nomadic mercenaries who do not intend to be inconvenienced by a computer disaster and who leave to find pastures new. Thus, recovery is always assumed to be faster and less expensive than it actually will be. It must always be accepted that in a disaster situation staff will resign and drift away to other jobs. New staff will have to be recruited and the learning curve will of course increase costs. Contract labour brought in to speed up reinstatement will also have a learning element to be estimated for and will always cost more than is expected. Costs are always higher than expected because bureaux, realising that a disaster situation exists, will capitalise by putting up their charges.

Computer Misuse

This type of insurance will cater for fraudulent or malicious activity or embezzlement on a company's computer. In this type of arrangement the computer is not destroyed. Whilst control measures and contingency plans are the most prudent methods of dealing with such problems, insurance has a large part to play. Some form of excess is usually required by the insurer. Thus the company insures against a £25,000,000 fraud and it may be required to carry an excess of £5,000,000. In other words, the insurer will take £20,000,000 of risk whilst the user must take £5,000,000. Premiums for this type of cover are in direct proportion to the controls that have been exercised and the amount of monies that are involved.

It makes sense for companies to insure computer fraud risks to a level that would not seriously harm their earning position in any financial year and then to cover themselves with an insurance above that level up to the maximum coverage available that they can afford. This combination must be attractive to the computer owner because it means that he can buy a higher level of insurance on an economic basis. Similarly, the underwriter will find this type of policy attractive since it means that the individual company is prepared to underwrite a very large amount of its own risk before it calls on the funds of outside organisations.

One of the main aspects of this type of cover is usually that someone must be named as causing a fraud and prosecution must occur. The principal exclusions are usually losses that are discovered twelve months after the event or where a company has employed an individual who has a past record of dishonesty.

The same causes usually apply where insurance cover is offered against computer abuse. For example, when an operator wipes tapes or discs. The individual must be named and some form of prosecution must follow.

Professional Indemnity Insurance

Professional indemnity is important for bureaux who have a responsibility to their clients for consequential losses, etc.

An important extension to cover with professional indemnity is the dishonesty of employees and the liability of associated or subsidiary companies.

The same principles in terms of excess apply to professional indemnity insurance as applied to fraud insurance.

Insurance Level Assessment

Re-creation costs are almost always wrongly assessed. Too much emphasis is put on the loyalty of employees who, at the worst, are nomadic mercenaries, so that recovery is always assumed to be faster and less expensive that it actually will be. In most disaster situations, staff will resign and drift away to other jobs if only because they will be required to work unsociable hours and alternative employment is plentiful. Contract labour that can be brought in to speed things up always costs more. Also costs are always higher than expected because bureaux, realising that a disaster situation exists, will capitalise by putting up their charges; usually because they have had to turn away other business to take on the emergency job. In the same vein, banks will increase their lending rates to the stricken company because they feel that their position is exposed.

The case study will examine methods of assessing re-creation costs. By far the more serious offence would be fraudulent activity or embezzlement on the company's computer which can dramatically curtail a company's earning ability. Whilst control measures and contingency plans are the most prudent methods of dealing with such problems, insurance must play a part. The ability to estimate and insure the size of the loss that could involve the destruction of a company must be high on the agenda of those with financial responsibility within company organisations.

As stated earlier, it makes sense for companies to insure computer fraud risks to a level that would not seriously harm their earning position in any financial year and then to cover themselves with an insurance above that level up to a maximum coverage available or that they can afford. This combination must be attractive to the computer owner because it means that he can buy high level insurance on an economic basis. Similarly, the Lloyds underwriter will find this type of policy attractive since it means the individual company is prepared to underwrite a fairly large amount of its own risk before it calls on the funds of outside organisations.

Insurance companies, of course, will only take this type of risk on when they are satisfied that the computer department is run efficiently and securely.

As with professional indemnity, the price paid for such insurance will be related to the company's turnover, the level of indemnity required and the level to which the company will self-insure.

Computer fraud and misuse is becoming a more fashionable policy with several insurers who now offer wording covering the subjects. These normally cover erasure, destruction or distortion of data or data carrying materials together with unjustifiable fraudulent and dishonest program manipulation, alteration or insertion of spurious data in computer systems.

Levels of Disaster Costing

There will always be at least three major levels of disaster. The first level is the classical "Boeing crashing into the building", where all information, computing facilities and personnel are destroyed. A lower level is the power failure or machine failure where one or two days processing are lost, but all back-up facilities are in existence, discs and tapes are secure and no personnel are injured.

Between these two levels of disaster lies the most probable and expensive disaster situation. This may very well be the type of disaster where a fire in the media library destroys all tapes and discs and a valid disaster plan is not in existence. Alternatively, it might be a case of maximum disruption being caused by a malcontent or an unbalanced employee. The individual working under prejudiced motivation destroys sensitive files and software or incapacitates the machine.

To return the system to normal working will require the assessment of seven major factors. In a pre-disaster situation it will be necessary to evaluate these in some depth. They are:

a. Personnel	Recovery times are a direct function of expertise, maturity and direction.
b. Back-up	The geographical location and availability of the machine must be a prime consideration. Supporting bureau machines must be taken into account.
c. Media Safety Systems	Non-suspect disc packs or remotely stored software packs will play an important role.
d. Systems, Program and Operator Documentation	The level and clarity of these systems will be an overriding feature.
e. Manual Systems	The ability to return to either whole manual systems or partial manual systems will be significant.
f. Manufacturer	The level of support that will be provided in terms of replacements or expertise.
g. Disaster Plan	The most significant part of the evaluation. Its existence can mean the smooth return, its non-existence could lead to bankruptcy.

Based on these factors it is possible to make an accurate assessment of the length of time required to get the system up and running again. Arbitrarily this might be:

Level 1 disaster .... 7 months to return the system.

Level 2 disaster .... 5 months to return the system.

Level 3 disaster .... 2 months to return the system.

It is assumed that critical systems which are essential to the organisation's well-being are in place before these time periods.

In the calculations several cost assumptions have to be made. The most important assumption is that in disaster situations people do not react out of the kindness of their hearts. If a machine is damaged or down then staff will be more expensive to find, computer time will be more expensive than was anticipated, money will be more expensive to borrow after the disaster and learning curves for new staff will be twice as long as expected. In terms of calculation the following assumptions should be made:

a. Contract staff are employed at rate plus 100%.

b. All weekend and overtime working is at cost plus 50%.

c. Only non-management personnel are paid overtime. Management personnel will be paid a bonus.

d. Hotels and food allowance for the non-management staff is 4 Star hotel rate per day. In Capital Cities or tourist centres it should be calculated at 4 Star rate + 40%.

e. Hotels and food allowance for management staff is 5 Star hotel subsistence rate.

f. Hire cars and taxis charge Company Expense Mileage Rate + 400%.

g. Computer time, which was budgeted at "n" per hour on "friendly machines" is now "2n" per hour and on bureau machines "5n" per hour and so on.

h. Agencies charge 25% of annual salary for staff they find.

j. Money is borrowed at 4% per annum above previous rate of interest, for the period of the disaster.

k. A statement of inflation must be made.

l. In any year there are 264 working days.

m. Learning curves for contract and new staff are assumed to increase former functions by 25%.

Example

A typical example of escalating costs is demonstrated by the following data taken from an actual survey, which approximately bears out the above assumptions:

Cost of single shift of operators   £420.50

Cost of single shift of contract
operators   £630.75

Weekend working, company employees, extra cost	£278.05
Weekend working, contract operators	£839.56

Re-input required from software documentation of 103,680,000 characters, allowing for time - wastage caused by finding data, sorting and affirming, answering queries etc. — 85.5 days

On three shifts. — 28.5 days

Machine rejection extended by 5% — 30.0 days

Input staff on contract are assumed to cost £35 per day with £5 commission and £5 bonus, or total cost per day of £45.

Using all 35 positions

Manual cost to recreate softwarein addition to normal costs — £94,500.00

Additionally, six tapes will need to be prepared containing master information. — £283,500.00

Manual system to monitor user departments, find information and documentation, all will be agency recruited and controlled by senior staff.

Cost per week of 25 staff working 6 dayswill be — £9,588.90

Allowing 30% learning curve in the first month and the need to have additional space @£2 per square foot per month, the total cost for a requisite four months will be. — £174,480.00

Operations staff are assumed to work weekends and additional staffs will be required at the manufacturer. A learning curve of 20% is assumed to apply in the first month. The staff will be assumed to revert to the new machine on delivery.

Additional cost	£109,928.00
Subsistence allowances, hotel etc.	£165,620.00
Travel costs at estimated £150 per day	£27,300.00
Management staff totals and subsistence costs	£4,480.00
Computer time at manufacturer/support organisation	£1,019,200.00

Non-management programmers who will have to evaluate processing and will work some twelve hours per day over this period — £177,606.00

Hotels and subsistence costs	£146,692.00
Hotels for management	£11,200.00

Miscellaneous travel costs at estimated value

£3,000.00

Auditors to head re-creation situation and monitor work — £60,000.00

Professionals to advise during the period of disaster re-creation from outside the company £60,000.00

Contract operators on back-up machine for three months and one week as minimum at a cost of £810.00 per shift

Weekend working at £1,078.00per shift

£305,214.00

Machine cost at unfavourable rates including learning curve periods £2,010,960.00

Learning curve of contract operator staff £76,302.00

Systems staff and hotels during the critical three month period and working extra overtime,estimated extra cost £63,840.00

Mileage between locations of hire vehicles £50,400.00

During this time 10% (or double normal turnover in staff) of all staff will leave and will have to be replaced.

Costs in agency commissions will be £149,300.00

Recruiting costs of senior management toestablish contract staff £4,000.00

Bonus payments to management £34,878.00

Additional maintenance costs for first and second shift workings £46,592.00

Progress mailings to customers, suppliers,press etc. @ 50p per letter and assumingfive mailings £30,000.00

TOTAL of data processing charges £5,136,578.00

By comparing the costs for the different levels of disasters it will be possible to work out the most likely situation to occur and to take financial cover for this eventuality. In the case of the study in question the most critical and most likely type of disaster would have cost the company £5,136,580 to recreate their computer system at a level comparable with the pre-disaster mode.

In this instance a company had actual cover for £1,500,000. If an averaging clause had existed in their policy and the disaster had occurred the total payment might have been £438,000, resulting in a single massive loss which may have caused the company to cease trading.

This calculation of a Single Loss Expectancy in this form can be extremely useful in determining the type of back-up arrangement that a company will use. For example, the costs entailed in a "hot-start" back up arrangement may be £1,900,000, a "cold-start" may be £3,400,000, a simple back-up arrangement may cost £5,000,000. It may be argued that a calculation of this type is irrelevant if insurance cover is in place. However, premiums have to be paid, staff recruited, unsociable hours worked, outside organisations used to recreate the system.

It will be evident that by evaluating the different levels of potential disaster the remedial course of action to be taken will be highlighted. Consequently, it will be possible to quantify the benefit that can be afforded by a given security measure, the cost involved and, as a result, the direct benefit that can be anticipated for a specific investment. Similarly it will be possible to obtain a recognition of all the potential problems that the business is exposed to through data processing and the most cost effective safeguards can then be selected.

Consequential Loss

This is much more difficult to calculate. Figures will need to be arrived at by contribution from the Financial Director, Marketing Director and Managing Director, since only the relevant director can know of the effect of prolonged disruption on investment plans, capitalisation, profits and future development plans.

Probably, the Sales Department will be able to make the most significant contribution in terms of customer loyalty and the anticipated loss of customers and profits, together with additional costs and investments necessary to re-secure the market area that the organisation currently enjoys. As a result a committee should be set up and chaired by the Managing Director to establish the probable level of consequential loss and ensure adequate insurance cover is taken.

Questionnaire

It is difficult to provide a questionnaire covering this area of loss control. This is especially so since the questionnaires included in the body of this book will highlight the threats and vulnerabilities to assets. However, the following questions may be of use in assessing the impact of a disaster on businesses:

1. What is the annual turnover of the business for the last five years? What is:

a.   Peak monthly turnover,

      b.   Percentages anticipated growth,

      c.   ROI,

      d.   Profit per annum,

      e.   Peak Stock Value,

      f.   Stock Turn?

2. What are the average purchases:

      a.   Peak,

      b.   Payment Rules,

      c.   Average Value of back order file,

      d.   Average length of time on file?

3. In terms of the sales ledger what are:

      a.   Average Monthly invoice value,

      b.   Average Statement run - when run,

      c.   Percentages payment or invoice,

      d.   Percentages payment or statement   1st

                                             2nd

                                           3rd

                                           4th

      e.   Average value of written off debt?

4. What level of interest is paid on loans?

5. What type of contingency plan exists? How effective is this? Has it been tested?

6. What is the level of user staff turn over? D.P. staff turnover?

7. What staff recruitment methods are used?

8. Which agencies are used for temporary staff? What are their charges?

9. What are the monthly or capital costs of:

> a. Contractors,
> b. Outside experts,
> c. Staff by grade,
> d. Hotels,
> e. Transport,
> f. Media,
> g. New communication lines,
> h. New ancillary equipment?

10. Availability of staff after hours?

11. What history of disasters exist?   What effect did they have?

12. In terms of capitalisation:
> a. What is the authorised and issued capital
> b. Is there a history of share capitalisation drops?

13. What is the yearly high and low of share values?

14. What is the level of dependency of subsidiary organisations on data processing?

15. What is the estimated level of loss, in the event of a disaster, on:

> a. Customer numbers,
> b. Work in progress,
> c. New product development,
> d. Losses of investment capital and ROI.,
> e. Computer functions (ATMs, Cryptography, Data base)?

16. What files will be lost, temporarily or permanently, because of encryption?

17. What will be the effect of the loss of management information on:

> a. Management,
> b. Customers,
> c. WIP,
> d. Investment?

The above questions will assist in calculating the loss in consequence of a disaster, since:

> (a) Shares will fall after a public scandal and historical information will assist in determining by how much.
>
> (b) ROI will reduce in a disaster
>
> (c) high interest rates may now obtain as the Bank may consider its position to be exposed.
>
> (d) debtors will not pay debts and Aged Debt Listings will increase.
>
> (e) loss of computers will impact on Stock Control and cause money to be tied up unnecessarily in stock, further increasing Consequential Loss.
>
> (f) customers will be lost to competitors, impacting Profits and requiring expensive PR and Sales activity to recover the market position.

The following questions, when combined with questions 5 - 11 will facilitate the calculation of the extra cost of working.

18. What are the supplier lead times for:

> a. Mainframes,
>
> b. Communications equipment,
>
> c. Peripherals,
>
> d. Media,
>
> e. Cabling,
>
> f. Stationery,
>
> g. Air-conditioning,
>
> h. Office equipment,
>
> j. Software,
>
> k. Application programs?

19. Back-up cost?

20. What is the value of software and programs?

> a.   Who supplied?
>
> b.   If in house, man-months to develop?

21. Location of:

> a.   Back up M/C
>
> b.   Hotels and Costs.

22. Policy for staff to work away from home?

Security Risk Management

16

Overview

Security risk management in computers falls into two categories, qualitative and quantitative. Which ever is used the underlying principle is the same. "Security" implies the protection of a system against all kinds of mishap or misuse. On all computer systems the threats fall into five categories:

1. Destruction of assets
2. Unauthorised modification or manipulation of information assets
3. Unauthorised disclosure of information assets
4. Denial of use of an asset
5. Fraud.

Fraud grows at 500% per year and conviction for this crime is of the order of 10,000 to 1 against. However, the less glamorous disclosure of secret information to competitors can have longer lasting effects on a company as can the destruction of the computer asset which can prejudice the survival of the company. So what can be done? The Computer Security expert will find that the techniques needed for defence are as complex and varied as the means of attack. Every part of the system matters:

People: recruitment, selection, training, control, procedures;

Security Procedures: audit, encryption, authentication, recovery, back-up, strategy;

Software: development, communications, tools, procedures, accountability;

Hardware: processors, peripherals, communications, terminals, libraries.

Yet from organisation to organisation every part will not be equally vulnerable nor will countermeasures be the same and never equally cost effective. The only way the Security expert can protect the computer system for the benefit of his company is by using proven risk management techniques. When these are applied to the security of computer operations they will encompass risk analysis, decision making and effectiveness review.

Computer security risk analysis should be structured to:

determine an organisations assets (people, software, hardware and procedures);

assess the nature and size of asset vulnerability to the five main threats (destruction, modification, disclosure, denial and fraud);

estimate the probability of the threat occurring;

estimate the single loss from the threat occurring;

estimate the annualised loss expectancy;

devise effective controls or safeguards;

establish a cost/benefit analysis;

select the most cost effective alternatives.

By using a structured risk management approach it will be possible to provide senior management with sufficient information to make sensible decisions based on quantitative evaluations of risk to countermeasure. It will also help to develop answers to the following questions:

How good is security now?

How good does it need to be?

What are the threats to assets?

What is the frequency of the occurrence of these threats? What measures can be taken to successfully reduce the impact and frequency of the threat occurring?

What will countermeasures cost?

What do countermeasures save?

What is the cost/benefit value associated with each countermeasure?

The process of Risk Analysis is shown below.

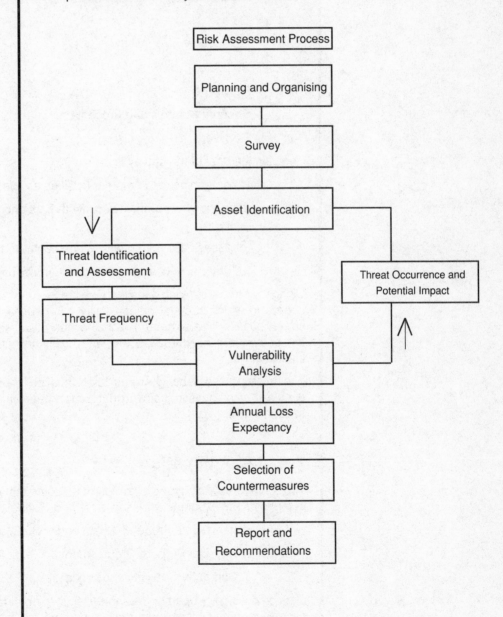

In each area of risk analysis it is necessary that the security level of procedures should be determined, safeguards should be documented and plans made for recovery. The likelihood of an undesired event happening is related to how well its effects have been anticipated and countermeasures implemented or documented.

The Security Risk Analyst will collect data by conducting a physical walk through of the existing computer facility and interviewing all the personnel involved with the computer operations.

In order to ensure that no asset is missed or potential vulnerability ignored a questionnaire will be used. The questionnaire must be tailored to each application and will differ from installation to installation. The organisation of the questionnaire will be time consuming but is an integral part of the planning and organising. Generally the following headings will always be constant:

> Personnel
>
> Accountability
>
> Data
>
> Operations
>
> Software
>
> Hardware
>
> Security Controls and Procedures
>
> Recovery.

The ultimate goal of the survey is to:

> (a) determine the computer facilities assets and their values;
>
> (b) identify all potential security threats and their likelihood of occurrence;
>
> (c) assess the vulnerability of the centre to the identified threats;
>
> (d) determine cost effective countermeasures.

Using the pre-determined questionnaire the Security Analyst will investigate the degree to which security responsibility has been assigned, understood and carried out. He will also determine the security of software and workflow controls and personnel procedures together with the history of failure in all aspects of the installation.

The notes that the Security Analyst takes must be retained and cross referred to each part of the questionnaire so that items entered into the risk analysis can be substantiated.

Asset Identification

There are three main types of computer resource that will have to be evaluated in terms of risk exposure and then protected. These are:

> 1. Intellectual Property (data and programs).
>
> 2. Physical Property (equipment and supplies).
>
> 3. Computer Services and Processes.

Data on physical property will be the easiest to obtain and can be arrived at by estimating capital losses and replacement costs. Intellectual Properties and

Computer Processes will present more abstract problems to the Analyst. The question that should be asked is: " How would the installation recreate files and software if there was an immediate disaster?" Costs to be included in the calculation are:

> Buying new software
>
> Recreating data from back up files
>
> Recreating data in house from source documents
>
> Validating software and data
>
> Determining customer account status
>
> Contracting DP operations outside the organisation.

Each administration centre should be encouraged to list replacement values of equipment, operations and resources and to arrive at a figure for loss as a consequence of disaster.

Threat Identification

Previous incidents or breaches of security are good indications of the types of threats that are relevant to the installation. Information on threats can be obtained from the following areas:

> 1. Security Office records
>
> 2. Computer logs
>
> 3. Operations re-run reports
>
> 4. Security software print-outs
>
> 5. User complaints
>
> 6. Staff turn over.

Comparisons with other similar installations will be useful in determining threats to the facility. Similar installations will usually have had similar problems and are certainly worth investigating on the installation being analysed.

Threat Frequency

Determining the threat frequency of occurrence is a process of continual refinement. Factors to be taken into consideration include:

> Crime rates in the area of the location
>
> Integrity and morale of computer staff
>
> Statistics of previous threats
>
> Business activities of the company
>
> Philosophy of computer staff
>
> Number and types of threats
>
> Number and type of countermeasures
>
> Effectiveness of countermeasures.

The threat frequency should always be shown as an annual figure and be subject to re-evaluation in the light of subsequent analysis.

Threat Occurrence and Potential Impact

Threats should be listed in order of magnitude or in the form of a criticality analysis. Computer security risk management is an iterative process. As more and more facts come to light the level of impact will change as may the frequency of occurrence, especially as existing countermeasures on other assets will have an effect on the asset under investigation. This will become apparent as the investigation proceeds.

Vulnerability Analysis

Having determined the threats by assets and the damage that may be caused by an unfavourable event or events a clear picture will begin to emerge of the elements that contribute to the system's vulnerabilities. After refinement these should be listed by vulnerability under one of the five threats already described. Within these categories the highest single loss expectancy will be listed first and others in order of reducing value.

At this stage it will also be necessary to determine the adequacy of existing countermeasures, safeguards and controls. These may be divided into three categories:

1. Physical:

>> Access controls

>> Fire and smoke detectors, extinguishers and suppressants

>> Metal detectors, package and briefcase inspections.

2. Administrative (written procedures):

>> Personnel policies

>> Security policies

>> Data adjustment and error correction procedures

>> Program development and control

>> Privileged software control.

3. Technical:

>> Activities log

>> User verification

>> Validation

>> Encryption.

Loss Expectancies

The evaluation of potential loss is the corner stone of security. Insurance cover, for example, is usually provided against a single loss expectancy. The hardware of an installation may have cost £100,000 and is insured for this amount since if it were destroyed by fire it would cost that much to replace. The insurers in calculating the premium know that a computer fire occurs once every 50 years. The Annual loss expectancy is therefore £100,000 divided by 50 years or £2,000 and if this is the annualised loss, their premium will reflect the number of instal-lations they cover and profit margin.

The important factors in insurance are the Single Loss Expectancy (SLE) and the Annual Loss Expectancy (ALE). The same is true of risk management.

Initially, adjectives may be used to describe loss and determine the criticality of a study. However, at some point, as far as is possible an accurate loss figure must be found

Selection of Countermeasures

Countermeasures should then be considered and carefully costed. The cost should be considered in respect of the reduction it brings about in the ALE to determine its utility value. The relationship between the value of the threat exposure and the cost of correction, together with the amount of their difference, will determine the priority of activity. The possible priorities which could be applied are:

> Correct immediately invariably with no cost penalty

> Excellent savings, activity on a priority basis

> Good saving, project to be created

> Low priority

> Action in the indefinite future

> Ignore - No action.

Even with countermeasures which show excellent savings it may take time to bring them into being. Clearly, delayed actions where a threat exists should be offset by insurance until remedial action can be taken. Good risk analysis programmes will provide reasonably accurate values for insurance purposes; the insurance later being reduced once the countermeasure is in place.

Qualitative Risk Analysis

In order to get an overview of the risk exposure it is usual to conduct a broad qualitative analysis first. Instead of using detailed financial values to calculate the value of the actual event an adjective is used, where the adjective defines a range of values.

Qualitative techniques are effective in producing a broad analysis ,a rough cut that highlights individual areas which are at major risk, and as a result can define starting points for remedial measures. These areas can then be quantitatively analysed. That is, monetary values can be applied to the "impact" to measure the cost effectiveness of counter measures.

Paper work is now vital. Every avenue explored must be documented so that logical assessments can be made at a later date. In qualitative analysis a Threat and Vulnerability Worksheet is used.

Qualitative Threat and Vulnerability Evaluation

A threat is defined as an event which could exploit a vulnerability or adversely affect the computer system.

Each vulnerability will be identified and evaluated on a work sheet. Where an overview survey is conducted the work sheets can form the basis of the report.

```
THREAT AND VULNERABILITY EVALUATION WORKSHEET

SHEET NUMBER: _____

1.  VULNERABILITY: _____

    _____

2.  DESCRIPTION OF
    VULNERABILITY:



    _____

3. THREAT:
Destruction / Denial / Disclosure / Modification / Fraud
    _____
4. IMPACT:



    _____
5. FREQUENCY:

6. A.L.E.(Adjective and estimate)
    _____
7. RATIONALE:



    _____
8. RECOMMENDED COUNTERMEASURES:
```

Threat and vulnerability work sheet.

Sheets should be serially numbered to allow later cross referencing, especially in the body of a report.

1. VULNERABILITY. This should describe the vulnerability that is going to be discussed. For example: "Back-up."

2. DESCRIPTION OF VULNERABILITY: This section will detail the vulnerability

to ensure that later there is no confusion. For example: "There is no arrangement to back-up the mainframe in the event of a disaster."

3. THREAT. The five threats are listed and it is only necessary to strike out the threats that will not come into being because of the vulnerability under reference.

4. IMPACT. This section should describe the effect on the company or the computer department if the vulnerability is exploited. For example: "In the event of a disaster that denies the company the computer system there will be considerable slippage before a back up site is found or replacement equipment delivered. The ensuing chaos will result in financial loss as a manual system is implemented and customers use the disaster as a means of extending their credit lines. Also, the absence of controls during the recovery period is an ideal time for fraud or espionage. The absence of a documented disaster plan will serve to exacerbate the situation."

5. FREQUENCY: This section is intended to record the statistical frequency of occurrence. If the vulnerability being examined was fire due to an aeroplane crash the statistical frequency of once in three hundred years might be shown.

6. ANNUAL LOSS EXPECTANCY (ALE). ALE is always shown as an adjective so the analyst and management can get a "feel" for the problem. An acceptable table of adjectives would be:

Very Low	Up to £1,000
Low	£1,000 to £10,000
Low/Medium	£10,000 to £50,000
Medium	£50,000 to £100,000
Medium/High	£100,000 to £500,000
High	£500,000 to £1,000,000

In this instance "Low/Medium" could be selected indicating the loss would be in the region of £10,000 to £50,000 every year.

7. RATIONALE. This will now describe how the threats will come to fruition. For example: "There is no back-up machine and no disaster plan. A fire or deliberate act of sabotage will mean that the company cannot process its data. All sales, purchases and stock movements will come to a standstill, creating a back log for future processing whilst an alternative site is found. Controls will be waived in an effort to get some form of data processing in place which could result in fraud, browsing or unintentional modification of data."

8. RECOMMENDED COUNTERMEASURES. All the countermeasures that will help to reduce the threat should be listed, even those that have been shown on other sheets against other threats. For example:

"1. Prioritise programs and determine acceptable minimum configuration. Decide on back-up and enter into a formal relationship with the owners of the machine.

2. Document recovery procedures.

3. Test these procedures and modify the plan in the light of the test."

An example of a Qualitative Study is shown in **Appendix A**. The Threat and Vulnerability Worksheets have been built into a report which is readily accepted by management.

The traditional computer security review has always tended to be subjective and to lean heavily towards the analyst's prejudices and areas of expert knowledge. Qualitative Risk Analysis in the computer environment moves away from this and produces values that will allow a Board of Directors to see the impact of existing weaknesses in computer security and the seriousness of a given situation and the potential losses to the organisation.

Quantitative Risk Analysis

The principles that applied in the qualitative study still apply except the impact must be quantified. If a Boeing crashes on an installation the loss will be the summation of hardware, software, recreation and consequential losses. This figure is the Single Loss Expectancy or S.L.E. from which the Annualised Loss Expectancy or A.L.E. is calculated.

Annualised Loss Expectancy (ALE)

It is usually impossible to investigate and know absolutely the impact of frequency of any identifiable event especially in the early stages of a study. At this stage estimates would have to be calculated and then later refined. Courtenay argued that the SLE should be expressed in terms of units of currency and the frequency of the occurrence should be expressed on an annual basis:

SLE	=	£10 let $i = 1$	Once in 300 years,	let $f = 1$
		£100 let $i = 2$	Once in 30 years,	let $f = 2$
		£1,000 let $i = 3$	Once in 3 years,	let $f = 3$
		£10,000 let $i = 4$	3 times per year,	let $f = 4$
		£100,000 let $i = 5$	Once per week,	let $f = 5$
		£1,000,000 let $i = 6$	Once per day,	let $f = 6$
		£10,000,000 let $i = 7$	Once per 2 hours,	let $f = 7$
		£100,000,000 let $i = 8$	Once per 15 mins,	let $f = 8$

It follows that annual loss may be approximately equal to the SLE divided by the frequency of the event.

However, because the exact impact and frequency cannot usually be specified with total accuracy, it is possible to associate the ALE as a product of the estimated "SLE in monetary units" and the "estimated frequency of occurrence." This produces the formula:

$$ALE = \frac{10^{(f+i-3)}}{3}$$

For illustration of the effect, the following table has been constructed inter relating the values of impact (i) and frequency (f):

Any combination of asset impact and frequency ratings which falls within the area marked with asterisks indicates either a calculation error or a major problem

	Values of Frequency (f)							
	1	2	3	4	5	6	7	8
1	*	*	*	*	£300	£3k	£30k	£300k
2	*	*	*	£300	£3k	£30k	£300k	£3m
3	*	*	£300	£3k	£30k	£300k	£3m	£30m
4	*	£300	£3k	£30k	£300k	£3m	£30m	£300m
5	£300	£3k	£30k	£300k	£3m	£30m	£300m	*
6	£3k	£30k	£300k	£3m	£30m	£300m	*	*
7	£30k	£300k	£3m	£30m	£300m	*	*	*

which demands immediate correction before proceeding with the risk assessment. However, for all normal circumstances a realistic figure will be calculated.

Values of impact and frequency should be filled in on an asset sheet from each intersection on the chart and a running total kept of the ALE attributable to each threat on the list of threats. Where more than one circumstance affects data modification, data destruction, data confidentiality, or processing availability the SLE (i) and frequency (f) values should be noted separately as an aid to deciding the resultant security measures.

A worksheet should always be completed, in exactly the same way and form as the one used in the Quantitative Method but in this methodology the SLE and calculated ALE should be shown. By quantifying the ALE it is now possible to determine the efficacy of countermeasures. An example of this form is shown on the next page.

Selection and Evaluation of Counter Measures

The next step in the risk management procedure is the selection of countermeasures. In selecting these it is recommended that the Countermeasure Evaluation Sheet is used which is shown below:

Section 1 contains a description of the proposed countermeasure. This is to facilitate cross references with the Threat and Vulnerability Sheets.

Section 2 holds the description of the countermeasure that is proposed.

Section 3 holds the cost of the countermeasure expressed as an annual figure. For example, a steel door on an entrance may cost £1000 but have a life and usefulness of 20 years, the annual cost would therefore be £1000/20 or £50.

Section 4 describes the threats that are affected by the countermeasures, and would again be abstracted from the relevant Threat & Vulnerability Sheet together with the current ALE. The Projected ALE is calculated with the security measure in position and the ALE savings is, of course, the difference between the two. The Return on Investment (ROI) represents the savings that can be expected from the countermeasure and is expressed as a ratio of total savings to cost of countermeasure. Total Savings is the addition of the savings by threat/ vulnerability that is affected by the countermeasure, since a countermeasure will often affect more than one threat.

Risk Management, in this sense, can become unnecessarily complicated since

```
┌─────────────────────────────────────────────────────┐
│                                                     │
│   QUANTITATIVE THREAT AND VULNERABILITY EVALUATION WORKSHEET │
│                                                     │
│   SHEET NUMBER: _____   │
│                                                     │
│   1.  VULNERABILITY: _____  │
│       _____ │
│                                                     │
│   2.  DESCRIPTION OF                                │
│         VULNERABILITY:                              │
│                                                     │
│                                                     │
│                                                     │
│                                                     │
│                                                     │
│       _____ │
│                                                     │
│   3. THREAT: _____ │
│   Destruction / Denial / Disclosure / Modification / Fraud │
│       _____ │
│   4. IMPACT:                                        │
│                                                     │
│                                                     │
│       _____ │
│   5. FREQUENCY: _____      S.L.E          │
│                                                     │
│   6. A.L.E. _____ │
│   7. RATIONALE:                                     │
│                                                     │
│                                                     │
│                                                     │
│       _____ │
│   8. RECOMMENDED COUNTERMEASURES:                   │
│                                                     │
│                                                     │
│                                                     │
│                                                     │
│                                                     │
└─────────────────────────────────────────────────────┘
```

Quantitive Threat and vulnerability work sheet.

```
COUNTERMEASURE EVALUATION WORKSHEET


SHEET NUMBER: _____

1.  COUNTERMEASURE: _____

   _____

2.  DESCRIPTION :




   _____

3. ANNUAL COST:

   _____

4. THREATS AFFECTED BY COUNTERMEASURE:
                                ALE

                    CURRENT      PROJECTED     ALE SAVINGS
   _____



   _____

5. ROI:



   _____

6. OVERLAPPING ADDITIONAL COUNTERMEASURES:
```

Countermeasure worksheet

not only does a countermeasure affect more than one threat, but there will be overlapping additional countermeasures.

Countermeasures should be listed, in the descending order of ROI. This will give the order of priority of corrective action.

Each additional countermeasure that is implemented will affect the overall security position and ALE. Changes in the ALE will effect the ROI values for each subsequent countermeasure. To adjust for this effect it is advisable to select the most cost-effective countermeasure first. The next countermeasure should be evaluated as if the first were already in place and the ALE savings and ROI values adjusted as necessary. This procedure is repeated for each countermeasure listed. Whilst the process sounds complicated in theory, in practice it is fairly simple.

Finally a plan of action and milestones for implementing the selected counter measures should be considered. When determining a proposed schedule of counter measure implementations. All counter measures with a ROI of greater that 2:1 should be considered for implementation. Less than this ratio they may be ineffective.

Presenting Analysis Results

Whichever method (Qualitative or Quantitative) is used to analyse an area, the Analyst, in presenting his results to Management, should remain aware that Management needs to know:

    a. WHAT is at risk?

    b. HOW likely is the occurrence?

    c. WHAT effect will it have?

    d. WHAT countermeasures can be installed?

    e. HOW MUCH will it cost?

The actual presentation of the results of a Risk Analysis is best done in the form of a report, summarising the findings of the analysis. The worksheets containing the detailed justification of the recommendations made in the report should be added as an appendix. Wherever possible the sheet numbers should be referred to when statements are made in the body of the report. For example: "Badge readers will provide a total savings of £29,700, see Threat & Vulnerability Sheet 2-28 and Countermeasure Sheet 11." This always enhances credibility and will invariably ensure that the recommendation will be well considered.

Example

In a survey of a financial institution it was found that there were messengers at the main entrance who had a good idea of who were employees and who visitors. However, this one security threshold was compromised during morning starting periods when large groups of people arrived simultaneously making it impossible for one man to monitor all arrivals and in the evening when no one was on duty. Additional vulnerabilities came to light when it was discovered that fire doors were used as general exits and staff could "tailgate" an entrance by waiting for someone to exit.

To complicate matters some one hundred contract programmers were employed who changed often and were unknown to the security guard; these came and left without let or hindrance. Additionally, the flat roof could be accessed from other buildings in the area and the roof door had a simple lock and was not alarmed. The final complication was that management disliked the idea of identification badges for staff and visitors. Thus anyone could gain entrance to the building and once inside move from floor to floor without difficulty.

The threats were clearly Disclosure, Destruction and Fraud. Disclosure because it would be possible to see VDU screens with confidential business information on them. This would have provided an intruder with information of value to competitors or even details of confidential "take-over" deals which would have been invaluable for "insider dealing".

Destruction because an outsider might try to damage equipment if they were mentally unstable or input spurious information to the data base out of malice. This would eventually have corrupted all files.

Fraud because it would be possible to use terminals left unattended, manipulating information for dishonest gain.

The first pass in analysing the situation would be to complete the Qualitative Threat and Vulnerability Sheet and get a "feel" for the problem.

The "filled in" document is shown *Page 224* and shows an ALE of "Medium". It was realised in the early stages that an unauthorised outsider gaining access to Stock Exchange takeover information would not only make money, but also cause public embarrassment to the company if the security breach became known. The exact impact was not known at this stage.

The frequency of the vulnerability was thought of as "daily" but this did not represent the frequency of attack and was consequently misleading. The ALE was shown as "Medium" which was perhaps realistic but none the less alarming. The sheet fulfilled its purpose by highlighting a critical fault and emphasising an urgent need for detailed investigation.

As the study progresses all sheets with "High" and "Medium" ALE will be evaluated as a priority, thus the qualitative analysis has provided a criticality analysis. The second time around it should be possible to accurately quantify the exposure. The sheet may now look like that on *Page 225*

Analysis of the situation showed that fraud up to £50,000 could be affected as a single loss. The manipulation of data to accomplish this showed a need for specialised knowledge and since other software recommendations were being implemented this was not considered a major threat.

Disclosure remained a real and large threat. Investigation in this area revealed that a public scandal due to a security lapse would lose ABC at least one major launch on the stock exchange or one medium size takeover impacting company income by at least £1,000,000. Clearly if it was "daily" the ALE would be £365,000,000! Historically, there had been outsider penetrations and investigation showed that in the ten year period that ABC had owned the building two major thefts had taken place without any form of forced entry. The frequency, until further refinement could show otherwise, was fixed at once in five years. The ALE thus became a serious £200,000.

The Countermeasure Evaluation Sheet is on *Page 226.* The number continues the reference trail. Costings of the countermeasures were as follows:

The effective life of the system was estimated at 4 years which gave an annual cost of £40,800/4 or £10,200.

SHEET NUMBER: 01

1. VULNERABILITY:Physical Access

2. DESCRIPTION OF
    VULNERABILITY:
    Destruction / Disclosure / Fraud

3. THREAT:

4. IMPACT:
Access to confidential information by third parties would result in loss of business or public scandal depressing the capitalisation value of the company.

5. FREQUENCY: Daily

6. A.L.E.(Adjective and estimate)   Medium

7. RATIONALE:
It is possible to walk from the streets to any part of the building and to exit again without serious hindrance.   An outsider repeatedly presenting himself would be taken as an employee. Browsing is possible.

Contractors pass from floor to floor with ease and without challenge.

Access is possible from the roof.

8. RECOMMENDED COUNTERMEASURES:
1. Code and card reader locks to be installed on entrances as follows:

a) first floor access from reception

b) lift exits on all floors

c) fire escape doors on all floors to be alarmed

d) roof door to be alarmed.
      2. Fire exits to be monitored by cctv.
      3. Main door to be locked at weekends. Side door to be used
      as entrance and to have a code and card lock.

4. Computer room and surrounding areas to have code and card locks.

5. Identification badges to be worn by all staff and visitors.

6. Contractors to wear colour coded badges.

1. VULNERABILITY: Physical Access

2. DESCRIPTION OF
     VULNERABILITY:

Poor physical access controls at main doors, between floors and at roof level.

3. THREAT:
Disclosure / Fraud

4. IMPACT:
Modification of data for fraudulent ends £50,000. Public scandal; loss of business and capitalisation £1,000,000

5. FREQUENCY:

6. A.L.E.

7. RATIONALE:
It is possible to walk from the streets to any part of the building and to exit again without serious hindrance. An outsider repeatedly presenting himself would be taken as an employee. Browsing is possible.

Contractors pass from floor to floor with ease and without challenge.

Access is possible from the roof.

8. RECOMMENDED COUNTERMEASURES:
1. Code and card reader locks to be installed on entrances as follows:

      a) first floor access from reception
      b) lift exits on all floors
      c) fire escape doors on all floors to be alarmed
      d) roof door to be alarmed.
2. Fire exits to be monitored by cctv.

3. Main door to be locked at weekends. Side door to be used as entrance and to have a code and card lock.

4. Computer room and surrounding areas to have code and card locks.

5. Identification badges to be worn by all staff and visitors.

6. Contractors to wear colour coded badges.

COUNTERMEASURE EVALUATION WORKSHEET

SHEET NUMBER: 01/2/1

1. COUNTERMEASURE:	New doors to lift areas equipped with a badge reader. Fire escape doors and roof areas to have cctv monitors.

2. DESCRIPTION :

The areas leading tothe lifts have glass doors with card reader and code locks. The main entrance will remain the same but doors off will have badge readers.

Alog of all entries and exits to be maintained.

Cards to have grading of access on magnetic stripe.

I.D.s to be worn at all times.

3. ANNUAL COST: £10,200

4. THREATS AFFECTED BY COUNTERMEASURE:

ALE

	CURRENT	PROJECTED	ALE SAVINGS
Disclosure of information	£200,000	£25,000	£175,000
Theft of property	£40,000	£8,000	£32,000

5. ROI: 20.29 : 1

TOTAL SAVINGS: £207,000

6. OVERLAPPING ADDITIONAL COUNTERMEASURES:

a) Locked main door at weekends

b) CCTV

c) Guard activity

Countermeasure evaluation sheet 01/2/1

Disclosure of information was now shown on this form as a direct transfer from 01/2 but it had now come to light that there had been test intrusions and on one occasion a picture, which was an investment by a pension fund, had been stolen and was worth £36,000 and on a second occasion a micro computer worth £4,000 was stolen. This now had to be added to the threats affected on an ALE calculation.

With the security system in place the frequency of penetration would become very protracted indeed and produced new projected ALEs. The difference between the two could produce total ALE savings of £207,000 for just £10,200 per annum or an ROI of £207,000/£10,200 of 20.29:1. Anything above 2:1 is worth considering!

In this instance a very conservative board of directors decided to make an immediate investment exactly as the Security Manager suggested!

Conclusion

The traditional computer security review has always tended to be subjective and to lean heavily towards the analyst's prejudices and areas of expert knowledge. Security Risk Analysis in the mainframe computer environment moves away from this and produces bottom line values by allowing management to readily see the impact of existing weaknesses in computer security and the potential losses to the organisation.

It also allows security personnel to consider almost all the potential threats rather than those which are more obvious. However, some will always get away. For example how could an analyst anticipate the fraud within a U.S. bank where a member of the public substituted his personal paying in slips for those left for public use in the bank's main hall and then when other peoples funds were credited to his account made off with the money? Perhaps less well than anticipating the fraud in a bank where the terminals faced walkways and were not automatically powered down when not in use. An enterprising janitor was able to post sums of money to his account and make off with the proceeds. This fraud would have been highlighted by a risk management study and counter-measures put in place in time to prevent a substantial loss.

To ensure that threats to each asset are considered, the following will serve as prompts to ensure that every asset is considered.

Examples of Assets

Hardware

    Central Machine

    CPU

    Main memory

    Input/output channels

    Operator console

Storage media

    Disks

    Tapes

    Streamers

    Cartridges

    Cassettes

I/O Devices

    Printers

    Card devices

    Terminals

    Gateways

    Disc and tape drives

Special equipment

    Data base machines

    Controllers

    File servers

Software

    Operating system

    Programs

    Applications

    Utilities

    Test programs

    Communications

Personnel

    Computer personnel

    Contractors

Users

Building staff

Administrative

Documentation

Operations

Procedures

Inventory

Physical

Environmental systems

Back up equipment

Supplies

Building

Data

Classified

Planning

Financial

Logistical

Personnel

Communications

Communications Equipment

Lines

Controllers

Front End Processors

Modems

Multiplexors

Interface Units

File Servers

Encryption Devices

Cables

Frame Rooms

Telephones

Case Study in Security Risk Management

JOSEPH BLOGGS & SON PLC.

Hardware	Two DEC VAX Mini Computers
	Two Nixdorf Front End Processors
	31 IBM-PC AT (One acts as an EFT terminal)
	25 NCR DMV (Word Processors)
Software	
	RSTS
	PC-DOS 3.2 +
	Remote Diagnostics

Applications Software:

FARM (A specialised pharmaceutical package)

GAP (A general accounting package)

CMOD (A specialised modeling package)

Various micro packages.

OVERVIEW:

Personnel

JBS has a computer establishment of 40 which will rise to 42 this year. Of these 34 are permanent, the balance being made up from outside contractors. The contractors are supplied by a nationally known Software House to meet programming and development deadlines. Contractors are accepted by the company as having been vetted by the Software House prior to appointment. Agency labour may also be used to meet shortfalls due to pregnancy leave, etc.

Staff turnover runs at 10%. Staff are required to work notice periods. Job descriptions do not exist and structured interview techniques are not used. References are sometimes taken up by telephone. There is a scarcity of computer staff in the area and much poaching. The Data Processing Manager adopts the view that he can quickly tell if a new employee is what he says he is from the quality of the work he produces. If there is doubt, the man is dismissed within days but the policy depends on the DPM's whim.

An agency, Comp Personnel Ltd., provide visual display operators when required. It is assumed that the background of these short term staff members has been verified by the Agency. Other short term vdu operators, for example foreign students during vacations, bring copies of job references with them. These are accepted at face value by JBS. Temporary staff can work on word processing and non sensitive ledgers .

Word processing staff, 28 of whom work outside the control of the computer department, are normally employed in lower grades and references are verified by the Personnel Department. In addition, recruitment is generally from the local farming community as a matter of policy.

During employment, staff backgrounds are not vetted to ensure that individual circumstances have not changed. 90% of staff belong to ASTMS, the white collar union. Pay is based on market demand and as such is high.

The smallness of JBS precludes a structured promotion tree for the computer department and promotion prospects for other employees are not good. The DPM was recently refused a seat on the Board.

The structure of the Computer Department is as follows:

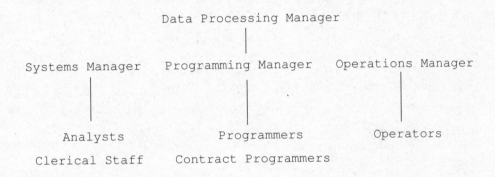

History

A two week strike was called in 1977. In 1985 a collusive fraud was discovered between warehouse men and the computer department involving £850,000 of stock. Recently, a hacker broke into the system but it is thought that this was a child who achieved very little by his intrusion.

The Computer Manager was appointed in 1985 following the fraud. She was recruited from outside the company. Up to that point she had worked for a competitor as a Chief Systems Analyst. Other junior managers within the department have been with the company for several years. However, the position of Systems Security Officer does not exist.

Operations

End of day back up runs are performed at start of day when the branches are put into off line mode and a back up copy is taken of the day's processing at the end of the working day. Copies of software and transactions are stored in a second building. Key files that are produced on the word processors are read into the data base of the VAX machines by a discreader located in the Word Processor Room. Files may be recalled from the computer memory by reversing the process. It is intended to replace this with direct links during the next twelve months.

Micro computer discs are stored in desks and filing cabinets. There are no detailed print outs of disc contents for recreation purposes and copying does not follow a recognisable pattern throughout the branches.

Great reliance is placed on the absence of computer knowledge within the branch offices in maintaining the integrity of the system. Additionally, contract and agency staff are not vetted by JBS; their expertise and ability to attack the system remains an unknown quantity. Post employment checks are not made on key employees to ensure that their personal circumstances have not altered.

Micro computers are located in branches to suit the users convenience and often face walk ways where members of the public can see the screens. When a machine is left unattended there is no time-out facility which would blank the screen or return it to a secure menu.

Physical Security

Physical security at the centre is good. However, in the branches it is possible to walk from the street into areas were terminals are accessing the mini systems.

Electronic Fund Transfer (EFT) & Major Financial Transactions

An EFT system is in use known as CHAPS. The Company constantly needs large monetary sums to complete purchases throughout Europe and South Africa and has a facility whereby it can transfer monies to 40 specified banks in various countries. Lloyds Bank have made recommendations on security. Their proposals depend on the initiator of the transaction holding a password which is entered at the time the transaction is set up and a second person holding a second password releasing the transaction after entry of a special transaction number held in a log by a third person. Three fold control should preclude fraud, especially when all three parties come from different sections or departments.

In JBS the Systems Manager holds both the transaction log numbers and the first password. A Senior Analyst holds the second password. Both are young and would have been described as ''bright young things'' by an earlier generation.

By agreement with Lloyds Bank a daily total of £2 million can be transferred without reference to the Board . All transfers are reconciled fortnightly by the Financial Director. When he is on holiday they are reconciled by internal audit on a weekly basis.

Financial transactions external to the banking system are via Telex and BACS. BACS transactions are produced for the payment of all bills and for the payroll. A tape is compiled once a month over a period of two days, when the Payroll Department input their totals and the Purchasing Department input details of the accounts to be paid that month. There is an upper limit of £10 million on this system. Once the transactions are complete the tape is demounted and waits for final approval by the Financial Director before being despatched by special messenger to BACS. At BACS a print out of every fiftieth item is made and the total for payment. This is then compared with the original hard copy. The information is written to tape in clear text and an authentication algorithm is not used. On a prearranged date all payments are made to the specific accounts in specified banks and JBS is debited by the appropriate amount.

Passwords

Rudimentary security measures are initiated by the DPM; these include issuing passwords to users. Passwords are given to managers for distribution to their staff, the issued password then becomes common to all operators within the branch. Passwords are four or five digits in length , memorable , alpha code. In addition a special password exists to edit accounts which is known to all senior personnel in the remote locations. Passwords are not related to the sensitivity of data and partial edit routines are available to general staff with full edit facilities available to senior staff. Activity logs are not maintained for branch usage.

Each user is allowed three access attempts before being dis-enabled. Having failed to access the system in three attempts an alarm is sounded on a Central Console from where the dis-enabled terminal is re-enabled. Forgotten passwords can only be obtained from the Branch Manager and are never given over the telephone. Passwords are automatically changed on a three month basis and when an employee leaves. No formal procedure exists for advising the DPM of leavers but JBS is thought by the DPM to be small enough for her to know when user operators leave because of the repeated meetings and telephone contact she has with Branch Managers.

Logs

Logs are maintained on the second VAX machine where development work is carried out and new programs are tested. The second machine, in a special area of memory, carries corporate models. These models cover future corporate buying patterns of raw materials and take over bids.

No non-computer based logs of micro discs are maintained. Thus there is no documented record of the number of discs in use, what they contain or who is responsible for them. There is also no Register of Micro Systems.

Micro computers are not fixed to the operating surface.

Communications

There are no back up modems for the tied lines except for a dial up line with the call number on the receiver.

Six branches communicate during the day with the Computer Centre. The system processes background information during the night and is on line to the branches in simplex mode.

Communications with the computer from the branches are not encrypted nor are they authenticated. Messages are always transmitted in clear.

The Frame Room has a plain windowless door that is often unlocked. The Patch Panel is also located in this room. There are no smoke or fire detectors.

Housekeeping

The Lower Computer Room, where systems testing takes place, is filled with boxes of paper, empty cartons, micro fiche tapes and bits of equipment not in current use. Micro fiche tapes are left in large quantities on top of the disc drive and tapes about to be used are piled on the CPU. A limited activity log is taken and stored on a daily basis but staff are unaware of its use and it is filed in copious quantity in the Computer Room. The DEC Engineers logs and manuals are also in the room as are the diagnostic discs which will accord the user total over-ride of security features.

The access port for remote software diagnostics is on the First Floor Computer. In this room discs that had been demounted were left on top of drives and the CPU. Staff drink tea in the room and there was evidence of smoking. At the time of the survey the door was propped open to facilitate the delivery of large manuals.

Contingency

The DPM has arranged full DEC VAX back-up with a Hot Stand-By at a remote bureau which offers this service to several DEC users. It is thought communications facilities are not possible. No documented Disaster Plan exists and as a result the back-up has not been tested.

The auditors estimated the time to recover after a major disaster as 120 days with three shifts running per day. This is regarded as alarmist and has been ignored by the DPM.

Security

Security Strategy has not been defined and a Security Manual for Information Processing does not exist.

Documentation

When the FARM, GAP and CMOD packages were bought, full user documentation was also supplied. Over a period of time programming amendments have been made and only rudimentary documentation added to the files.

No formal documentation exists of Program Development or Program Standards, although it is hoped to rectify this in the next year or so.

Case Study

1. Examine the major threats to the VAX systems by drawing up Threat and Vulnerability Sheets.

Qualitative values should be used:

Very Low	Up to £1,000
Low	£1,000 to £10,000
Low/Medium	£10,000 to £50,000
Medium	£50,000 to £100,000
Medium/High	£100,000 to £500,000
High	£500,000 to £1,000,000

Frequency of Occurrence will be determined by historical frequencies. Where these are unavailable the following, taken from actuarial evidence in the U.S.A., will apply:

Major disaster e.g.

Boeing crashing on installation:1 in 300 years

Major fire: 1 in 40 years.

Major storm damage: 1 in 120 years.

Major theft: 1 in 30 years.

Major vandalism: 1 in 35 years.

System crash: 1 in 6 months.

Major operator error: 1 in 4 months.

Communication line failure: 1 in 2 months

2. List the most critical vulnerabilities and determine a schedule of events to correct these.

Possible Solutions

The following pages are composed of Threat and Vulnerability Worksheets based on the study. At this level they represent little more than a Criticality Analysis which would prioritise work for a Quantitive Risk Management Analysis. However, they are a real basis for evaluating countermeasures and assessing impact.

At this level a vulnerability that is present on a daily basis implies that the threat might occur on a daily basis also. This is not necessarily the case but it does serve to emphasise the importance of countermeasures in that situation. Consequently the frequency of occurrence in that type of instance is to emphasise the urgency of the situation. Later refinement will remove this frequency and fix it at a more realistic level.

SHEET NUMBER: 01

- -

VULNERABILITY   Unauthorised Access - CHAPS

- -

DESCRIPTION OF
VULNERABILITY:

Insertion of illegal data. Situation is dominated by closely knit
small group.

- -

THREAT: Fraud

- -

RATIONALE:

Total control of the system rests with one individual who holds both
the sequential log and half the requisite authority. The other half
is held by an analyst or in her absence by a stand in from within
the department. Thus with minimum collusion a substantial fraud could
be initiated.

- -

IMPACT:

Loss of funds up to the daily allowed payment
total. Public loss of confidence should such a fraud become
public knowledge, depressing share values.

- -

S.L.E: Very High

ESTIMATED FREQUENCY OF OCCURRENCE: Once in twenty years

A.L.E: Medium

- -

RECOMMENDED COUNTERMEASURES

Peer audit, i.e. verification of the transaction carried out by a person
not employed by Group Treasury.

The sequential log to be held by a third party, ideally this should
be the Audit Department, who would issue numbers against a known
transaction and from time to time verify the complete transaction.

Staff used in peer audits to be rotated.

SHEET NUMBER: 02

VULNERABILITY: Unauthorised Access - BACS

DESCRIPTION OF
VULNERABILITY:

Embezzlement by altering the BACS output.

THREAT: Fraud

RATIONALE:

Fraudulent entry to BACS tape after payment lists are produced and before transmission to BACS Computer Centre.

IMPACT:

Loss of funds.   Loss of confidence should such a fraud become public knowledge, depressing share values. Loss of monies if the fraudster transferred monies to a personal account and left.

ESTIMATED FREQUENCY OF OCCURRENCE: Once in twenty years

A.L.E: Medium

RECOMMENDED COUNTERMEASURES

1. Authentication algorithm to be used once the final input has been made to the tape. Procedures to be in place to verify the data signature on the tape prior to transmission.2. Rigorous recomparison of tapes with BACS output.

```
SHEET NUMBER:   03
-------------------------------------------------------------------

VULNERABILITY: External staff
-------------------------------------------------------------------

DESCRIPTION OF

VULNERABILITY:          External  staff not subject to the high level of
screening  that should apply to JBS employees.


-------------------------------------------------------------------

THREAT:        Destruction , Denial , Disclosure , Modification , Fraud


-------------------------------------------------------------------

RATIONALE:

Cleaning  staff  have unlimited access to areas  where  sensitive data
is processed and are relatively unsupervised.

Contract staff process sensitive data and do not have the same level of
screening as JBS staff.

Temporary vacation staff do not have appropriate screening.


-------------------------------------------------------------------

IMPACT

Loss of sensitive data with possible impact on the capitalisation of the
Group.
-------------------------------------------------------------------

ESTIMATED FREQUENCY OF OCCURRENCE: Once in five years

A.L.E: Low/Medium
-------------------------------------------------------------------

RECOMMENDED COUNTERMEASURES

1. Cleaning staff, Contractors and all temporary staff to be screened
as part of a standard security procedure before any contract is given
or employment offered.

2. Contractor to hold insurance indemnity to compensate the JBS  Group
for  breaches  of ethics or criminal activity.

3.  All micro manuals to be locked away at night.

4. All outside staff to be subject to the same disciplines as regular
employees.
```

SHEET NUMBER 04

VULNERABILITY: Personnel standards

DESCRIPTION OF

VULNERABILITY: There is a very low establishment and anabsence of personnel standards. Staff loyalty must be questioned in view of the activities of the previous Managing Director and Financial Director and the levels of support that they received.

THREAT:

Destruction / Denial / Disclosure / Modification / Fraud

IMPACT: Loss of profits due to inability to cope with

ADP needs. Loss due to accidental or deliberate acts.

FREQUENCY: Once in 20 years   A.L.E. Medium

RATIONALE: The production of essential personnel cont-

rols has never occurred. The organisation became disastrously dependent on two key members of staff and remains dependent on one.

RECOMMENDED COUNTERMEASURES

1. Define long term computer strategy.

2. Document procedures in the form of a manual since there is no personnel department. This document should cover:

a) hiring procedures;

b) assigning procedures;

c) termination procedures,

d) job descriptions,

e) grievance procedures.

3. Having installed a new computer system new staff to use it should be considered whose loyalties and previous activities are not suspect.

SHEET NUMBER: 05

VULNERABILITY: Lack of Security Strategy Plan

DESCRIPTION OF
VULNERABILITY:

Due to the absence of a Security Strategy Plan there is no defined
thrust in ADP systems security.

THREAT:

Fraud, Disclosure, Modification, Destruction, Denial

RATIONALE:

The Group are vulnerable to '' state of the art '' penetration and
amateur penetration. No provision has been made for even rudimentary
systems security requirements let alone forsystems life cycle security
requirements.

IMPACT:

Potential fraud. Unnecessary costs to rectify the situation. Possible
loss due to unauthorised modification of data.   Disclosure of
confidential information to interested third parties.

ESTIMATED FREQUENCY OF OCCURRENCE: Evident daily; of the order of

once in 15 years.

A.L.E: High

RECOMMENDED COUNTERMEASURES

1. Produce a Strategy Plan linked to precise budgets ensuring high
levels of flexibility which in turn will provide adequate business
processing with high security thresholds.

2. Security Strategy Plan to be introduced by

Board of Directors to demonstrate their interest in security.

3. A Group Security Manual to be developed from the Security Strategy
to be used by all staff and again introduced by the Board of directors.

VULNERABILITY: Software standards

DESCRIPTION OF

VULNERABILITY: No documented standards exist covering software development in-house or by an external group.

THREAT:

Destruction / Denial / Disclosure / Modification / Fraud

IMPACT:

Unauthorised access to systems.

FREQUENCY: 1 in 25 years   **A.L.E.** Low/Medium

RATIONALE:

The absence of procedures and low establishment means there can be little management control over software development.

RECOMMENDED COUNTERMEASURES

1. Define ADP Strategy.

2. Produce standards to cover all development.

3. Define requirements of bought-in packages.

SHEET NUMBER: 06

- -

VULNERABILITY: Contingency Plan

- -

DESCRIPTION OF
VULNERABILITY:

Absence of a contingency plan

- -

THREAT:

Denial of service

- -

RATIONALE:

There is no detailed contingency plan yet the loss of facilities would
have an adverse effect on the company.

- -

IMPACT:

Unnecessary high costs and delays in implementing a back up or support
arrangement.

- -

FREQUENCY OF OCCURRENCE: 1 in 10 years

A.L.E: Low

- -

RECOMMENDED COUNTERMEASURES

1. Produce Contingency Plan with several different scenarios of disaster
levels detailing staff responsibilities.

2. Consideration to be given to machine and operating system
standardisation to facilitate back up.

3. Consideration to be given to a network in line with 2. above.

4. Exercise Contingency Plan to ensure it will work.

SHEET NUMBER: 07

VULNERABILITY: Poor Housekeeping Procedures

DESCRIPTION OF
VULNERABILITY:

Very poor housekeeping procedures exist in respect of the micro computers in use.

THREAT:

Destruction , Denial , Disclosure , Modification , Fraud

RATIONALE:

Poor disc copying and storing procedures could result in loss or damage to discs or the theft of data. With ''state of the art'' criminals this lack of security would present an opportunity to steal information.

discs are stored in desks in certain cases and in all cases in the same room. A fire would thus result in the loss of information and the labour cost in creating it.

Terminal procedures are also weak and provide opportunity for browsing.

Back-up tapes are stored in the same room in the same building and where these are stored in a safe this is fire proof but not heat proof.

IMPACT:

Unnecessarily high costs in recreating files and the possibility of providing information to the unscrupulous.

ESTIMATED FREQUENCY OF OCCURRENCE: 1 in 25 years.

A.L.E: Medium

RECOMMENDED COUNTERMEASURES

1. A Security Manual to be produced and introduced with Board level backing. Management Audit to ensure that the micro computer users conform to the Manuals' requirements.

SHEET NUMBER: 08

VULNERABILITY: Screen Procedures

DESCRIPTION OF

VULNERABILITY: Screens face walkways

THREAT:

Disclosure , Modification , Fraud

RATIONALE:

Unauthorised access to the system could be gained without any evidence of the access having taken place.

Passers-by are able to browse and see confidential information and also learn the form in which data must be input.

IMPACT:

Disclosure of confidential information. Inability of staff to monitor a third party's unauthorised activities on their terminals.

Loss of security.

ESTIMATED FREQUENCY OF OCCURRENCE: 1 in 15 years.

A.L.E: Low

RECOMMENDED COUNTERMEASURES

1. The logging of activities is essential for the security of the system. To achieve this economically it will be necessary to implement a standardised system with logging software.

2. Screens should not face areas where casual visitors have walking access. Micros to be disabled after a specific period of inactivity by returning the system to the first menu.

3. Log on attempts to be restricted to three after which the micro is disabled.

4. All access activities to be logged and audit trails provided to identify individual activity.

5. Document micro procedures.

6. Instil security consciousness in personnel so that micros are always logged off or left in menu mode when not in use.

SHEET NUMBER: 09

VULNERABILITY: Unauthorised Access; Passwords

DESCRIPTION OF

VULNERABILITY:Password administration and use

THREAT: Destruction , Disclosure , Modification , Fraud

RATIONALE: Passwords are issued and controlled by users, not by a central administrator. Passwords bear no relationship to the sensitivity of the information to be protected and there is no defined policy on passwords.

IMPACT: All systems must be regarded as insecure. As a result any staff member could, in theory, access other members files gaining access to sensitive data for illegal use.

ESTIMATED FREQUENCY OF OCCURRENCE: 1 in 12 years.

A.L.E: Medium/Low

RECOMMENDED COUNTERMEASURES

1. A network system would facilitate centralised control and administration of passwords and employee accountability .

2. Specific password procedures should be developed and documented in a computer security manual. These must include the following procedures:

   a) Passwords to be changed every 30 days.

   b) Passwords to be formally released by Security Manager in a sealed envelope.

   c) Password procedures to be published.

   d) Access to sensitive levels of data to generate a detailed log of activity.

   e) Passwords not to be displayed on screens.

   f) Passwords to be alpha numeric.

   g) Repeated log on failures to be advised to Security Officer for action.

   h) Automatic removal of leavers passwords.

   j) Passwords to be unique to the individual.

SHEET NUMBER: 10

- -

VULNERABILITY: Overall security oversight absent

- -

DESCRIPTION OF
VULNERABILITY:

No Systems Security Officer

- -

THREAT:

Destruction , Denial , Disclosure , Modification , Fraud

- -

RATIONALE:

Absence of a Security Officer with responsibility for computer systems
has created a high level of vulnerability.

- -

IMPACT:

Unnecessary vulnerabilities and system weaknesses leading to an unlawful
attack on one or all of the systems.

- -

ESTIMATED FREQUENCY OF OCCURRENCE: 1 in 16 years.

A.L.E: Medium

- -

RECOMMENDED COUNTERMEASURES

1. Appointment of Security Officer with responsibility for all computers
and communications. Reporting to Security Manager.

SHEET NUMBER: 11

VULNERABILITY: Unauthorised Access; Communications

DESCRIPTION OF
VULNERABILITY:

Tap on external lines

Tap on line in Frame Room

THREAT:

Disclosure

RATIONALE:

Passive tapping on a dedicated line could result

in the disclosure of company sensitive information.

IMPACT:

Public scandal; loss of Group capitalisation value

Financial loss.

ESTIMATED FREQUENCY OF OCCURRENCE: 1 in 12 years

A.L.E: Medium

RECOMMENDED COUNTERMEASURES

1. Use of ''black box'' encryption on all external transmissions.

2. Use of partial field encryption by software.

3. Access to Frame Room to be monitored and window to be cut in door
to allow visual monitoring of all activity in the Frame Room.

Life Cycle Security

17

Introduction

Computer system security is a continuing function commencing with the system specification through the design, development, implementation, acceptance and operation stages to the final phasing out and commissioning of a replacement system.

A computer system has four specific phases in its life cycle. They are:

1. The Initiation Phase
2. The Development Phase
3. The Operational Phase
4. The Final Phase.

The **Initiation Phase** covers the period when the general requirements and the specification of the system are defined.

The **Development Phase** covers the period when the system is defined, designed, programmed and tested.

The **Operational Phase** commences when the system has been accepted and goes into use.

The **Final Phase** covers the period from the commissioning of a replacement system through to the final taking out of use of the obsolescent system.

Throughout each of these phases it is imperative that security implications are considered in the context of a defined Security Strategy, that the appropriate security measures are planned and built in, that the security procedures are properly carried out, that the security controls are continually reviewed in the light of their efficacy, changing threats and the system's development and that the lessons learned are carried forward into the replacement system.

Security concerns, which are different at each stage, should be an integral part of the entire planning, development and operation of a computer application. It is recognised that there will be trade-offs between security and other requirements and that these may not always be resolved in favour of security. However, all security concerns must be carefully costed on a risk management basis before being discounted in favour of another benefit or requirement. It must always be borne in mind that the retrofit of security measures can be expensive.

The following examples illustrate the many facets of security requirements to be encountered in the different phases:

Initiation Phase. The objectives and general requirements of the system are usually defined and documented during this phase and system designers will evaluate alternative approaches to the target system. Based on feasibility studies, a decision in terms of system direction is usually made.

If security is discounted for the sake of expediency at this stage the feasibility studies and related cost benefit analyses will be distorted and become inaccurate.

Development Phase. Programming and testing continue apace and the activity on different systems may very well overlap.

If security is now neglected the results may be dire. However, it is possible to make logical decisions on controls, both in terms of security and software development, to achieve economic and practical levels of security.

Operational Phase. Systems have been accepted and the organisation has become fully dependent on the computer system to fulfill its objectives. At the start of this phase security must be in place and also operational controls must be enforced in the day to day operations.

Any revision of security measures must be based on proven risk management methods. Selected security improvements must be implemented on a planned and coherent basis. Repeated small modifications are likely to make the computer application more complex and, as a result, less reliable.

Final Phase. Very little new work is undertaken at this time and the view is usually held that if deliberate or accidental damage has historically been of low frequency and small impact the same will be true of the future. This may be correct but generally the old system will be running in parallel to the new and experienced staff may well decide to experiment with the potential of the old system, especially if they are employed on a temporary or contract basis.

Existing security measures should not be ignored during this phase but must be carefully costed and show high value benefits before any new measures are implemented. Internal audit must be regarded as a continuing first line of defence until the new system is implemented and the old phased out.

Planning Security during the Initiation Phase

Corporate security strategy should be defined and in existence at this very early stage, especially as there is a danger that security and integrity concerns may be neglected until the nature of the system is clearly defined. This will lead to systems whose basic characteristics are inconsistent with security objectives and may result in security problems for which there is no cost effective solution.

The following must receive the Security Officers attention:

- a) Source data
- b) Separation of duties
- c) Restricted interfaces
- d) Identification verification
- e) Facility security
- f) Security Risk Management.

Source Data

Source data must be accurate and complete enough to support its intended uses. Clearly, serious harm can result from maliciously introduced errors.

It is probable that the computer system will mirror the existing manual system and this will make the assessment of the impact of errors relatively easy. If new data sources are to be used or the data is to be used for new purposes then a detailed study will be required.

Software that automatically validates data must be considered. In assessing the use of proprietary software a risk management study must be conducted for each application system.

Separation of Duties

The structure of the computer function must be such that two or more independent people are involved in all critical and important actions. Thus peer reviews will be carried out by programmers and two operators will always be on duty when second and third shift operations are involved.

As far as possible, data collection and the initiation of transactions must stay in the hands of user departments.

Restricted Interfaces

Provision must be made to restrict users to limited forms of access to the system. Data accuracy will be impossible to maintain if several users can update a master data file.

Security requirements must be planned with the computer and user departments. At this stage it will be possible to determine data sensitivity and the principles of ownership of data. Once this has been done the Guardian will determine who has access to his data and what form the access will take. The Custodian will then take responsibility for administering the access requirements and the Security officer will ensure the process is compatible with the Corporate Security Strategy.

Where persons outside the organisation will be served by the application even query rights to the data base should be examined for consistency with security and privacy requirements.

Identity Verification

This will be one of the Security Officers main concerns. It is possible that former systems which are now taken onto the new system did not require user identification. If the system is being transported in total then the same laissez-faire ease of access may apply.

The Security Officer must check every application to ensure that identification procedures are in place commensurate with the value of the data to be protected.

If dial-up lines are incorporated into the communication net work then a real threat will exist of hackers or other unauthorised people gaining entry to the system. Adequate thresholds must be in place to prevent this eventuality.

Facility Security

The Security Officer will need to ensure that Operational Controls, Personnel

Procedures, Recovery procedures, Contingency Plans and Physical Security measures are in place, that they are adequate and tested for weaknesses.

Security Risk Management

A table of Assets must be built up at this stage. Each Asset must have a list of vulnerabilities, countermeasures, anticipated frequency of attack and the annual loss expectancy of such an attack. It will be the Security Officers responsibility to continually update the security data base.

The impact of the following must be examined in depth:

        a) Inaccurate data

        b) Falsified data

        c) Disclosed data

        d) Lost data

        e) Unavailable data.

Inaccurate Data

This is where data or programs become corrupted with errors and the system continues to function producing "creeping corruption".

The Security Officer must estimate the potential impact of the actions that may be taken as a result of the erroneous data being accepted as authentic. In producing the equation consideration should be given to the impact of a few serious errors and the cumulative effect of a series of small errors.

Falsified Data

The Security Officer must consider the effect of an individual or group of individuals falsifying information in order to gain some advantage. It should be assumed that the falsification is undetected by manual methods. The study should estimate the probable financial impact over a period of time, either from pecuniary loss, public embarrassment and loss of confidence, or the destruction of the data base and consequent denial of the facility.

Disclosed Data

The study must also examine the effect of scandal following the disclosure of sensitive information. In the case of public companies this will embrace the effect on share capitalisation.

The side effects of the data being confidentially disclosed to interested third parties and not necessarily discovered must also be considered. An example of this would be mail lists or customer lists being passed to competitors.

Lost Data

This will also be a consideration for insurance purposes. An accurate estimate must be made if data or programs used by the application system are destroyed or corrupted. It should be assumed that back up versions are unavailable or unusable and data must be reconstructed manually. An estimate should also be made of the financial implications of reconstruction from old data copies.

Unavailable Data

This occurs when a system has gone down and has not been brought up on another system. Again this is an important insurance consideration as well as a valuable risk analysis study.

The analysis of all five situations must be supplemented by estimates of frequency. Unfortunately, during this initial stage there will not be an historical record of major and minor failures nor will it be possible to estimate accurately the frequency of disasters since the effectiveness of undesigned controls must be hypothetical. However, as a starting point, a rough estimate must be made of the likelihood of failure drawing on background from other installations and published statistics.

The figures produced will start the data base of security related events and set a level of priority to security measures.

Management Considerations.

Strategy will have been determined and documented at the earliest stage in the Initiation Phase.

The Security Manual, as an extension of the strategy Document, will start to be be produced by the Security Officer. Items to be considered at this early stage will include:

> a) Physical security including access restrictions
>
> b) Software development procedures and standards
>
> c) Library procedures
>
> d) Personnel procedures
>
> e) Requirements for sub-contractors
>
> f) Loss control
>
> g) Recovery and back-up
>
> h) Disaster plans.

At this time risk management techniques will have been standardised and will support the requirements of the developing Security Manual.

Building Security during the Development Phase

Effective management of the development activities associated with this stage is the prime way to improve security and keep costs to a minimum. If the software development effort is poorly organised and depends on debugging of programs for its quality control, then software controls are almost certainly inappropriate and development costs are likely to be very high.

The Security Officer in conjunction with data custodians must determine basic software requirements and the software to be used for this purpose. For example, screen 'time out' facilities, access logs and violation alarms. The decisions about what security provisions are needed and the extent to which they are enforced by software, need to be documented and included, if not already present, in the Security Manual.

Programmers should not be expected to identify the security concerns that arise from a user's application. This must be defined by the Data Custodian and written into the Security Manual. Internal auditors should be used to evaluate the security controls, once these are in place, and to recommend modifications. This should be the subject of a risk management analysis to determine any security trade-offs against system efficiency.

Selection of requisite software modules should be a joint function between the Security Officer and the Data Custodian. Similarly, the selection of algorithms and data structures should be defined by the Data Custodians under advice from the Security Officer.

Some requisite controls can be enforced by both software and physical and administrative procedures. For example, data integrity can be checked by human review or by automated bounds and consistency checks. Normally the Security Officer will select automated controls because of their reliability, consistency and low cost once implemented. However, the Security Officer will need to determine the danger of the incompleteness of the chosen controls or if they can be bypassed in anyway. Once this has been evaluated as at an acceptable level, the controls must be incorporated in the very early design stage of new or developing systems.

Definition of Security Requirements

The Security Officer will need to identify each job function related to the application system. He will also need to consider each job function which relates to the application in a different way as defining a different interface to the system. This will also include interfaces to other automated systems. The Security Officer will systematically,at this stage, include the following critical job functions:

> a) Source data collection
>
> b) Input preparation
>
> c) Data entry
>
> d) Output dissemination
>
> e) Data base administration
>
> f) System security planning and control
>
> g) Internal audit
>
> h) Application program maintenance
>
> j) Archival or back up data storage
>
> k) Computer operations
>
> l) System programming.

The Security Officer having defined the Application System Interfaces will also need to document the responsibilities associated with each individual who will interact with the application system through the interface. He will also need to define the constraints on the use of each interface to preserve security. This will be incorporated into the Security Manual where this is appropriate.

This will also apply when the system interacts with another system. The Security

Officer must not assume that the other automated system is trustworthy but must determine the degree to which they are untrustworthy and, if appropriate, take the necessary steps to make them secure.

Risk management will again play its part by considering the consequences of errors or deliberate malpractice occurring in the use of the interface.

It will also be necessary for the Security Officer to identify management and administrative controls that will be available to ensure the interface is used correctly.

Separation of Duties

The Security Officer will need to examine all the interfaces at this stage to ensure that the security exposures will be minimised even if the interface is misused badly.

During the Expansion Phase well defined separation of duties will greatly reduce costs, especially as the ability to check individual actions will supplement personnel screening activities. This is particularly important when outside contract labour is used.

System Availability

Having assessed the effect of the loss of the system, albeit temporarily, during the Design and Development Phase, during the Expansion Phase it will be necessary for the Security Officer to monitor the situation on a continuing basis. Support mechanisms for a brand new system may be totally inappropriate at this stage. Systematic testing of Contingency plans and back-up resources will be imperative. The testing will generally require the modification of documented plans.

User needs will also require monitoring by the Security Officer. The growth of the system may mean that earlier assumed levels of acceptable disruption are no longer acceptable. Availability requirements may well be more rigorous and as a result more expensive.

Changes to application programmes during this phase must not be permitted unless they have been approved and developed as an official modification to the system. Strong and proven System and Programming Standards must be in place. In addition to administrative standards and controls the following will be considered at this stage:

       a) Unnecessary programming

       b) Restricted User Interfaces

       c) User Friendly Systems

       d) Shared Computer Facilities

       e) Isolation of Critical Code

       f) Back-up and Recovery

       g) Use of available Controls

       h) Design Review

       j) Peer Review

       k) Program Library

       l) Documentation of Security-related Code

m) Programmer Association with Operational System

n) Redundant Computation

p) Test and Evaluation.

Each project or part of a project will be controlled by pre-defined procedures. This will prevent excessively complex design which cannot be correctly implemented, maintained or audited.

Unnecessary Programming

The Security Officer must ensure that procedures are in place to prevent users getting unneeded programming capability because of incorrect or weak terminal interface procedures. No one should be able to by-pass controls imposed by the operating system. If a user is able to execute his own program this should be highlighted by the system since he may well have the ability to by-pass any security control.

Individuals who may enter programs from terminals direct to the system must be kept to a minimum. Clearly, this is a privileged operation since the individual could enter a Trojan Horse or a Logic Bomb. Consequently strong logging procedures must be in operation.

Restricted User Interfaces

These must be tailored at this stage to the users specific requirements. The greatest threat to the system occurs when the users are given unnecessary access to a general purpose programming language since it will then be extremely difficult to analyse all the ramifications of user actions. The Security Officer should understand the user's needs and ensure that interfaces are designed to meet these needs as simply as possible and with no unnecessary capabilities.

User Friendly Systems

The more user friendly the system is the more vulnerable it may become. However, if the interfaces are easily understood, it will discourage users from by-passing controls. System responses must be clear and easily understood by the user.

The Security Officer should ensure that access to non-sensitive files and programs does not require the user to enter excess information or answer repeated questions. However, access by users to sensitive data and programs, albeit with restricted authority, will deserve detailed thought by the Security Officer, since users may neglect or bypass controls they consider cumbersome. In this instance default options might be made available.

All access requirements must be documented in an operations manual and appear or be cross-referenced in the Security Manual.

Shared Facilities

During this stage of the systems life cycle it is possible that development work and live processing will continue "side by side" on the computer. In the interests of security this is always undesirable and as far as possible programme development activities should be excluded from the machine that runs the application.

The Security Officer must continually monitor the situation by risk analysis models. It may be that at this stage of development it will be more economical to run very sensitive applications on a separate computer. In terms of hardware performance small computers are now as cost effective as larger machines; however, the Security Officer will need to take into his risk management equations other costs, such as communications, software etc., before coming to a decision.

Isolation of Critical Code

Critical code and programs will be listed by the Security Officer in the Security Manual. Use of code or programs will require specific authority and detailed logging of activities. If appropriate, automated controls can be used to protect sensitive modules. These may include:

    a) Checksums on the object code to detect unauthorised changes

    b) Hardware protection states

    c) The use of "read only" memory when security related code resides in a fixed area of memory

    d) Use of security kernels.

In this latter case all code that is relevant to security is isolated from the bulk of software. However, this approach will require operating systems and software to support the function together with guarantees that security controls are invoked at the appropriate time. To reach a decision in the use of security kernels the Security Officer, Computer Manager and User Committees must be in agreement on its desirability. The risk analysis would need to be carefully calculated and agreed.

Details of secure kernel activities would be documented separately from the Security Manual but cross-referenced in it.

Back-up and Recovery

Contingency planning consists of the advance plans and arrangements to ensure continuity of the critical functions of an applications system. The plans, developed by the Security Officer, will include total or partial stoppage of operations or destruction of the data base or facility.

With appropriate contingency planning, facilities can be restored after a few hours. However, this presupposes that repeated testing and evaluation has continued during the life of the systems.

As the systems grow it may well be that system availability will not accept even a few hours of discontinued service. The Security Officer will then need to give consideration to automatic back-up and recovery mechanisms.

Use of Available Controls

The operating system will generally provide a variety of controls. These may not be called into use initially and it will be the Security Officers' responsibility to ensure that they are called into use when required rather than allowing application controls to be specifically written.

N.B. *All reviews must be documented.*

Design Review

The entire security plan should be reviewed by a group of experts who have not been part of the design effort. It is especially necessary to review all decisions which cannot be altered during the life cycle of the installation.

Peer Review

During the Expansion Period there will be repeated requests for program patches and alterations. The Security Officer must document peer review procedures and ensure that they are implemented. At least one other programmer will be required to review the new code to the point of understanding it completely and being made equally responsible with the original programmer.

Program Library

Rigorous controls will be necessary as new program modules near completion, especially once review and testing has begun. The program library will catalogue and control access to all versions of program modules as they are developed.

The program library should:

      a) record all accesses and modification to program modules;

      b) enable current and previous versions of code to be   compared;

      c) permit only authorised persons access to program modules.

Audits of activities should be conducted on a non-routine basis so that staff cannot anticipate periods of activity.

Documentation of Security Related Control

Program documentation is imperative and will be needed for security when software controls are reviewed for effectiveness, especially if they are to remain effective after software maintenance activities. The Security Officer must define and identify security related modules or sections of code.

Programmer Association with the Operational System

This will be a constant area of review by the Security Officer during the Expansion Period of the system. Having helped develop the system, programmers must not be in a position to receive benefits from the system when it becomes operational. Peer Reviews will help to eliminate this feature but conspiracy can defeat this protective measure unless activity logs are used; even then it will be essential that operation controls do not make it easy for programmers to use earlier code insertions.

Redundant Computation

Critical computations should be checked by redundant processing to verify the correctness of results. This will include the recalculation of a critical result by an alternative method, reasonableness and consistency checks and the examining of extra attributes in a retrieved data item to ensure that the data item found was the one searched for. The effectiveness of these checks depends on the experience of the programmer and should be fully documented.

Test and Evaluation

The Security Officer must have a test plan for security. A test plan should describe what is to be tested and what tools will be used. It must include tests that identify the system's response to any abnormal, unusual, unlikely and illegal circumstances that may exist during processing.

The "Static Evaluation" of code will represent one form of continuing testing and verification of the system. Portions of the source code will be evaluated to determine if they implement the design specifications and are free from errors. This will always include critical sections of code.

Ideally the test will be conducted under the supervision of the Security Officer using teams of independent third parties. At this time Penetration Studies should also be considered, to identify weak controls.

Alternatively "dynamic Testing" may be considered. This involves executing the application system with test data and comparing the results with those that were expected. During this type of testing the Security Officer should ensure that production data files or other important files are off-line to prevent destruction or revelation of their contents.

Software tools available to the Security Officer include:

      a) Source Code Analysers

      b) Program Analysers

      c) Flaw hypothesis.

These must receive the same level of security as critical code and remain in the custody of the Security Officer.

Testing of the system must continue during its lifetime and be visible to members of staff.

Management Considerations

The Security Manual, which must be complete at the beginning of this stage, will need to be specific and not contain generalities. All requirements must be based on the evaluation of threats and vulnerabilities combined with risk analysis studies.

Alterations to the Security Manual in the form of refinements may continue as this stage progresses. For example, whilst requirements definition logically precedes all other development activities, in practice there is a large overlap, and many requirements may be modified or clarified during the remainder of the development. The Security Officer must establish procedures so that requirements can be modified in an organised and controlled way.

The Security Manual will give detailed attention to:

      a) data validation, consistency and reasonableness checks;

      b) requirements for identification and verification, including basic techniques;

      c) data ownership , access and authorisation;

d) journalling and monitoring of variance activities;

e) encryption of communications, on and off-line storage;

f) programming requirements;

g) user operational requirements;

h) test and evaluation.

Maintenance of Security during the Operational Phase

Following the Development Phase, the Operational Phase is the longest period of the life cycle. This is the time when development is limited and very few new systems are proposed. The organisation is completely dependent on the facility and there are few teething troubles or system failures. Controls that were embedded in the two earlier stages are generally providing the expected protection and values within the security risk management model change very little. However, security measures should not be relaxed during this stage and there are a series of procedures and practices that can be introduced to supplement software controls. These will include the control of data during input, off-line storage and dissemination of output, enhanced employee procedures, software modification and hardware maintenance.

Control of Data

This is a continuing necessity and falls into three parts:

    a) Input Verification

    b) Data Storage

    c) Output Dissemination.

Input Verification is the process of ensuring accurate transcription of source data to machine readable form. If input errors are not detected during transcription they may be propagated through the data base causing creeping corruption. The processing of erroneous data can also cause unanticipated control flow paths to be taken in the application software leading to program halts or even to bringing the application system down.

Techniques to ensure the veracity of data will include the use of check digits and control totals. These fall within the domain of users and the Security Officer should ensure that they are not subverted or ignored because familiarity with the system has bred contempt.

Data Storage and management must remain a security priority during this stage. Storage data that is subject to accidental or intentional modification, destruction or unauthorised modification and disclosure will effect the installations ability to recover in a disaster situation.

The Security Officer must ensure that there is strictly controlled access to the storage area. Media should only be released to authorised personnel and the storage and organisation of information should be such that access to specific sensitive data does not mean access to all sensitive data.

The movement of data storage media outside the off-line storage area must be accounted for at all times. The media log must include as a minimum:

   a) Identification information

   b) Destination

   c) Authorised signature

   d) Estimated return time.

The storage of information off site will have been decided in the Expansion Phase as will the use of encryption for sensitive data. However, the Security Officer must continue to monitor the process to ensure that sufficient up-to-date programs and code are stored off site to efficiently facilitate recovery goals.

Output dissemination controls of sensitive data helps to ensure continued protection of the data after it leaves the computer. Printout should be carefully separated and labelled. Procedures must be in place for its destruction after use to prevent unauthorised browsing.

Data is easier to steal in this form and at this stage in the life cycle. The following measures should be implemented:

1. Logging Receipts

   Numbers of copies should be limited. All   editions of copies should be numbered. Authorised   signatures should be required before copies are allocated.

2. Distribution

   Methods for distributing copies of sensitive data should be documented and adhered to.

3. Labelling

   Each page of sensitive output should be marked with an appropriate sensitivity classification.

Employment Practices

The Security Officer, jointly with the Personnel Manager, must monitor hiring procedures of staff who will be involved with the facility. References must be checked and personnel screened.

Within the facility the Security Officer should ensure that duties are separated, vacations are made obligatory, jobs are rotated regularly, limitation of levels of funds to be handled by individuals is imposed and strict control of physical access is maintained. Termination of employment procedures must be followed and all staff must receive a level of security training.

Modifications to Software

When programming is undertaken during this stage it will only exceptionally be large scale work and the already documented controls of new development work will apply. With minor work, code reconciliation must always take place where new and old code are compared and the differences retained for specific periods of time. Modified software must be subject to the same testing as was the original.

Hardware Maintenance

When Preventive Maintenance occurs, procedures must be in place to demount sensitive data for the duration of the maintenance. Areas of memory should be zeroised, especially where the data has been processed. This is vital where remote diagnostics are used.

Security Manual

This will be updated as necessary during this period and attention will be given to the risk management model to update it on a periodic basis. Data bases grow in size during this period as do the number of users and careful attention must be given to these two factors.

Security in the Final Phase

At this stage in the system life cycle a decision will usually have been made on the new system and the old is being run just long enough to move systems across to the new machine.

Any new decisions on security measures will now require high value justification which will usually not be available unless there is a threat of total disaster or fraud or large value public embarrassment through disclosure of confidential data.

If the new system is being developed alongside the old, the Security Officer will ensure that functions are separated and that strong personnel policies are in place. These policies will especially apply to sub-contractors.

Internal audit will now play a strong role in ensuring that controls and procedures are followed despite the age of the system. This is very important during this stage since all security and design efforts will be concentrated on the new system.

Once a date is known for the final transfer, other installations which depend on this installation for back-up, should be advised of the impending change.

The Security Officer and User Groups must come to a joint decision on the length of time that data and software should be archived.

Questionnaire

Initiation Phase

Source Data:

1. Will the data supplied to the ADP system be accurate and complete enough to support its intended use without harmful side effects?

2. Will the new system use new data sources or present data for new purposes?

3. Can users be adequately identified and be held accountable for their actions? How?

4. Are user interfaces with the system sufficiently restricted? How?

5. Do the boundaries between ADP and related manual activities provide maximum separation of duties and independent review? How?

Project:

1. Were standards laid down for the project?

2. Which departments authorised which projects?

3. What standards exist for monitoring and supervising the progress of projects?

4. Does a steering committee exist for the project?

5. Are outside contractors or consultants used at this phase?

6. Have the company's auditors been involved?

7. Have interfaces with existing systems been evaluated?

Risk Analysis:

1. What methodology is in use?

2. Has an evaluation been made of the impact of:
   a) Inaccurate data?
   b) Falsified data?
   c) Disclosed data?
   d) Lost data?
   e) Unavailable data?

Development Phase

1. Has a security manual been produced? Does it contain non- specific terms?

2. Is there adequate definition of what software must do?

3. Is each job function clearly defined?

4. Is each job function which relates to the application system in a different way clearly defined as a different interface to the system?

5. What management and administration controls are available to ensure the interface is used properly?

6. Are the requirements of those using the interface realistic?

7. Has the system error tolerance been defined?

8. Are the interfaces defined from the viewpoint of:
   a) Data input?

   b) Communications?

   c) Data output?

   d) Description of data?

9. How is it ensured that the functional specification meets the requirements of users?

10. Is the system user friendly?

11. Can users execute their own programs?

12. Are computer facilities shared?

13. Does program development continue concurrently with normal processing?

Sensitive data:

1. Are check sums used to detect unauthorised changes?

2. Does security related code always reside in a fixed area of memory?

3. Does the operating system provide and use:

   a) User's identification?

b) Authorisation matrices?

c) Journalling of activities in the operating system?

4. Does program documentation exist of security related code that:

  a) implements security controls?

  b) performs critical processing?

  c) accesses critical or sensitive data during its execution?

Program practices:

1. Are peer reviews used?

2. Does the program library:

  a) permit only authorised persons to access program modules?

  b) record all access to program modules?

  c) associate control data such as record and byte counts with program modules to facilitate the detection of changes?

  d) compare current with previous code versions?

3. Are programmers in a position to receive benefits from the operating system?

Test and evaluation:

1. Have the tests established that the system is:

  a) reliable?

  b) meets it specification?

  c) meets user requirements?

  2. Does a documented test plan exist?

3. Are static evaluation techniques used to establish the security of the system?

4. Is dynamic testing used?

Operational Phase Security

1. What methods are used for error detection:

    a) Check digits?

    b) Control totals?

2. What data storage policies exist?

3. What are the policies of access to storage areas?

4. What user authorisation policies exist?

5. How is storage media logged? Does the log contain:

    a) identification information?

    b) destination?

    c) authorisation?

    d) estimated time of return?

6. What policies exist in output control? Is confidential data marked? If so what labelling is used?

7. What security training policies exist?

8. What policies exist for the modification of existing software?

9. How are changes documented?

10. How long is old code retained?

11. How long are before and after images retained?

12. Is the same testing applied to the new code as the old?

13. Is the contingency plan up to date and effective? Have the following been identified:
    a) Critical functions?
    b) Alternative sites?
    c) Manual replacement of limited processing?
    d) Back up data?

Appendix A

This report is based on an actual case study and was prepared by Control
Risks Information Technology Limited for purposes which include use by
the client's legal advisers in the contemplation of legal proceedings.

It has been included to show what can happen when security is lax and when
directors begin to take advantage of the system for personal profit. All
names have been changed.

This report should not be copied or reproduced in any way without reference
to Control Risks Information Technology Limited.

CONTENTS

CHAPTER 1

MANAGEMENT SUMMARY

1.0 INTRODUCTION

This management summary sets out the terms of reference for the study, the method of operation, conclusions and recommendations.

Details of the threats and vulnerabilities are contained in the Work Sheets at Appendix A. These have been analysed and assessed and the results have been grouped in the succeeding chapters as follows:

Chapter 2	Strategy
Chapter 3	Vulnerability of micro-computers
Chapter 4	Personnel
Chapter 5	Documentation
Chapter 6	Software and Data Classification
Chapter 7	HOBS

Chapter 8 - The Way Forward, proposes in broad terms a logical programme to implement a strategy designed to upgrade the security of the West Cross Group Plc. computer systems.

1.1 TERMS OF REFERENCE

Control Risks Information Technology Limited agreed to provide a security overview study for The West Cross Group Plc. and the following became the terms of reference:

a) To carry out a computer security survey on the series of PCs located in Moorside House , Coomb Down. Security would be examined to determine the potential or actual threat of fraud or embezzlement. The study would also examine the threats of:

> Disclosure of confidential information
> Destruction of the system
> Denial of service
> Unlawful modification of data.

b) To define the immediate requirements needed to establish an acceptably secure system and make recommendations for the improvement and maintenance of the security of the system.

1.2 METHOD OF OPERATION

Control Risks Information Technology Limited conducts its reviews using its own comprehensive and exhaustive questionnaire to reveal possible areas of vulnerability. This questionnaire was used as far as practicable. Where vulnerabilities were discovered, investigations were conducted in depth to determine the nature of the countermeasures which should be considered.

Threat and vulnerability worksheets were drawn up and this report is structured around the summary of those documents. Copies of these worksheets are at Appendix A.

1.3   ACKNOWLEDGMENTS

Throughout the review Control Risks Information Technology Ltd. received the fullest co- operation from the members of West Cross Group Plc. and would like to thank all those concerned for their help and the information they supplied. The following members of the Group were interviewed.

> Mr. Ian Doe
> Mr. Sven Thomas (of Research Business Systems)
> Ms. Dorothy Davis
> Ms. Soraj Nair

1.4   BACKGROUND

The West Cross Group is a growth company and the installation of the computers has generally come about by accident rather than design. The company has begun to use a system of micro computers which should increase the overall efficiency of the departments. There has not been any level of standardisation.

Micro computers were generally bought and used under a policy known to Mr.David King who has since left the Group. Security is token and systems efficiency is low.

To remain competitive with a low office establishment West Cross Group must determine an overall computer strategy followed by a security strategy, since once the former has been resolved the latter can be implemented economically and with maximum protective efficiency.

The policy adopted by Mr.King has resulted in an absence of procedures necessary for the Group's well-being and security.

1.5 FRAUD POTENTIAL

Computer related fraud needs five condition for its consummation:

a) Monetary availability
b) System vulnerability
c) Opportunity to commit the act
d) Available technical resources
e) Ability to commit the act.

Whilst a detailed study could not be conducted because of time constraints all five conditions are present in the West Cross Group systems. Two of the conditions being present would normally provoke concern.

Personnel loyalty might be a redeeming countermeasure. However, the gentleman responsible for the systems,Mr.King, has a history of deceit by knowingly being involved for a lengthy period of time with companies operating contrary to Group interest.   Mr.Ian Doe has since been responsible for the computer systems and he was also involved with these companies.

Therefore, the redeeming feature of staff integrity and loyalty must be ignored. Since the five basic weaknesses are present the system must be regarded as compromised until it is proved otherwise.

1.5 AREAS OF CONCERN

All the existing micro computers are open to misuse. Unlawful manipulation of systems for personal gain may very well have occurred.

Future plans and development demand that stricter security measures must be drawn up and implemented. This can only be achieved by formulating a computer strategy to cover the next five year period, defining user requirements and producing an operational requirement against which hardware and software can be matched. Security strategy must be defined and documented.
Once defined it must be implemented. The characteristic pattern of a growing company where trusted and key personnel produce systems with a minimum of controls, audit trails and documentation must become a thing of the past.

The value of the company data is recognised by senior management and there is concern that this should not be corrupted. However, there is not a corresponding awareness of the principles of system security among other members of staff. Consequently, proper security measures will signifi-cantly reduce the possibility of illegal manipulation of data.

The installation is not secure in any accepted sense of the term. This may be due to either incompetence through lack of understanding or deliberate intent for gain. In Mr.King's case ignorance of computer systems must be ruled out since he has had for some considerable time, it is understood, a company owned computer in his home which he has used to increase his knowledge. His understanding is now at such a level that he has, apparently, gone into partnership in the computer market place with Mr.S.Wyne (Mr.Wyne was a once a contractor to the Group).

A programme of corrective measures required to enhance the security of the system is listed below:

IMMEDIATELY

Implement the security measures for HOBS defined by the Bank of Scotland and reiterated in their letter of the 22nd July 1987. Whilst Mr.Thomas is working on site and until a totally new policy is in place, Mr.Thomas should play a part in this process, possibly taking oversight of security.

DURING THE NEXT TWO MONTH PERIOD

The following represent a requirement to prevent fraud and ensure that the information processing system is secure:

        a)   Define Corporate Micro Strategy.
        b)   Define Security Strategy.

        c) Produce an operational requirement based
on a) and b).
        d) Produce a Security Manual.
        e) Appoint member of staff as a Computer Security Officer
on a part-time basis.

FROM TWO MONTHS TO FOUR MONTHS

The following should be implemented:

        a) Install a new system.
        b) Rationalise staffing.
        c) Classify data.
        d) Implement security measures.

At the end of both periods a detailed security risk management study should
be conducted to determine the efficacy of the work done and the next stages
of activity, if any, that are required to conform with the Strategy Plan.

CHAPTER 2

STRATEGY

The growth and development of micro systems within the Group has been piecemeal and uncoordinated. Security thresholds are extremely weak and bear no relationship to the level of sensitivity of data they are designed to protect. (Reference Threat and Vulnerability Sheet 10). As the systems stand, very little can be done to produce true secure processing and a radical re-think of policy is necessary, especially as the Group will become more and more dependent on information processing for its future successful business activities.

Most of the equipment in use is no longer ''state of the art'' and some is quite old. Meaningful and cost effective security would be very difficult to implement and could not be produced to a satisfactory standard because of the dissimilar software and operating systems.

It is recommended that the schedule of replacement should be brought forward with a minimum of delay and that consideration be given to a network system. A network system will provide uniformity of control, activity logs, logical access restrictions and audit trails. It will also allow a Systems Security Officer to enter systems and monitor activities, an impossibility at present. The Security Officer will be able to implement secure password procedures, again an impossibility with the present system.

There are an increasing number of micro based systems that are capable of supporting several concurrent users, for example, baseband LAN systems. These systems have advanced hardware which support multiple processor estates, virtual memory addressing and other hardware features that are needed to provide adequate user isolation and security. Such systems, irrespective of their size, are functionally the equivalent of multi-user mini computer and main frame systems. It follows that they support users with security requirements similar to those in the West Cross Properties Group and that appropriate levels of protection are available.

A feasibility study to determine the most suitable and cost effective solution is recommended which should include a Security Strategy Plan to be incorporated into the operational requirements, where appropriate, and submitted to suppliers for tender. The Security Strategy Plan would become part of the overall Computer Strategy. (Reference Threat and Vulnerability Sheet 03).

Once formulated the plan should be introduced to staff by a member of the Board. Strategy and security must be seen to emanate from the Board of Directors to ensure credibility with other members of staff, especially in the current atmosphere of laissez faire. (Reference Threat and Vulnerability Sheet 03)

It is recognised that a Strategy Plan will require a detailed study and a knowledge of available hardware and software. However, without a defined strategy, fraud would be very difficult to prevent on any future system. (Reference Threat and Vulnerability Sheet 02)

The Security Strategy must include the following:

- Data classification
- Access controls and password policy
- Output controls
- Password administration
- Terminal policy
- Manual controls of source documents
- Contingency
- Environmental and physical security.

Due to the history of dishonesty in the Group, the fact that it was common knowledge within the office when it was happening and the difficulty of securing the existing systems, it is recommended that the definition of computer strategy should be given a very high priority. Once completed it should be implemented with a minimum of delay.

CHAPTER 3

VULNERABILITY OF GROUP MICRO COMPUTERS

The three principle threats that are evident within the installations are the following:

1. Embezzlement and fraud
2. Disclosure of confidential or sensitive information
3. Deliberate data manipulation.

When ''partner'' frauds have been evident it is not unusual to find other frauds being effected by junior employees. Additionally, some staff appear to divide into King and Williams camps and are of uncertain loyalty to the Group.

That these three threats may not have been consummated to date does not limit or reduce their future impact. Opportunities for misuse and abuse exist within the existing system and when the attractiveness of the goal is equalled by the vulnerability of the system then the probability of illicit acts is increased to a dangerous level.

PASSWORDS

Passwords were controlled and issued by users. This has now changed with Mr. Thomas changing passwords daily. However, even this measure, appropriate though it is, is insufficient to guarantee security. This would not matter if the information being processed was not key to the company's trading and if it were possible to link passwords to the level of classification of data being processed. Until this is possible all systems must be regarded as insecure. (Reference Threat and Vulnerability Sheet 09).

Appropriate password requirements can only be implemented in a new and upgraded system. Passwords should be controlled and released to users by the Security Manager.

LIBRARY ACTIVITIES

Copying discs gives rise to concern. Back up copies appear to be taken and would be sufficient to partially recover most of the systems. However, there are no detailed print outs of disc contents for re-creation purposes and copying does not follow a uniform pattern throughout the different systems.

There is also no documented record of the numbers of discs in use, what they contain and who is responsible for their safekeeping.

Fire is a major threat to the discs. In the main discs appear to be stored in desks or cabinets, which would be lost in case of fire. (Reference Threat and Vulnerability Sheet 11)
Recovery in the event of fire is problematic since there is no Disaster Plan in existence and even the sketchy contingency arrangements that exist have not been tested or exercised regularly. (Reference Threat and Vulnerability Sheet 06)

SCREEN PROCEDURES

The nature of stand alone micros does not facilitate the logging of access and individual activity within the system. Thus no one is accountable for his actions and nor can an illegal activity be monitored by third parties or auditors. This again is a strong argument for a more sophisticated system. (Reference Threat and Vulnerability Sheet 08).

The procedures for operating the various micro computers are weak and must be strengthened. This can be effected by a logical approach to security. For example, there is no '' time out'' facility on the micros ; that is no facility exists whereby a micro which has not been used for a specified time either blanks its screen or returns to a secure menu. Thus unattended micros are open to abuse by unauthorised personnel. It is recommended that only three access attempts are permitted to each micro. After three attempts the micro should be disabled and, ideally, a central micro console alarmed.

It is also recommended that for the more sophisticated system proposed software to audit access to the system should be considered. Printouts of unusual activity could then be automatically obtained without the necessity of the Security Officer making detailed examination of vast quantities of print out to check for anomalies. However, this should be considered on a cost effective basis after a detailed risk management study should the proposed system be bought.

All micro screens should face away from walk ways to prevent casual browsing by passers-by. Additionally screens that have no input for 4 minutes should be programmed to return to the opening menu. This will prevent unattended VDU's from being tampered with.

Micro computer power is the way forward for West Cross Property Group but a higher level of security consciousness is necessary. Terminal or screen procedures must be documented and be included in the Security Manual.

FIRE

Even a small fire could have disastrous consequences. All staff should, therefore, be trained in the use of extinguishers and the protection of discs and files in an emergency. Regular fire drills including evacuation of the area and implementation of appropriate security measures should be carried out.

CHAPTER 4

PERSONNEL

The defined and documented procedures for interviewing, vetting, employing and terminating employment of staff need to be produced. This may very well prove to be the corner stone of security. A periodic re-appraisal of vetting should be carried out on senior and other staff involved with corporate finances during their employment to ensure that life styles have not inexplicably changed. (Reference Threat and Vulnerability Sheet 04)

An individual, possibly Mr.Thomas should take responsibility for micro computer security. When a system is being developed security is always regarded as a counter productive element and almost invariably ignored. However,for the future, it is recommended that micro security should become a specific function within the Group under the direction of a part time System Security Officer; a part time function is suggested since the work would never merit a full time appointment.

The System Security Officer should, if possible, be divorced from the existing and future staff. This function should rest sensibly with Mr.Thomas although it is recognised that his function is temporary.

There is a general lack of security awareness among the Company's staff in the field of micro computers which might possibly be corrected by security training. The Systems Security Officer, once appointed, should be responsible for conducting training seminars for all members of staff on a yearly basis. He should be supported by senior members of the Group in this venture.

It follows that the Security Officer should establish an information security policy and document this. This will identify the types of information requiring protection and specify the control measures which will apply to each type of information.

As already stated existing staff seem to fall into loyalty groupings. A new system, once established and operating could be serviced by totally new members of staff eliminating this very serious problem and producing a new esprit de corps.

CHAPTER 5

DOCUMENTATION

There is an absence of documentation within the various elements of the Group. This needs to be corrected in the first instance by a Strategy Plan linked to security. This should be backed by a Security Manual which will define security with a view to protecting the assets of the Group. It is recognised that there is a resources problem within the company and that it may be necessary to use a third party organisation to produce these documents.

There is no documented Contingency Plan to meet disasters and no back up arrangement. This gives rise to concern. Statistically the United Kingdom has more computer fires than any other country and whilst the recognised probability is one fire in every thirty three years none the less the organisation should protect itself by documenting a contingency plan.

The documented Contingency Plan should take into account the following features:

> a) Personnel: Recovery time is a direct function of expertise, maturity, the availability of additional outside staff and direction.

> b) Back up: The location and availability of a support machine or support bureau.

> c) Media safety: Nonsuspect media packs or remotely stored discs will play an important role.

> d) Documentation: Systems, program and operation documentation.

> e) Manual system: The ability to return to whole or partial manual systems

> f) Supplier: The level of support provided in terms of replacement or expertise.

The Contingency Plan, once in existence, should be reviewed periodically and specifically after modifications and additions to the system and as a result of regular tests.

CHAPTER 6

SOFTWARE AND DATA CLASSIFICATION

SOFTWARE

No standardisation of operating systems exists preventing interchangeability of machines.

The Nominal Ledger receives direct postings. The use of a Property Management Package providing audit trails and controls was ignored. Only one individual, Mr. Doe, now knows exactly when and what items fall due. Previously this knowledge was shared by Mr. King.. The weakness is obvious; the Group is key personnel dependent and lacks efficient control of its affairs.

Other applications programs are dominated by word processing using Wordcraft.

Program alterations have been made by Mr. Wyne at Mr. King's request. No normal documentation exists on these changes and Mr. King is now in business partnership with Mr. Wyne. This gives rise to concern.

Full Edit facilities are generally available allowing not only read and write privileges but delete and change privileges. This will allow anyone familiar with the system to remove data without the normal safeguards and procedures.

Other inputs to the system are from source documentation. The system is not in good order since there are minimal controls from a computer stand point.

A clean start with a new system is the only economic and secure approach to this situation.

(Reference Threat and Vulnerability Sheet 05).

DATA CLASSIFICATION

In order to produce cost effective access controls the company must first decide on the value of its data. For example some types of data have a definite monetary value whilst other data have a value related to the need to prevent disclosure or misuse.

The data stored and processed by the company is of many types. The level of sensitivity of the data varies from publicly available information to data which should only be seen by specifically authorised members of staff (for example password information). The development of the Group has increased the need to classify the level of sensitivity of certain items of data and has certainly increased the need for careful application and protection measures.

The main aims of data classification should be:

> a) to identify the data stored or processed by the computer systems;
>
> b) to identify the levels of sensitivity of the data;
>
> c) to identify the Data Owner and Custodian of each entity;
>
> d) to propose a way of categorising the data, so that the sensitivity of the data may be recognised and appropriate levels of protection be provided.

Security controls would then be related to this classification system. (Reference Threat and Vulnerability sheet 10).

CHAPTER 7

HOBS

The controls on the Prestel line to the Bank of Scotland have largely been ignored and because of this the service has been temporarily suspended. Currently, the identifier and passwords are written together in a staff guide book. As a result dual control functions have been lost. (Reference Threat and Vulnerability Sheet 01).

The following is a quotation from a letter from the Bank of Scotland dated 22nd July 1987 and filed in the Groups' Banking File:

> ``...it has been brought to our attention by our HOBS Desk that you are one of the few organisations that allows one individual total access to the system.
>
> It has been our experience in the past that most business users allow many people to view the information available and at least two people accessing together to make inter account transfers and bill payments.
>
> The obvious benefits from this additional staff member being required is that it prevents abuse of the system and unauthorised transfers.''

To set a new payment procedure into the system requires written notification from the client company and an acknowledgment from the Bank. To suppress copies of the two written communications and later delete the payment system from the Banks Prestel system would be easy and would facilitate illegal transfers of money.

If the auditors, as has been stated by members of Group staff, are only interested in the final reconciliations rather than the mechanics of reconciliation then it would be easy to remove monies from accounts, use it and later return it in time for audit.

Additionally, the accounting system is muddled. The confusion that exists may be in position to intentionally discourage those trying to audit bank reconciliations and this possibility could not be discounted at the time of the survey.

Certainly, the existing system must not continue to exist and it is recommended that the identifier should be changed and the new number given privily to Mr.Thomas for input at transmission time until new standards are brought into effect.

CHAPTER 8

THE WAY FORWARD

The Group do not have the ability to implement full systems security with the present equipment or staff. This means they will remain vulnerable to the misuse and abuse of the micro systems by existing staff, ex-employees or knowledgeable outsiders. The Group should be prepared to commit expenditure, as a matter of urgency, to defining and documenting strategy and procuring adequate hardware and software to meet their needs.

Having taken this step attention must be given to data classification. Following this, access, input/output and operations controls should be defined depending on the classification of the data. Until this is accomplished there is an unacceptable level of vulnerability.

It is recognised that it will take the Board some time to bring the accepted recommendations into being. For this reason it is suggested that an outside independent organisation, should be used to assist in these projects and to train staff in the various projects requirements. The skills acquired will thus remain within the Group and its interests will be safeguarded on a continuing basis.

It is suggested that for the time being Mr.Thomas should take over the role of Systems Security Officer and be involved in each step of the development.

Staying with the existing systems and security thresholds is highly dangerous; weaknesses exist which can be expensively exploited for individual gain and some would affect the Group both financially and in its commercial and Stock Exchange ratings.

APPENDIX A

THREAT AND VULNERABILITY WORK SHEETS

A full security risk management study was not attempted because of the mixed nature of the individual units. Thus the work sheets in this section define a category of threat caused by a specific vulnerability. The estimated frequency of occurrence is thus approximate and based on historical or statistical data gleaned from other installations.

Impact is a description of what may be expected if the threat is consummated. This will produce some sort of financial loss which is usually expressed as a Single Loss Expectancy (SLE). In this study the Annual Loss Expectancy (ALE) has been used as a guide to a Criticality Analysis which categorises the priority of countermeasures. For convenience the ALE has been expressed as an adjectival value except in certain specific instances. Adjectives are graded as follows:

Very Low	Up to £1,000
Low	£1,000 to £10,000
Low/Medium	£10,000 to £50,000
Medium	£50,000 to £100,000
Medium/High	£100,000 to £500,000
High	£500,000 to £1,000,000

SHEET NUMBER 01

VULNERABILITY: Unauthorised Access - HOBS

DESCRIPTION OF
VULNERABILITY:
Insertion of illegal data. Situation is dominated by closely knit
small group of unknown loyalty.

THREAT: Fraud

RATIONALE:

Total control of the system rests with one individual who holds both the
sequential log and half the requisite authority. The other half is held
by his female assistant. Both are aware of the complete procedure to enter
data via HOBS. Procedures for establishing and removing accounts into
which money is to be paid would not be difficult to circumvent.

IMPACT:

Loss of funds either permanently or short term.
Public loss of confidence should such a fraud become public knowledge,
depressing share values. Loss of monies if the fraudster transferred
monies to a personal account and left.

ESTIMATED FREQUENCY OF OCCURRENCE: 1 in 5 years
A.L.E: High

RECOMMENDED COUNTERMEASURES

1.Peer audit, i.e. verification of the transaction carried out by a person
not employed in the section responsible for input. For example Mr.Thomas.
2.The identifier number to be held by a third party, ideally this should
be a board member who would input numbers against a known transaction and
from time to time verify the complete transaction.
3.Implicit confirmation of Bank of Scotland policies and recommendations.

VULNERABILITY: Computer Strategy

DESCRIPTION OF
VULNERABILITY: There is an absence of organised development of the computer facility which has lead to unacceptable vulnerabilities.

THREAT:
Destruction / Denial / Disclosure / Modification / Fraud

IMPACT: Financial loss through disorganised development.
Financial loss through fraud.
Financial loss through the disclosure of confidential information to third parties.

FREQUENCY: 1 in 18 years   **A.L.E.** Not available

RATIONALE:
The Group has no defined computer strategy linked to business strategy, computer development cannot be logical and controlled nor can the Group make rigorous use of the resources employed.
Weaknesses of the highest order exist in an already vulnerable department.

RECOMMENDED COUNTERMEASURES
1. Define Computer Strategy and link this with security strategy through the system life cycle. The Strategy to embrace:
              - Policy in respect of Information Processing
              - Proposed schedule of implementation
              - Personnel policies
              - Usage of Information Processing
              - Security strategy
              - Source documentation policies and controls.

SHEET NUMBER: 03

VULNERABILITY: Lack of Security Strategy Plan

DESCRIPTION OF
VULNERABILITY:
Due to the absence of a Security Strategy Plan there is no defined thrust in ADP systems security.

THREAT:
Fraud, Disclosure, Modification, Destruction, Denial

RATIONALE:

The Group are vulnerable to `` state of  the   art ``
penetration and amateur penetration. No provision has been made for even rudimentary systems security requirements let alone for
systems life cycle security requirements.

IMPACT:

Potential fraud. Unnecessary costs to rectify the situation. Possible loss due to unauthorised   modification of data.   Disclosure of confidential information to interested third parties.

ESTIMATED FREQUENCY OF OCCURRENCE: The effect of the absence
of an overall Security Strategy is evident daily. 1 in 10 years.
A.L.E: High

RECOMMENDED COUNTERMEASURES

1. Produce a Strategy Plan linked to precise budgets ensuring high levels of flexibility which in turn will provide adequate business processing with high security thresholds.

2. Security Strategy Plan to be introduced by Board of Directors to demonstrate their interest in security.

3. A Group Security Manual to be developed from the Security Strategy to be used by all staff and again introduced by the Board of directors.

SHEET NUMBER 04

VULNERABILITY: Personnel standards

DESCRIPTION OF
VULNERABILITY: There is a very low establishment and an
absence of personnel standards. Staff loyalty must be questioned in view
of the activities of the previous Managing Director and Financial Director
and the levels of support that they received.

THREAT:
Destruction / Denial / Disclosure / Modification / Fraud

IMPACT: Loss of profits due to inability to cope with
ADP needs. Loss due to accidental or deliberate acts.

FREQUENCY: 1 in 25 years.   **A.L.E.** Medium

RATIONALE: The production of essential personnel controls
has never occurred. The organisation became disastrously dependent on two
key members of staff and remains dependent on one.

RECOMMENDED COUNTERMEASURES
   1. Define long term computer strategy.

   2. Document procedures in the form of a manual since there is no
   personnel department. This document should cover:
        a) hiring procedures;
        b) assigning procedures;
        c) termination procedures,
        d) job descriptions,
        e) grievance procedures.

   3. Having installed a new computer system new staff should be
   considered to use it whose loyalties and previous activities are not
   suspect.

SHEET NUMBER 05

VULNERABILITY: Software standards

DESCRIPTION OF
VULNERABILITY: No documented standards exist covering software
development in-house or by an external group.

THREAT:
Destruction / Denial / Disclosure / Modification / Fraud

IMPACT:
Unauthorised access to systems.

FREQUENCY: 1 in 20 years   **A.L.E.** Low/Medium

RATIONALE:
The absence of procedures and low establishment means there can be little
management control over software development.

RECOMMENDED COUNTERMEASURES

    1. Define ADP Strategy.

    2. Produce standards to cover all development.

    3. Define requirements of bought-in packages.

SHEET NUMBER: 06

VULNERABILITY: Contingency Plan

DESCRIPTION OF
VULNERABILITY:
Absence of a contingency plan

THREAT:
Denial of service

RATIONALE:

There is no detailed contingency plan yet the loss of facilities would
have an adverse effect on the company.

IMPACT:
Unnecessary high costs and delays in implementing a back up or support
arrangement.

FREQUENCY OF OCCURRENCE: 1 in 10 years
A.L.E: Low

RECOMMENDED COUNTERMEASURES

1. Produce Contingency Plan with several different scenarios of
disaster levels detailing staff responsibilities.

2. Consideration to be given to machine and operating system standardisation to facilitate back up.

3. Consideration to be given to a network in line with 2. above.

4. Exercise Contingency Plan to ensure it will work.

SHEET NUMBER: 07

VULNERABILITY: Poor Housekeeping Procedures

DESCRIPTION OF
VULNERABILITY:

Very poor housekeeping procedures exist in respect of the micro computers in use.

THREAT:
Destruction , Denial , Disclosure , Modification , Fraud

RATIONALE:

Poor disc copying and storing procedures could result in loss or damage to discs or the theft of data. With ``state of the art'' criminals this lack of security would present an opportunity to steal information. discs are stored in desks in certain cases and in all cases in the same room. A fire would thus result in the loss of information and the labour cost in creating it.
Terminal procedures are also weak and provide opportunity for browsing. Back-up tapes are stored in the same room in the same building and where these are stored in a safe this is fire proof but not heat proof.

IMPACT:
Unnecessarily high costs in recreating files and the possibility of providing information to the unscrupulous.

ESTIMATED FREQUENCY OF OCCURRENCE: 1 in 22 years.
A.L.E: Medium

RECOMMENDED COUNTERMEASURES

1. A Security Manual to be produced and introduced with Board level backing. Management Audit to ensure that the micro computer users conform to the Manuals' requirements.

SHEET NUMBER: 08

VULNERABILITY: Screen Procedures

**DESCRIPTION OF
VULNERABILITY:**
Micro access not logged
Screens face walkways

THREAT:
Disclosure , Modification , Fraud

RATIONALE:

Unauthorised access to the system could be gained without any evidence
of the access having taken place.
Passers-by are able to browse and see confidential information and also
learn the form in which data must be input.

IMPACT:
Disclosure of confidential information. Inability of staff to monitor
a third party's unauthorised activities on
their terminals.
Loss of security.

ESTIMATED FREQUENCY OF OCCURRENCE: 1 in 10 years.

A.L.E: Low

RECOMMENDED COUNTERMEASURES

1. The logging of activities is essential for the security of the
system. To achieve this economically it will be necessary to
implement a standardised system with logging software.

2. Screens should not face areas where casual
visitors have walking access. Micros to be disabled after a
specific period of inactivity by returning the system to the
first menu.

3. Log on attempts to be restricted to three after which the micro
is disabled.

4. All access activities to be logged and audit trails provided to
identify individual activity.

5. Document micro procedures.

6. Instil security consciousness in personnel so that micros are
always logged off or left in menu mode when not in use.

SHEET NUMBER: 09

VULNERABILITY: Unauthorised Access; Passwords

DESCRIPTION OF
VULNERABILITY:
Password administration and use

THREAT:
Destruction , Disclosure , Modification , Fraud

RATIONALE:

Passwords are issued and controlled by users, not by a central
administrator. Passwords bear no relationship to
the sensitivity of the information to be protected and there is
no defined policy on passwords.

IMPACT:
All systems must be regarded as insecure. As a result any staff member
could, in theory, access other members files gaining access to sensitive
data for illegal use.

ESTIMATED FREQUENCY OF OCCURRENCE: 1 in 5 years.
A.L.E: Medium/Low

RECOMMENDED COUNTERMEASURES

1. A network system would facilitate centralised control and administration of passwords and employee accountability .

2. Specific password procedures should be developed and documented
in a computer security manual. These must include the following
procedures:

a) Passwords to be changed every 30 days.

b) Passwords to be formally released by Security Manager in a sealed
envelope.

c) Password procedures to be published.

d) Access to sensitive levels of data to generate
a detailed log of activity.

e) Passwords not to be displayed on screens.

f) Passwords to be alpha numeric.

g) Repeated log on failures to be advised to Security Officer for
action.

h) Automatic removal of leavers' passwords.

j) Passwords to be unique to the individual.

SHEET NUMBER: 10

VULNERABILITY: Data Classification System

DESCRIPTION OF
VULNERABILITY: Micro computer data is not classified according to its confidentiality or sensitivity. Access to data is not controlled according to its classification.

THREAT:
Disclosure , Modification , Fraud

RATIONALE:
Access to data is uniform and often not sufficiently restricted. Too much reliance is placed on passwords that are known to several staff members.

IMPACT:
Unauthorised access could allow ''browsing'' through data preparatory to fraud or malicious or accidental modification of data.

ESTIMATED FREQUENCY OF OCCURRENCE: 1 in 12 years.
A.L.E: Medium

RECOMMENDED COUNTERMEASURES

1. Classify each item of data according to its level of sensitivity or confidentiality.

2. Classification to become part of Security Manual.

3. As each system is specified or developed controls will be implemented as defined in the Security Manual Classification Section.

```
SHEET NUMBER   11
------------------------------------------------------------------

VULNERABILITY:   Library Controls
------------------------------------------------------------------

DESCRIPTION OF        Non existent library controls
VULNERABILITY:


------------------------------------------------------------------

THREAT:
Destruction / Denial / Disclosure / Modification / Fraud
------------------------------------------------------------------
IMPACT:            Loss or removal of tapes and discs could
cause  maximum   disruption,  modification   of data and financial
loss.
------------------------------------------------------------------
FREQUENCY: 1 in 5 years                A.L.E. Low


------------------------------------------------------------------
RATIONALE:          Discs and tapes,  including  back up,  are
stored in the computer room.    Their loss would cause maximum
disruption and denial of facilities.


------------------------------------------------------------------

RECOMMENDED COUNTERMEASURES

      1. Implement library log.
      2. Essential or critical data and programs
      to be stored off site.
      3. Document security policy.
```

Job Description of a Security Officer

The general terms of reference for a typical Security Officer would be as follows:

1. To act as the company's computer Security Officer with overall responsibility to establish and administer the security policies. ADP security encompasses the physical, personnel, communications, hardware, software, contingency planning, risk management and any other security aspects contributing to the protection of the total system, site or operation.

2. Duties of the security officer would include:

    a. Advising senior management and user management on all aspects of computer security including networks and micro computers;

    b. Ensuring compliance with security policies, including the identification of types of security for data handled, transmitted or stored;

    c. Controlling risk analysis studies and recommending corrective measures;

    d. Directing and controlling the testing of all contingency plans;

    e. Ensuring that computer installations conform to the requirements of the data protection act;

    f. Providing security training;

    g. Assisting in the investigation of security violations;

    h. Ensuring proper management of user passwords and any other security data.

    i. Controlling and managing computer misuse and abuse investigations.

    j. Co-ordinate Validation and Verification of software and application programs.

Skills Required

The Security Officer should have detailed knowledge of security in the data processing environment. However there should be equal paths of organisational knowledge, security instinct and an ability to work with people. A high degree of trustworthiness is implied.

Although hard to obtain the ideal Security Officer would have approximately the following background:

a. At least five years experience within a computing environment;

b. An acquired knowledge of security ;

c. At least two to three years experience of the organisation for which he works;

d. The ability to isolate problem areas quickly;

e. The ability to work with people. The individuals should have demonstrated effective and cooperative natures in working with other individuals within their own departments.

Seniority

Ideally the Security Officer should report to a board member in order to have the right level of security back up. To report below this level will inhibit performance and may result in investigations being inhibited.

Selection

The selected Security Officer will be in a position of total trust with access to all systems. Before the position is offered a complete screening should be performed by an outside organisation. The screening should be repeated every eighteen months.

Job offers should be contingent on favorable reports.

TYPICAL BARRIER TIME DETAILS

BARRIER	ACTION	TOOLS	TIME (mins)
3M FENCE			
Chain Link	Climb		
	Cut through	Bolt Cutter	0.5
Expanded Metal			
3"x1 1/2"x1/16"	Cut through	Bolt Cutter	2.5
		Oxy/A Torch	2.0
Weld Mesh			
75x25x3cm	Single	Bolt Cutter	2.1
	Double	Bolt Cutter	3.9
		Oxy/A Torch	3.2
	Climb	Ladders	2.4
WALLS	Ladder-Padding		0.15
4" Reinforced Concrete	Hand		5-7
8" Reinforced Concrete	Hand		10-20
Timber + Gypsum	Hand		2-3
· + Expanded Metal	Hand		8-10
Single Brickwork	Hand		2-3
Double Brickwork	Hand		4-7
4" Reinforced Block	Hand		2-3
+ Expanded Metal	Hand		8-10
8" Concrete Blocks	Hand		4-6
+Filled Fibrous Concrete	Hand		25-30
12" Reinforced Concrete Block	Hand		20-25
ROOF			
Tiles/Slate	Hand		1.0
+ Weld Mesh	Hand		10-12
Metal Deck 1/16"	Hand		5-7
DOORS			
Softwood Panel Frame	Pry open	Hand	0.25
Hardwood	Pry open	Hand	0.45
1/16" Steel Plate	Cut	Hand	3-5
1/14" Steel Plate	Cut	Torch/Bar	5-7
WINDOW			
Glass 1/14" Tempered	Axe		0.05
Wired	Axe		0.2
Laminated	Axe		0.5
Plyglass	Axe/Saw		1-2
Weldmesh	Bolt cutters		2-4
1/2" M.S.Bars	Bolt cutters		3-5
SHUTTERS	Bolt cutters		15-20
BARBED TAPE AND			
CONCERTINA COIL	Lay Over	Ladder/Board	0.3
		Bolt Cutters	0.7
RUN WITH TOOLS 100 METERS			0.3
CRAWL WITH TOOLS 100 METERS			1.3

These figures have been reproduced courtesy of Group4 Security Services, Broadway, Worcestershire.

BARRIER PENETRATION BY A 1 TON TRUCK

BARRIER	RESULT	VEHICLE	NOTES
3' ``V'' Ditch	Stopped	Immobilised	Could be bridged with planks
10'x 3'Ditch	Stopped	Slight damage	
4' Concrete Blocks	Stopped	Extensive damage	
Guardrail	Penetrated	Serious damage	Vehicle could still be used
Embedded tires	Stopped	Minor	
4' Embankment + Concrete Blocks	Stopped	Extensive damage	
Angled Steel	Stopped	Front wrecked	
Chain link	Penetrated	Minor	
Chain link with cable	Stopped cable held	Minor	
Vee Fence	Stopped	Extensive damage	

For most installations it is possible to time an attack and to raise the threshold of security. Lorries present the most successful terrorist weapon since they can strap telegraph poles on the back and reverse at high speed into walls. Afterwards the lorry can be used as a climbing frame and initial get away vehicle. It follows that there should be no areas where lorries can get up to speed; access roads should have gates and sleeping policemen, as well as many turnings to prevent unwelcome visitors getting up speed.
Car parks, which offer cover for intruders, should also be sited away from the computer building. Closed circuit televisions should have good views of car parks, main entrances, roofs and the sides of the building.

These figures have been reproduced courtesy of Group4 Security Services, Broadway, Worcestershire.

Glossary of Terms

These terms may not be used by security managers/officers during their normal activities with computers. However, the Glossary contains additional explanations of terms used in the text.

Whoever is responsible for security or systems audit will require a good knowledge of computer security terminology. As far as is practicable the terms used in this manual have been repeated and defined in this section. However other terms have been added for reference purposes.

Access
The ability of a user to communicate with (input to or receive output from) an Automatic Data Processing System (ADPS); or have entry to a specified area. This definition does not include those persons (customers) who simply receive products created by the system and who have no communication or interface with the ADPS or its personnel.

Access Category
One of the classes to which a user, a program, or a process in an ADP system may be assigned on the basis of the resource or groups of resources that each user, program or process is authorized to use.

Access Control
The process of limiting access to the resources of an ADP system only to authorized users, programs, processes, or other ADP systems (in computer networks). Synonymous with Controlled Access, Controlled Accessibility.

Access Control Mechanism
Hardware or software features, operating procedures, management procedures, and various combinations of these designed to detect and prevent unauthorized access and to permit authorized access to an ADP system.

Accountability
The quality or state which enables violations or attempted violations of ADP system security to be traced to individuals who may then be held responsible.

Accreditation
The authorization and approval, granted to an ADP system or network, to process classified or sensitive unclassified data in an operational environment. Accreditation will be made on the basis of a certification of competent authority that designated technical personnel have examined and verified that design and implementation of the system meet pre specified technical requirements for achieving adequate data security.

The authorization and approval, granted to an ADP system or network to process sensitive data in an operational environment, and made on the basis of a certification by designated technical personnel of the extent to which design and implementation of the system meet pre specified technical requirements for achieving adequate data security.

Active Wiretapping
The attaching of an unauthorized device, such as a computer terminal, to a communications circuit for the purpose of obtaining access to data through the generation of false messages or control signals, or by altering the communications of legitimate users.

ADP
Automatic Data Processing

ADP Environment

Any area in which ADP functions are performed, including central computer facilities, peripheral devices and I/O devices outside the single controlled area, and remote terminal facilities.

ADP Facilities

The physical resources, including structures or parts of structures, which house and support data processing capabilities. For each computer installation designated as a data processing installation.

ADP Security

Measures required to protect against unauthorized (accidental or intentional) disclosure, modification, or destruction of ADP systems and data, and denial of service to process data. ADP security includes consideration of all hardware/ software functions, characteristics, and /or features; operational procedures, and access controls at the central computer facility; remote computer and terminal facilities, and the management constraints, physical structures and devices; and personnel and communication controls needed to provide an acceptable level of risk for the ADP system and for the data or information contained in the system.

The measures required to protect against unauthorized (accidental or intentional) disclosure, modification or destruction of data (classified, personal, sensitive, business) and loss of the ability to process data. The ADP security program is concerned with, but not limited to, honest human errors and omissions, dishonest and disgruntled employees, fire, water damage (leaking pipes, flood, fire fighting, storm, etc.), espionage, sabotage of equipment, software, equipment and processing time, loss of electrical power, communications lines and air conditioning, indirect theft or fraud through manipulation of data, windstorm, earthquake, emanations, loss or degradation of processing capability and software deficiencies.

ADP Security Plan

The overall plan for providing security throughout the life cycle of automated project or program, ADPS or facility. The plan documents the operational requirements, security environment, hardware and software configuration(s) and interfaces; all security procedures, measures, and features; and, for ADPS, the contingency plans for continued support in case of a local disaster. The plan represents the baseline for the risk analysis.

Annual Loss Expectancy

The ALE of an ADP system or activity is the estimated yearly dollar value loss from the harm to the system or activity by attacks against its assets.

Application Software (Functional)

Those routines and programs designed by or for ADPS users and customers to complete specific, mission oriented tasks, jobs, or functions, using available ADP equipment and basic software. Applications software may be either general purpose packages or specific application programs. Except for specific packages that are bought in from outside vendors, application packages are usually developed in house by employees or contract staff.

Asset

An asset is any software, hardware, personnel resource, information, communications hardware or software or administration within an ADP system of activity.

Attack

A realisation of a threat. The frequency of the threat will depend on such factors as the location,value and type of information processed. The level of protection proposed for an asset will not effect the frequency of attack only the impact. That an attack is made does not mean that it will succeed. The success of the attack depends on the vulnerability of the system and the effectiveness of the counter-measures.

Audit

An independent review and examination of system records and activities in order to evaluate the efficacy of system controls and audit trails.

Audit Trail

A chronological record of system activities which is sufficient to enable the reconstruction, review and examination of the activities surrounding or leading to each event of a transaction from its inception to output of the final result.

Authentication

a. The act of verifying the eligibility of a node, terminal or individual to access specific information.

b. A measure designed to provide protection against fraudulent transmissions by establishing the validity of a transmission.

Authenticator

a. The means used to identify or verify the eligibility of a terminal or node to access specific categories of information.

b. A symbol, a sequence of symbols, or information arranged in a predetermined manner and inserted in a message or transaction for the purpose of authentication.

Authorisation

The granting of access rights to a user or process to an asset.

Back up Procedures

The provisions that are made to recover data and programs and to restart the DP facilities after a disaster or failure, usually on an alternative machine.

Bandwidth

A characteristic of a communication channel, usually the amount of information that can be passed through it in a given time period and usually measured in bits per second or bauds.

Bell Lapadula Model

A formal model of computer security policy that describes a set of access control rules. In this model, the entities in a computer system are divided into abstract sets of subjects and objects. The notion of a secure state is defined and the system is then found to be secure. The Bell-Lapadula model is just one method of authentication: others exist.

Bogus Message

A message sent for some purpose other than its content and which may consist of dummy data groups or meaningless text.

Bounds Checking
Testing of computer program results for access to storage outside its authorised limits. It is synonymous with memory bounds checking.

Browsing
Searching through data to find information without necessarily knowing the format of the information being sought.

Call Back
Used to identify a terminal dialing into a system. The line is disconnected and the computer calls the accessing terminal back.

Cartridge
A tape system of storage used on microcomputers to increase the backing memory.

Cipher Group
A group of letters or numbers (usually five in number) used in encrypted versions of messages.

Cipher System
A system in which cryptopgraphy is applied to plain text elements.

Ciphertext
Unintelligible text or signals produced through the use of cipher systems.

Cipher Text Auto-Key
A cryptographic logic which uses previous cipher text to produce key.

Compromise
The exposure of clandestine personnel, installations or other assets, or of classified information or material, to an unauthorized person.

Compartmentalisation
a. The isolation of the operating system, user programs, and data files from one another in main storage in order to provide protection against unauthorized access by other users or programs.

b. The breaking down of sensitive data into small, isolated blocks for the purpose of reducing risk to the data.

Compromise
An unauthorized disclosure or loss of sensitive defense information.

Computer Network
A complex consisting of two or more interconnected computers.

Computer Security
The protection resulting from all measures designed to prevent deliberate or inadvertent unauthorized disclosure, acquisition, manipulation, modification, or loss of information contained in a computer system, as well as measures designed to prevent denial of authorized use of the system.

Confidentiality
A concept that applies to data that must be held in confidence and that describes the status and degree of protection that must be provided for such data about

individuals as well as organizations.

Contingency Plans
A plan for emergency response, back-up operations, and post-disaster recovery maintained by an ADP activity as a part of its security program. A comprehensive consistent statement of all the actions (plan) to be taken before, during and after a disaster (emergency condition), along with documented, tested procedures which, if followed, will ensure the availability of critical ADP resources and facilitate maintaining the continuity of operations in an emergency situation.

Controlled Access
The process of limiting access to the resources of an ADP system only to authorized personnel, users, programs, processes, or other ADP systems (as in computer networks).

Cost-Risk Analysis
The assessment of the costs of potential risk of loss or compromise of data in an ADP system without countermeasures versus the cost of providing countermeasures.

Countermeasure
Any action, device, procedure, technique, or other measure that reduces the vulnerability of an ADP system or activity to the realization of a threat.

Covert Channel
A communication channel that allows a process to transfer information in a manner that violates the system's security policy. See also: Cover Storage channel, Covert Timing Channel.

Covert Storage Channel
A covert channel that involves the writing of a storage location by one process and the reading by another, either directly or with the assistance of the Trusted Computing Base.

Covert Timing Channel
A covert channel in which one process signals information to another by modulating its own use of system resources (e.g., CPU time) in such a way that this manipulation affects the real response time observed by the second process.

Critical ADP Resources
Those resources that must be protected because their compromise, alteration, destruction, loss, or failure to meet objectives will jeopardize the accomplishment of the organisation's functions.

Cryptoanalysis
The steps and operations performed in converting encrypted messages and plain text without initial knowledge of the key employed in the encryption. Its purpose is to evaluate the adequacy of the security protection that it is intended to provide, or to discover weaknesses or vulnerabilities which could be exploited to defeat, or lessen that protection.

Cryptographic System
The documents, devices, equipment, and associated techniques that are used as a unit to provide a single means of encryption (enciphering or encoding).

Cryptography

The art or sciences concerning the principles, means, and methods for rendering plain text unintelligible and for converting encrypted messages into intelligible form.

Cryptology

The field that encompasses both cryptography and crypto-analysis.

The science which deals with hidden, disguised, or encrypted communications. It embraces communications security and communications intelligence.

Data

Numbers or text characters which require Interpretation in a certain Context in order to become Information, hence the term 'raw data'.

Data Base

A file of data so structured that appropriate applications draw from the file but do not themselves constrain the file design or its content. The Data Base is accessible to various subsystems and departments in an organisation such as the Accounts Department, the Marketing Department, Sales and so on.

DBMS (Data Base Management System)

The management system under which the various Users of a system and their Subsystems are integrated so that they can all access the same Data Base for different purposes and at different levels of access.

Data Confidentiality

The state that exists when data is held in confidence and is protected from unauthorized disclosure. Misuse of data by those authorized to use it for limited purposes only is also considered to be a violation of data confidentiality.

Data Encryption Standard (DES)

An unclassified crypto-algorithm published by the National Bureau of Standards in FIPS PUB 46 for the protection of certain U.S. Government information.

Data Integrity

The state that exists when computerized data is the same as that in the source documents and has not been exposed to accidental or intentional modification, disclosure, or destruction.

Data Processing Activity (DPA)

Any facility, room, or building housing ADP equipment and/or storage media.

Data Security

The protection of data from accidental, unauthorized, intentional, or malicious modification, destruction, or disclosure.

Data Storage and Retrieval System

A computer system which performs the functions of storing, processing, retrieving and routing information to the query terminal. Such functions are sometimes referred to as Data Base Management System.

Decrypt

To convert, by use of the appropriate key, encrypted (encoded or enciphered) text into its equivalent plain text.

Dedicated Mode
The operation of an ADP system such that the central computer facility, the connected peripheral devices, the communications facilities, and all remote terminals are used and controlled exclusively by specific users and groups of users for the processing of particular types and categories of information.

Downsizing
The push to replace older, larger computer systems with newer, smaller, networked PCs.

Dump
A list of the contents of the memory, registers, and buffer areas of a configuration.

Duress Alarm System
A mechanical or electronic device which enables personnel on duty to alert an agency, usually security police, for the purpose of obtaining immediate assistance without arousing suspicion.

Eavesdropping
The unauthorized interception of information-bearing emanations through the use of methods other than wiretapping.

Encryption

     a. **End-to-end** encryption. Encryption of information at the origin within a communications network and postponing decryption to the final destination point.

     b. **Link-by-link** Encryption. The application of on-line crypto operations to a link of a communications system so that all information passing over the link is encrypted.

The invertible coding of data through the use of a transformation key so that the data can be safely transmitted or stored in a physically unprotected environment.

Encryption Algorithm
A set of mathematically expressed rules for rendering information unintelligible by effecting a series of transformations to the normal representation of the information through the use of variable elements controlled by the application of a key.

End-to-End Security
The protection of information passed in a secure telecommunications system by cryptographic or other method point of origin to point of destination.

Fail Safe
The automatic termination and protection of programs or other processing operations when a hardware or software failure is detected in an ADP system.

Fail Soft
The selective termination of affected non-essential processing when a hardware or software failure is detected in an ADP system.

Fault
A condition that causes a device or system component to fail to perform in a required manner (e.g., a short circuit, broken wire, an intermittent connection).

File Protection
The aggregate of all processes and procedures established in an ADP system and designed to inhibit unauthorized access, contamination, or elimination of a file.

Firmware
A method of organizing the ADP system's control hardware in a microprogrammed structure rather than as wired circuitry such that the method falls in neither the software nor the hardware systems. The firmware or microprogramming handling security and related control functions shall be alterable only within the Central Computer Facility and only under conditions that are controlled by specific personnel. It must not be alterable by users or by software.

Floppy
A disc used in a micro computer so called because of its flexible nature. As distinct from a Hard- or Winchester Disc.

Front End Processor
A computer associated with a host computer that performs pre-processing functions. It may perform line control, message handling, code conversion, error control, data control, data management, and terminal handling.

Full Maintenance
All diagnostic repair, modifications, and overhaul.

Functional Testing
The portion of security testing in which the advertised features of a system are tested for correct operation.

Garbled
An error in transmission, reception, encryption, or decryption which changes the text of a transmission or any portion thereof in such a manner that it is incorrect or un-decryptable.

General-Purpose System
A computer system that is designed to aid in solving a wide variety of problems.

Handled
Data stored, processed or used in an ADP system or communicated, displayed, produced or disseminated by an ADP system.

Handshaking Procedures
A dialogue between a user and a computer, a computer and another computer, a program and another program for the purpose of identifying a user and and authenticating his identity, through a sequence of questions and answers based on information either previously stored in the computer or supplied to the computer by the initiator of dialogue. Synonymous with password dialogue.

Hard Disc
Also known as a Winchester disc. A sealed magnetic storage device which can either have removable cartridges, or in the smaller sizes found on Microcomputers, fixed discs. Capacities range from 20Megabytes up to 400Megabytes.

Hardware
Physical equipment such as mechanical, magnetic, electrical, or electronic devices used in the configuration and operation of an ADP system. This term

is synonymous with ADP equipment and includes:

(1) General and special purpose digital, analogue and hybrid computer equipment;

(2) Components which are used to create, collect, store, process, communicate, display or disseminate classified information;

(3) Auxiliary equipment such as data communications terminals, source data automation recording equipment, data output equipment (e.g., printers, plotters and computer output microfilmers) either cable-connected or self-standing, used in support of computer equipment;

(4) Electrical accounting machine (EAM) used in conjunction with or independent of computers.

Hardware Security
Computer equipment features or devices used in a ADP system to preclude unauthorized (accidental or Intentional) modification, disclosure or destruction to ADP resources.

Host
A uniquely addressable computer system that is available through the network. The local host provides service to local onsite users. The remote host provides similar services to local users through the network.

Identification
The process that enables, generally by the use of unique machine-readable names, recognition of users or resources as identical to those previously described to an ADP system.

Imitative Communications Deception
The introduction, by unauthorized parties, of signals or traffic which imitates valid messages into communications channels, to deceive authorized users.

Impersonation
An attempt to gain access to a system by posing as an authorized user. Synonymous with Masquerading.

Inadvertant Disclosure
Accidental exposure of sensitive information to a person not authorized access.

Incomplete Parameter Checking
A system fault which exists when all parameters have not been fully checked for correctness and consistency by the operation system, thus making the system vulnerable to penetration.

Individual Accountability
Measures to positively associate the identity of a user with his access to machine and the material he accessed. This will normally include a time in and out.

Information Flow Control
A concept requiring that information transfers within a system be controlled so that information in certain types of objects cannot, via any channel within the system, flow to certain other types of objects. See also: Covert Channel and Bell Lapadula.

Integrity
The capability of an ADP system to perform its intended function in an unimpaired manner, free from deliberate or inadvertent unauthorized manipulation.

Key (Cryptographic)
A sequence of symbols or electrical or mechanical equivalents which, in cryptosystems, is combined with plain text to produce cipher text.

Key-Auto-Key
A cryptographic logic which uses the previous key to produce the new key.

Key Generation
The origination of a key or of a set of distinct keys.

A device or algorithm which employs a series of mathematical rules to deterministically produce a pseudo-random sequence of cryptovariables.

Key List
A printed series of key settings for a specific cryptonet at a specified time, which is produced in list, padded, or tape form.

Key Tape
A paper, mylar, or magnetic tape containing the key for a specific cryptonet at a specific time.

Keyword
Synonym for Password.

Least Privilege
This principle requires that each subject in a system be granted the most restrictive set of privileges (or lowest clearance) needed for the performance of authorized tasks. This limits the damage that can result from accident, error or unauthorized use.

Masquerading
An attempt to gain access to a system by posing as an authorized user.

Memory Bounds
The limits in the range of storage addresses for a protected region in memory.

Memory-mapping Registers
Registers which are used for translating symbolic or virtual storage addresses into absolute storage addresses.

Mimicking
Synonym for Masquerading.

Mode of Operation
The security environment and method of operating an ADP system. There are three modes of operation:

a. **Dedicated.**
The user has control of a central computer facility, its connected peripheral devices, and all remote terminals exclusively for the processing of a particular type(s) and category(ies) of sensitive material. All users of the system are cleared for, and have access authorization for, all material in the ADP system.

All storage media are either purged or removed from the computer and, together with other output, safe-guarded as appropriate to its classification or sensitivity before resuming processing in a less restrictive mode.

b. **Controlled.**

Reliance is placed upon various security controls and counter measures to permit operation of an ADP system in a mode of operation which is less restrictive than dedicated and more restrictive than multilevel. Examples are:

1) *Compartmented.* Utilization of a resource sharing computer system for the concurrent processing or storage

      a) Of two or more types of sensitive compartmented information,

or

      b) Of any type of sensitive compartmented information with some other kind of information. System access is afforded personnel holding TOP SECRET clearances, but not necessarily all the sensitive access approvals that are involved. Storage areas containing compartment information are purged before continuing processing, and outputs may require special handling.

2) *System High* or *Benign Environment.*

Information of different levels of classification or special category designations are processed simultaneously in the same computer system with security controls commensurate with those prescribed for the highest classification being processed. In this mode all data processed, along with any outputs generated, will be considered to be of the highest security classification.

c. **Multilevel Security Mode.**

A mode of operation using an operating system which provides a capability that permits various levels and categories or compartments of material to be stored and processed in an ADP system. In a remotely accessed resource sharing system, the material can be selectively accessed and manipulated from various controlled terminals by personnel having different security clearances and access approvals.

Multiple Access Rights Terminal

A terminal that may be used by more than one class of users; for example, users with different access rights to data.

Multi-Level Secure

A class of system containing information with different security classifications that simultaneously permits access by users with different security clearances and needs-to-know. The system prevents users from obtaining access to information for which they lack authorization.

Multiprocessing

The operating system's provision of multiple concurrent processes to multiple interactive users.

Multiprogramming

The technique by which the Operating System shares the resources of the computing system among several resident user programs. The idea behind multiprogramming is that the Operating System keeps more than one user program resident in main memory at a time.

Mutually Suspicious
Pertaining to the state that exists between interactive processes (subsystems or programs) each of which contains sensitive data and is assumed to be designed so as to extract data from the other and to protect its own data.

Need-to-Know
The necessity for access to, knowledge of, or possession of classified or other sensitive information in order to carry out official duties.

Network
This is the interconnection of two or more ADP central computer facilities that provides for the transfer or sharing of ADP resources. The ADP network consists of the central communication links, the front-end processors, and the telecommunications systems.

Object
A passive entity that contains or receives information. Access to an object potentially implies access to the information it contains. Examples of objects are: bits, bytes, words, fields, records, blocks, pages, segments, files, directories, programs, processors, network nodes, etc., as well as video displays, keyboards, clocks, printers, etc.

One-Time Cryptosystem
A cryptosystem employing keying variables which are only used once.

One-Time Pad
A manual, one-time cryptosystem produced in pad form.

Operating System (OS)
An integrated collection of service routines for supervising the sequencing and processing of programs by a computer. Operating systems control the allocation of resources to users and their programs and play a central role in assuring the secure operation of a computer system. Operation systems may perform input-output, accounting, resource allocation, compilation, storage assignment tasks, and other system related functions (synonymous with Monitor, Executive, Control Program, and Supervisor).

Operations
The working of the computer. Operating Staff load media and remove output at correct moments in time. They are also responsible for dynamic configuration control.

Password
A protected word or string of characters that identifies or authenticates a user for access to a specific resource such as a data set, file, record, etc.

Penetration
The successful and repeatable extraction of information from a protected data file.

Personal Data
Data about an individual. This may include individual history or hand, voice or retina prints.

Physical Security
The protection of a material entity (property) from disruption and is concerned

with measures designed to safeguard personnel, to prevent unauthorized access to equipment, facilities, material and documents, and to safeguard them against espionage, sabotage, damage and theft.

a. The use of locks, badges, and similar measures to control access to the central computer facility.

b. The measures required for the protection of the structures housing the central computer facility from damage by accident, fire, environmental hazards, loss of utilities, and unauthorized access.

Piggy Back
Unauthorized access to an ADP system via another user's legitimate connection.

Plain Text
Intelligible text or signals that have meaning and that can be read or acted upon without the application of decryption.

Print Suppress
To eliminate the printing of characters in order to preserve their secrecy, for example, the characters of a password as it is keyed by a user at an input terminal.

Privacy Transformation
Synonym for Encryption Algorithm.

Privileged Instructions
a. A set of instructions generally executable only when the ADP system is operating in the executive state.

b. Special computer instructions designed to control the protection features of an ADP system.

Protected Area
An area housing one or more ADP systems, including communications equipment, remote computer facilities, terminals or peripheral devices, which is continuously protected by physical security safeguards and access controls.

Public Key Cryptography
A type of cryptography in which the encryption process is publicly available and unprotected, but in which part of the decryption process is protected so that only a party with knowledge of both parts of the decryption process can decrypt the cipher text.

Purging
a. The orderly review of storage and removal of inactive or obsolete data files.

b. The removal of obsolete data by erasure, by overwriting of storage, or by resetting registers.

Randomiser
A random bit generator which produces patterns used to modify the key variable of crypto-equipment to establish a unique point on the key cycle at which encryption is to begin.

Read Access

A fundamental type of access in which the only flow of information is from the object to the subject.

Real Time Function

A response to a penetration attempt which is detected and diagnosed in time to prevent the actual penetration.

Recovery

The restoration of the ADP facility or other related assets following physical destruction or major damage.

Remote

A general term encompassing several categories of equipment connected to an automated message processing exchange. This term includes remote terminals and remote Data Processing Installations.

Remote Terminal

A terminal which is connected to and functionally related to a computer system.

Residue

Data left in storage after processing operations, and before degaussing or rewriting has taken place.

Responsible Person

A member of user staff, who is not necessarily computer erudite but takes responsibility for terminal, micro computer and document security at a local level. Generally, he will contribute to a local security Handbook, maintain logs of activity with sensitive data and carry out local training.

Resource

Anything utilized or consumed while performing a task. The categories of resources are: time, information, objects (information containers), or processors (the ability to utilize information). Specific examples are: CPU time; terminal connect time; amount of directly-addressable memory; disc space; number of I/O requests per minute, etc.

Resource Sharing

In an ADP system, the concurrent use of a resource by more than one user, job, or program.

Restricted Area

Any area, access to which is subject to special restrictions or controls for reasons of security or safeguarding of property or material.

Risk

An assessment of the probability that an entity will successfully attack a particular system. A risk is an evaluation of:

    a. A vulnerability.
    b. A threat.
    c. The probability of occurrence.
    d. The impact.
    e. The countermeasures which may be taken.

Risk Assessment

An analysis of system vulnerabilities to establish an expected loss from certain events based on estimated probabilities of the occurrence of those events. The purpose of a risk assessment is to determine if proposed countermeasures are adequate to reduce the loss or the impact of loss to an acceptable level.

Risk Management

An element of managerial science concerned with the identification, measurement, control, and minimization of uncertain events. An effective risk management program encompasses the following four phases:

1. Risk Assessment, as derived from an evaluation of threats and vulnerabilities;
2. Management Decision;
3. Control Implementation; and
4. Effectiveness Review.

Scavenging

Searching through residue for the purpose of unauthorized data acquisition.

Scenario

An outline of a sequence of events aimed at attacking an ADP system or leading to an accidental breach of security.

Security Audit

An assessment of the system of controls that ensure the continuity and integrity of the environment as defined by management. An assessment of the reasonableness of these controls is achieved by examining and evaluation controls over system access, accuracy, and availability.

Security Kernel

A localized mechanism, composed of hardware and software, that controls the access of users (and processes executing on their behalf) to repositories of information resident in or connected to the system. The correct operation of the kernel along with any associated trusted processes should be sufficient to guarantee enforcement of the constraints on access.

Seepage

The accidental flow, to unauthorized individuals, or data or information, access to which is presumed to be controlled by computer security safeguards.

Sensitive ADP Resources

Those resources that must be protected because their compromise, alteration, destruction or loss will adversely affect the security of the business, personal, or other data/information. This includes information used to manage sensitive resources.

Small Computer System

A physically small, programmable, computer system that costs under £30,000 to purchase and has its own power supply, chassis or mounting cage, control console, and possibly input and output devices. Also, it can be operated in the stand-alone mode, or under operator or stored program control and will perform a meaningful, complete, and predetermined processing sequence. It is usually installed in a laboratory or office environment. Examples are word processing equipment, graphics display terminals, and other intelligent display terminals, with or without peripheral devices.

Snapshot
A dynamic printout of selected data in storage or working memory that occurs at breakpoints or checkpoints during computing operations or on operator command.

Spoofing
The act of inserting a false instruction or false data into a data communications transmission with the intent that it appears valid at the receiving equipment (e.g., a computer).

System High Mode
Utilization of an ADP system to process or store sensitive compartmented information, when the total system, to include the central computer facility and all of its connected peripheral devices and remote terminals, are secured in accordance with the requirements for the highest classification level and for all types of sensitive compartmented information processed or stored; and all users with access to the system will have a valid TOP SECRET clearance and access approvals for all sensitive information stored or processed by the system.

System High Security Mode
A mode of operation in which all personnel having access to the ADPS have a security clearance, but not a need-to-know, for all material then contained in the system. An ADPS is operating in the system high security mode when the central computer facility and all of its connected peripheral devices and remote terminals are protected according to the requirements for the highest classification of material then contained in the system. In this mode, the ADPS design and operation must accordingly provide for some internal control of concurrently available classified material in the system on the basis of need-to-know.

System Integrity
The state that exists when there is complete assurance that under all conditions an ADP system is based on the logical correctness and reliability of the operating system, the logical completeness of the hardware and software that implement the protection mechanisms, and data integrity.

System Software
System software consists of the operating system and associated system software, including assemblers, input-output control systems, interpreters, compilers and other utility programs that are not keyed to particular user requirements (i.e., considered user application software). Where security functions are executed by a Data Base Management System, it also requires protection as system software.

Tampering
An unauthorized modification which alters the proper functioning of equipment or systems in a manner which degrades the security it provides.

Telecommunications
Any transmission, emission, or reception of signs, signals, writing, images, sounds, or other information by wire, radio, visual, or any electromagnetic systems.

Telecommunications Centre

A facility, normally serving more than one organization or terminal, responsible for the transmission, receipt, acceptance, processing and distribution of incoming and outgoing messages.

Teleprocessing Security

The protection that results from all measures designed to prevent deliberate, inadvertent, or unauthorized disclosure, acquisition, manipulation, or modification of information in a teleprocessing system.

Teleprocessing System

Integrating communications and ADP equipment primarily for achieving a remote-processing capability.

TEMPEST

A de-classified short name referring to investigations and studies of compromised emanations.

Terminal Identification

The means used to establish the unique identification of a terminal by an ADP system.

Threat

A threat is any circumstance or event with the potential to cause harm to the ADP system or activity in the form of destruction, disclosure, ad modification of data, or denial of service. A threat is a potential for harm. The presence of a threat does not mean that it will necessarily cause actual harm. Threats exist because of the very existence of the system or activity and not because of any specific weakness. For example, the threat of fire exists at all facilities, regardless of the amount of fire protection available.

Threat Monitoring

The analysis, assessment, and review of audit trails and other data collected for the purpose of searching out system events which may constitute violations of data security.

Time-Dependent Password

A password which is valid only at a certain time of the day or during a specified interval of time.

Time-Sharing

Technique employed by current generation operating systems to support multiple concurrent user programs for very short periods of time, usually in a simple round-robin fashion, in an attempt to distribute processor time evenly among all users desiring service.

Top-Down Design

The decomposition of system design decisions through a succession of refinements, from the more general to the more specific.

Top-Level Specification (TLS)

A non-procedural description of system behaviour at the most abstract level. Typically a functional specification that omits all implementation details.

Traffic Analysis
The study of communications characteristics which are external to the encrypted texts.

Traffic Flow Security
The protection that results from those features in some crypto-equipment that conceal the presence of valid messages on a communications circuit. Usually by causing the circuit to appear busy at all times, or by encrypting the source and destination addresses of valid messages.

Transmission Authentication
A procedure whereby a station may establish the authenticity of its own transmission.

Trap Door
A condition existing in the system software or hardware which can be triggered to subvert the software or hardware security features. Basically there are two kinds of trap doors: First, the condition is triggered by something internal to the system; second, a condition is triggered by an external input to the system (e.g., a remote terminal or application program input message).

Trojan Horse
A computer program with an apparently or actually useful function that contains additional (hidden) functions that surreptitiously exploit the legitimate authorizations of the invoking process to the detriment of security. For example, making a "blind copy" of a sensitive file for the creator of the Trojan Horse.

Trusted Computer System
A system that employs sufficient hardware and software integrity measures to allow its use for simultaneous processing of multiple levels of classified and/or sensitive information.

Trusted Computer Base (TCB)
The totality of protection mechanisms within a computer system, which are responsible for enforcing a security policy. It creates a basic protection environment and provides additional user services required for a trusted computer system. The correct operation and integrity of the TCB must be independent of the actions of anything not within the security perimeter for the system.

Trusted Path
A mechanism by which a person at a terminal can communicate directly with the Trusted Computing Base. This mechanism can only be invoked by the person on the Trusted Computing Base and cannot be imitated by untrusted software.

Trusted Software
The software portion of a Trusted Computing Base.

User Identification
A plain text or computer language set of characters that uniquely identifies any authorized person, office, or staff agency who may directly use and receive products or services from a computer system.

Validation
That portion of the development of specialized procedures, tools, and equipment needed to established acceptance for joint usage by one or more components or their contractors.

Verification
Informally, a clear and convincing demonstration that software is correct with respect to well-defined criteria, such as a security model. In a formal context, verification refers to the mathematical demonstration of consistency between a formal specification and a security model (design verification) or between the formal specification and its program implementation (implementation verification). The phrase "formally verified" generally implies that computer-assisted techniques have been employed in the verification effort.

Virtual Memory
A memory organization which allows programming for a very large memory, although the physical memory available in the processor is much smaller, by automatically swapping required memory segments.

Virus
A spurious program that can infect other programs by modifying them to hold copies of itself. It is self replicating and attaches itself to a host in the form of a program or data object for the purpose of concealing and then transporting itself to another domain.

Index

Index

Index

Index